BATTLE TESTED

JAMAL BYRD

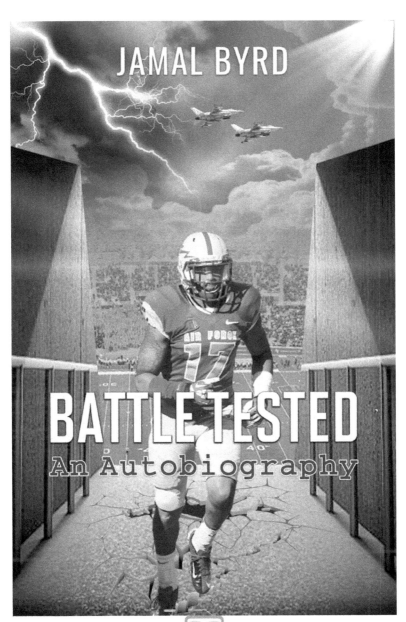

JAMAL BYRD

BATTLE TESTED
An Autobiography

Books to Hook
PUBLISHING

First Paperback Edition November 11, 2022
Kindle Edition November 11, 2022

Cover design by Nash Welch and Nusrat Awan.

ISBN 978-1-959039-25-9 (paperback)
ISBN 978-1-959039-23-5 (eBook)
ISBN 978-1-959039-24-2 (audiobook)

All Scripture quotations are from the King James Version Bible.

Printed in the United States of America.

Books to Hook Publishing, LLC.

Books to Hook
PUBLISHING

CONTENTS

PREFACE   vii

FOREWORD   x

CHAPTER ONE: FAMILY TIES   1

    DETROIT RAISED   1

CHAPTER TWO: THE SANDBOX   6

    PEAKS AND VALLEYS   8

CHAPTER THREE: BORN TO BALL   19

    UNFORGETTABLE MOMENTS   22

    HIGH SCHOOL GRIDIRON   27

    BALLIN' ON THE COURT   33

    CONCRETE JUNGLE   45

CHAPTER FOUR: FLY, FIGHT, AND WIN   56

    STUDENT ATHLETE   62

CHAPTER FIVE: THE AIR FORCE ACADEMY   70

    SILVER LINING   121

CHAPTER SIX: THE FRUITS OF MY LABOR   149

    BREAKING GENERATIONAL CURSES   159

    PROGRESS IS THE PROCESS   164

    HE WHO FINDS A WIFE   173

    PANDEMONIUM   190

TRIUMPH OVER TRIALS   192

BLESSINGS ON BLESSINGS   199

A STAR WAS BORN   206

BEAUTIFUL STRUGGLE   213

HIGHLY FAVORED   216

PLANTING NEW ROOTS   219

CONCLUSION   224

NOTES   226

ABOUT THE AUTHOR   244

PREFACE

I composed this work to give God the glory for my success. I live as a follower of God, giving everything and all that I am to him. I consider myself a walking testimony, and it is my conviction that a special calling on my life has led me to share my gifts and experiences with the world through the power of words. I thank God for the journey he's guided me through because it made me the man I am today. My distress in the valley and my blessings on the mountain are all owed to him. God's hands have never wavered in my life and I would not be here without him.

This autobiography highlights the hardships I've endured throughout my life, cultivating perseverance. I aspire to motivate people all over the world. Through my experiences, readers can realize that they can achieve their dreams and do whatever they set their minds to. Having gone through life facing perpetual adversity including countless injuries, disunion, alcohol abuse, anger, social pressures, and more, I've learned that life's battles are inevitable. Adversity distinguishes those who survive and choose a better life through God, living in his provision. By publicly sharing my life journey and tribulations, I hope to convey the beauty in the struggle and the power of God's grace.

I authored this for the small-town athlete who's been overshadowed. The one who's been overlooked and hasn't received the notoriety he or she deserves. This book is not only to serve as stimulation, but to discourage the lack of recognition from negatively affecting their psyche and using it as a catalyst to fuel their drive, as I did.

This is for the inner-city boy or girl with influences pulling them in the wrong direction. I encourage you to stay on the right path and lead instead of following. I want the reader to know that they do not have to succumb to the dead ends of a negative environment, but they can overcome their shortcomings and use them to their advantage. God always provides a way out. The path of promise is uncommon and will make you seem peculiar to most. Society shows that distinction is not always embraced and is most often ostracized. The world didn't like Jesus, but that didn't block him from his purpose, so don't let anyone stop you from executing yours.

In highlighting differences, I place a spotlight on some of the racial issues I've confronted, like many other minorities, and how they impacted my life. It is also intended to convey that suffering racism should not be an excuse for complacency or failure, but to give strategies on how to deal with this phenomenon. Racial discrimination continues to plague this nation and can only be resolved through the changing of hearts, love, and open and honest discussions.

I aim to embolden the one who is afraid to completely give themselves over to God. The straight and narrow path taken to follow Jesus is not cool, especially in today's agnostic society. The popularity shortfall with humans does not begin to measure up to the bounty of taking the leap of faith to serve God; our reward in Heaven will always be greater. In fact, making the decision to walk with the Lord will be the best choice you can ever make. I pray that you too will come to this understanding throughout my book.

I'd like to thank my Lord and Savior, Jesus Christ, for giving me both the idea and ability to compose this book. I want to thank my beautiful wife, Shaianne, for supporting me throughout this new endeavor and for always bringing out the best in me. Thank you to my first child, Malachi, who inspires me without even knowing it. I'm thankful for my immediate family: my mother Shawn, my brother Darius, and my father Ernest, especially for their direct contributions to my work. My extended family has also played a tremendous part in my life: all my aunts, uncles, and cousins, chiefly the ones in Tacoma. I greatly appreciate my cousin and editor, Yuri Kenan, who polished my book from top to bottom, and my sister-in-law Joy Randle who helped review my novel. I want to express gratitude to each of my friends I grew up alongside in Tacoma. All my teammates who I played ball with in college and met at the Academy, and all the great people I met in the military. I'm appreciative to the city of Tacoma for the influence it's had and the opportunities it's provided for me. I would like to offer thanks to every one of my coaches, teachers, trainers, and physicians who have invested in and assisted me over the years. Last, but not least, I want to thank anyone who has ever believed in me, backed me in any way, or attended any of my games.

FOREWORD

By Zach Banner
6-year NFL Veteran
USC Alumni

When Jamal had told me he had written a book, I thought to myself, "He probably wrote a short story about major milestones. Perhaps he has drafted a few chapters and wants me to read them over as a second set of eyes." But when he specified "autobiography," I had no idea that he'd spent the last three years writing a full-length novel. So, when I received my advanced readier copy, I smiled because once again, Jamal Byrd had shown that there are no limitations to the things he's capable of.

I have been friends with Jamal since attending Giaudrone Middle School in 2005. You will soon read about the details of the neighborhoods in Tacoma, Washington that we grew up in. I am the same age as his little brother, Darius, so we were both two grades younger than Jamal. When Jamal and his friends were in eighth grade and we were in sixth, we idolized them and did everything we could to be around them. We wanted to dress like them, act like them, and one day, be like them. But my parents were aware of the things that Jamal will explain in this book: we were surrounded by gang violence, and it had started to become a reality in our school.

I didn't finish middle school at Giaudrone because my mother decided to transfer me to Gray Middle School, on the other side of town. Gray had its own problems with adolescent gang violence as well, but it was closer to my aunt's house. Thus, I was protected by my four older cousins, instead of being by myself. I tell you this story because I had only watched Jamal from afar for the next several years as we attended to separate high schools. In Tacoma, when someone is exceptional in sports and being recruited by colleges, every athlete hears about it. So, I wasn't shocked in high school when I learned that my middle school idol was going to play for Air Force. I was so proud of him. He survived Tacoma, alive, healthy, and educated. The standard for the rest of the Byrd family had been set.

Jamal's story is still being written even after the publication of this book. He has become a great man, leader, friend, husband, and most importantly, father to my Godson Malachi. I am blessed to have him as one of my best friends in life, and I can't wait to see all the other amazing things he will do. As you read this book, I implore you to pay attention to how similar his story is to other minority boys and girls who grow up in the inner city. Please focus on how he details his life and displays how he started life like a lot of our youth in American society. He persevered through so much as a kid, teenager, and still does as an adult. After you're done reading this amazing book about my brother, I urge you to hand it to a kid or adult of a similar background so they can be inspired to weather their storms and one day, write a story about how they dominated in life.

CHAPTER ONE

FAMILY TIES

"Shoot it, Mal, shoot it, Mal!" Vence and Antonio implored me before I drained the game-winning shot. Immediately after the ball went through the net, my parents picked my brother and I up and told us they needed to talk. Upon arriving at home, they promptly sat us down on the living room couch. From the intense pain in my mother's eyes and the distinctive look on my father's face, I could discern something dreadful had transpired. Initially, they explained how much they loved us and that we hadn't done anything wrong, so we shouldn't feel bad or responsible. Using soft tones and slow speech, they expressed that occasionally relationships didn't work out between adults. Darius and I exchanged uneasy glances as our suspense skyrocketed. Suddenly, they dropped the bomb: *they were getting a divorce.* We were appalled as our entire world had just imploded. The most astonishing consideration was that everything seemed perfectly fine between them; they did a superb job of masking their predicament. This calamity would be the genesis of a series of dramatic changes for me and would alter my life forever. Yet, they hadn't even expressed the whole story; the vile particulars would be revealed thereafter.

DETROIT RAISED

My mother, Cardia Vershawn Clark, was born on July 19, 1968. She grew up in the '70s and '80s in the rough streets of Detroit, also known as "Motor City," Detroit's prime claim to fame. The auto industry flourished in Michigan for several reasons, but one of the simplest explanations is that key innovators just happened to live there. Henry Ford was born on a farm in nearby Greenfield Township, and Ransom Olds settled in Lansing in 1889. These two would be two of the most important pioneers in the industry by the turn of the 20th century.[1]

Detroit has a darker side it's widely known for as well, meriting the murder capital crown numerous times over the last century. Motor City is home to the Italian mafia and many celebrated drug lords. The 1967 Detroit riot: the second-largest civil disturbance in modern U.S. history took place only a year before my mother was born.

By the time my mom graduated from Kettering High School on Detroit's eastside in 1986, she was well versed in her environment's happenings. She'd observed Detroit's crime and even encountered it first-hand. Growing up in poverty, survival mode was the default approach to raising children. Consequently, her mother, Helen, took the risk of selling narcotics to provide for her children. This income supplemented her insufficient state-provided income. Thus, it wasn't long before my mother was exposed to a life of crime. Accordingly, the traffic of customers inside Helen's home made her a prime target for armed robbery. My mother was just a child when assailants burglarized her home at gunpoint, extracting drugs, money, and household items. This incident frightened my mother and made her rethink her living conditions.

Helen was not a terrible person by any means. She was simply a product of her environment. Helen's mother and grandmother had both been bootleggers during the prohibition era and lived promiscuous lifestyles, trickling down to her. Helen had a great sense of humor and loved to play board games. Her career choice was no short to my mother. She gave her daughter plenty of love and attention when she was a child, and she always put her children first. Helen splurged on her children every Christmas, providing them with tons of toys. She bought her children outfits each holiday and ensured they were sharply dressed. She also showed my mother a lot of affection, which is why my mom was so tender with my brother and me growing up.

My mother grew up with two older siblings, her sister Toni, and brother Robert. Toni picked on her a lot, and they often clashed as children. Toni was regularly tasked with looking after my mother, who is several years younger, which was more of a chore to her than a bonding experience. Contrarily, in adulthood, the two sisters evolved into inseparable siblings, even raising their families together. Robert, on the other hand, was her protector from the beginning. He ultimately died from stomach cancer while I was only a few years old, thus my memories of him are very faint. Regrettably, he wasn't the only loss in my early childhood. Helen not only exposed and indulged in marijuana with my mother while she was a teenager, but she struggled with alcohol abuse as well. Her alcohol addiction piloted a severe drinking problem that would eventually lead to her demise. In 1994, Helen died from Cirrhosis of the liver, just like her mother, while I was only two years old. Cirrhosis is a late stage of scarring (fibrosis) of the liver caused by many forms of liver diseases and conditions, such as hepatitis and chronic alcoholism.[2] The latter being the case for my grandmother. So, unfortunately, I don't recall my interaction with her.

My mother's father, Cordell, and a fraction of his side of the family also fell victim to Detroit's depravity, indulging in alcohol, drugs, crime, and consequently, prison. My grandfather did his best for his daughter as well, but his ability to provide cohesion for her was simply lacking. Detroit's negative influences were just so difficult to overcome. Cordell too meant well but capitulated to misdeeds while my mother was a child. He has since turned things around and is a loving father and grandfather. He's even conquered alcoholism through the help of Alcoholics Anonymous. Cordell has always been into fitness, fashion, and stylish cars. His exercise program over the last few decades has allowed him to exhibit a body builder frame into his 70s. Cordell has always furnished my brother and I with solid advice over the years via all the wisdom he has amassed, which we are truly grateful for.

Nevertheless, the instability and inconsistency of Cordell and Helen's presence allured my mother to live with her aunt. This allowed her to attend high school with her favorite cousins and escape her impoverished neighborhood. Even in a destructive environment with little encouragement, my mom still performed well in school. She was a quiet and soft-spoken child who often went out of her way to avoid conflict. She was a swift learner and typically grasped discipline by observing other's mistakes, although she netted her fair share of trouble. So much so that our cousin Terrance called Toni and told her that my mother had been misbehaving. Toni, who had moved to Colorado several years prior, invited my mom out to visit in hopes of redirecting her behavior. During her trip, my mother became a Christian while attending church with Toni, and never moved back to Detroit.

My father, Ernest William Byrd II, had a much different upbringing. He was the son of Awbrazenda Wells and Ernest Byrd Sr. His parents divorced when he was just only years old, causing him to bounce around after his mother left. But that did not reduce his youth. My father stated he had an excellent childhood and was spoiled, mentioning Christmas was great and full of presents. He also expressed that he was able to travel around the country at a young age, which is why he still loves to take road trips today. By the time my dad reached the sixth grade, Ernest Sr., received full custody of him. Ernest Sr. soon remarried a young lady named Barbara, a very small, yet strong black woman. My dad loved Barbara right away and got along with her extremely well.

Education was a priority on my father's side of the family. My dad maintained quality grades throughout his youth, good for acceptance into Cass Technical High School, one of Detroit's most prestigious schools.[3] Awbrazenda worked at General Motors before earning a bachelor's degree and his father was a lifelong Chrysler employee. Following his graduation from Cass Tech in 1981, Ernest Jr. attended Henry Ford Community College. There he studied heating and air conditioning; subjects he'd focused on in high school. Meanwhile, he also worked at Pizza Hut to earn money while attending school.

Sadly, he was not generating enough income to get his own place, so he acquired a second job at McDonald's. Ernest would go from one job to the next in between his studies. Even still, he could not afford a place of his own. Over time, my father grew frustrated with his work integration with school.

While he did not attain an associate degree from Henry Ford, he did receive a certification in heating and air conditioning and would go on to pocket a third-class license in air conditioning. After my dad expressed his employment irritation to one of his buddies, his friend suggested the military as an option. My dad was not interested in the Marines and did not like the jobs in the Army. He was, however, fond of the jobs in the Air Force, hence he decided to do an early enlistment in July of 1983, joining in January of 1984.

After basic training, he spoke with his leadership and was able to secure an air conditioning job. Being that he was from Detroit, my father selected bases in the Midwest on his dream sheet. To his dismay, his first tour landed him at Peterson Air Force Base (AFB) and the United States Air Force Academy (USAFA) in Colorado

Springs, Colorado. His new cultural scenery took a lot of getting used to coming from Detroit, especially now that he was the only Black person in his field.

After settling into Colorado, my dad found his way to Israelite Church of God in Christ. Israelite is a great church that was once led by the late founder and Bishop, Roosevelt Dunn. On my mother's visit to Colorado, this is where she would meet my father. While attending the same church, my father got to know my mother and ultimately led her to Christ. Though from very different backgrounds, their relationship flourished. They began dating and married one year later. From humble beginnings of a one bedroom, they would soon need more space as Helen would be coming to reside with them. Not so much after my grandmother came to live with them did they have to upgrade dwellings once more as I, Jamal Elijah Byrd, made my entrance into the world.

CHAPTER 2

THE SANDBOX

I was born on April 28, 1992, at the USAFA hospital. After being discharged from the hospital, my mom lessened her work schedule at her hair salon to part-time, shifting from five days a week to three to care of her newborn child. When I was three months old, my dad deployed to Saudi Arabia, and by the time he returned six months later, I was already walking and talking. Upon my second birthday, my dad received his next tour, sending us to Guam for two years.

Too young to appreciate the scenery, the only thing I remember about Guam are the geckos. They were everywhere, and we often found them inside our home, scaling the walls. In Guam, my mother stopped working at salons altogether because they charged a 50% commission. Rather, she decided to do hair from home and continue taking care of me. Making more money working from home allowed my mother to keep her hair in luxurious styles that women would awe and rave about around town. Consequently, she single-handedly promoted her own business by marketing herself; that's how she generated clientele in the new location. A few months after being in Guam, my little brother, Darius Davon Byrd, was born on August 19, 1994. Following his birth, my dad received his final and permanent duty station at McChord AFB, just outside of Tacoma, WA.

Tacoma is a mid-sized city, and the third largest in Washington behind Seattle and Spokane. Tacoma, one of 23 cities in Pierce County, is in western Washington, 30 miles south of Seattle. It is home to 220,000 people with a diverse makeup broken down into 58.0% White, 12.8% Hispanic, 11.2% Black, 9.4% two or more races, 6.1% Asian, 1% American Indian, 1% Pacific Islander, and 0.5 percent other.[4] Tacoma is home to the sixth largest port in the U.S. and is known as the "City of Destiny" because of its location to deep port waters and quick access to railroad service back in the 1800s.[5]

The move to Tacoma created a setback for my mother as the state of Washington required her to obtain a state specific Beautician License, although she was far more educated and experienced than any of the courses. Thus, she made the executive decision that it would be more beneficial to be a stay-at-home mother, rather than continue working. Moreover, she preferred to be at home with her two young children and avert paying a babysitter. Now that she'd stopped working, my parents orchestrated a way to survive on one income; hence, they budgeted appropriately and lived within their means.

As Darius and I grew older, we did everything together. We got along most of the time, and never let anything come in between us. At no time did my mother let us fight, and she always ingrained we were all each other had. When horseplaying I was often too rough with Darius and ended up hurting him. I would either tell him not to cry and snitch or threaten to beat him up if he did; Darius rarely ever told. Nevertheless, he was the victim of my mischievousness many times; I was too scared to own up to my actions and kept quiet when it came time to confess, repeatedly resulting in Darius having to pay for my mistakes and getting both of us a whooping. Spankings were our standard form of punishment, which did a suitable job of correcting our behavior. Aside from that, Darius agrees our childhood was a bit sheltered, but it was also pleasant and stable during our early years.

Darius was always more into music than I was. He was exceptionally talented on the drums and knew how to play the piano well. He even played the drums at church for several years. Growing up, he owned toy drum sets he learned to play on. Because of his talent and dedication, my parents eventually bought him a real one. We also loved playing sports and video games with and against each other. Our basketball games were extremely lopsided because I was always so much bigger than Darius, but it made him better in the end.

Personality-wise, Darius and I had many similarities, with only a few differences. One of our distinctions was that Darius was far more timid than I was. I was more willing to test the waters of our parents by seeing how much I could get away with. Darius learned from my misbehavior through observation and evaded the same blunders. He was scary in a sense because he did not want any trouble. I called him a "mama's boy" because he always seemed to be up under her, receiving what I perceived as favoritism. I don't know if it was on purpose or not, but I believe my mother showed Darius partiality because she was also the youngest child, so she knew what it was like to be in his shoes.

All-in-all, we were a close-knit family growing up. My dad brought home the bacon as an Airman, and my mother maintained the home. We didn't have much money growing up while living on my father's enlisted income, but we weren't poor. As a child, I thought we were pretty well off because we still had nice things and even traveled from time to time. We went to church every Sunday, had family game nights, played video games together, and were well supported by our parents in all our sports endeavors. My mom was strict, but my dad was zero tolerance, and we knew he meant business.

PEAKS AND VALLEYS

I have always been an intellectually advanced person. As a stay-at-home mom, my mother had ample time to spend with my brother and I during our childhood. Although she only held a high school degree, she was brilliant and preached the power of education from the beginning. She spent an endless amount of time with us on our academia to include letters, numbers, words, colors, animals, the full spectrum. We were completing activities and workbooks almost every day before we even started preschool. The repetition paid off; my mother said, "I was a very quick learner and grasped things almost instantly." She described my learning ability as exceptional.

In 1996, my mom was anticipating my fourth birthday so I could start preschool. To her surprise, my grade school indoctrination was delayed because I was too advanced. I was given an exam to gauge my knowledge level and tested at a kindergarten level and was told I did not need preschool. Thus, my schooling was deferred a year, and my mother did not get the break she desired. Despite that, she continued to work on my intellect.

Once I finally started elementary school the following year, it was a breeze. I was usually the first one done with my assignments, a trend that would continue throughout grade school. This would also work against me at times. Socially, I would follow mom's advice to avoid most confrontations, "Don't talk about anyone's mother, bother their food, or play with their money." Overall, I was a pretty good kid in school. My behavior was tied to the fear my parents instilled in me if I acted up. I was also threatened with punishment for any grade lower than a B, a feat that would never take place during my grade schooling.

I was on the honor roll every year in elementary school. Finishing my work before classmates meant I was regularly met with boredom, generating the urge to socialize; I liked to joke around and have fun. This prevented my classmates from finishing their work and was one of my teacher's areas of concern during parent-teacher conferences. In fact, I was so astute early on, that in second grade, my Christmas story was published in the local newspaper. My teacher, Mrs. Woodard, thought my paper was excellent enough that she elevated it for recognition. My parents were so proud of my work. Considering my intelligence mixed with Whitman's poor quality of education, elementary school was a piece of cake. It was also full of new encounters. In third grade, I experienced my first natural disaster.

It was February 28, 2001, and I was quietly completing a writing assignment in class. Before I knew it, the ground was rumbling with enormous intensity, and the room was shifting from side to side like a tree on a windy day. As the highly frightening earthquake quivered, Mr. Carlson rapidly instructed us to take shelter underneath our desks. While under the table, I could hear classroom materials falling, and some of my classmates crying and screaming. I was also weeping at the concern we'd all perish. The ground seemed to tremor endlessly before coming to a halt.

The 6.8 magnitude earthquake was a terrifying incident. Prior to arising, we were directed to remain under the desks in the event of an aftershock. Back at home, our house did not suffer any damage. At worst, things had just fallen or were shuffled around. The rest of Pierce County wasn't so fortunate. On the day of the earthquake, Washington State declared a state of emergency. The next day, Governor Gary Locke requested federal assistance and estimated the economic consequences at $2 billion.[6] That occurrence was the highlight of my third-grade year. Fourth and fifth grades were less eventful environmentally and more of the same academically.

Aside from my heightened behavioral issues, Giaudrone middle school was similar scholarly. I sustained my parent's grade requirements and had fun after completing my coursework. I also maintained my honor roll standing. Giaudrone was a new middle school constructed in 2003. It was an upgrade accompanied by twice the number of students as elementary school, 78% of them being minority. With its central inner-city location, Giaudrone was also a below-average institution. It is currently ranked 1,859 out of 2,052 schools in the state of Washington.[7]

Midway through my sixth-grade year, I experienced the most tragic event of my life. I remember the episode like it was yesterday. My parents loved each other and seemed to be a great match. They had their disagreements like any married couple, but for the most part they got along very well. That's what made the story even more staggering. Prior to the family meeting, we were told my dad was doing field training for a couple of weeks on base. This was common, so Darius and I didn't think anything of it straightaway. In actuality, my dad had been staying at an apartment because my mother discovered he'd had an affair while he was on a year-long overseas tour. As a Christian woman, my mother does not hinge on divorce as an outlet. She places her confidence in God, forgiveness, and working things out with her spouse. My mother's belief system meant she would sustain her marriage if my father asked for God's forgiveness and was liberated from his fault, but he insisted on a divorce. He had fallen for another woman and decided to leave his family to be with her. We were informed he would be moving cross-country to Alabama to live with her after his military retirement.

My world was shattered. At age 11, I had never experienced pain of that magnitude; emotionally, I still haven't. The fact that my dad could leave his family for another woman was crushing. I could not believe what was happening, let alone comprehend why. Afterwards, I portrayed normalcy while around others, but deep down inside, I was traumatized. This triggered my display of a cold exterior as I became numb to the emotional pain. So, I was glad he moved away because I hated him at the time and never wanted to see or talk to him again.

This situation would be the conception of a whole new Jamal, an angry and guarded one. Divorce disrupts the child's perceptions of social reality. It confronts the child with loss and the need to reorder internal representations of familiar external patterns. Concepts of roles of father and mother and perceptions of the permanence of relationships must be revised. The rationale for divorce is usually not clear to children. The news of separation may come as a surprise even if the child knows that the parents are unhappy. Divorce is a cognitive puzzle for the child, bringing dissonance and inconsistency to the child's social and affective world. To deal with loss and to rearrange the disrupted perceptions demands time and energy that must be withdrawn from the work of the schoolroom and from social interaction with peers.[8]

At such an influential age, my father's departure caused an immeasurable amount of agony, bestowing the mindset that anyone could leave if my own father did. Instantly, I began putting up a wall fortified with steel and concrete so that no one would ever hurt me like that again. I refused to allow anyone to get close to me for a long time, and this policy has impacted my relationships until this day. Anytime I was threatened with someone not wanting to talk to me again, I wasn't bothered because I didn't permit myself to care enough. I became introverted. Even when it came to dating, I was nonchalant about breakups to prevent being wounded.

During a divorce, children often feel frustrated, afraid, and confused. They can carry these emotions throughout their teenage years and well into adulthood.[9] After the divorce, it seemed like anger was the only emotion I showed. I became a furious kid. A study discovered, controlling for social class, that boys in divorced families manifested significantly more maladaptive symptoms and behavior problems than boys in intact families. One explanation for boys' greater difficulties in adjusting to parental divorce is that typical post-divorce living arrangements are quite different for them than for girls. While custodial mothers provide girls with same-sex role models, most boys must adjust to living without same-sex parents. In examining boys and girls living in intact families and in different custodial arrangements, it was found that few effects could be attributed to family structure per se, but that children living with opposite-sex parents (mother-custody boys and father-custody girls) were not as well-adjusted on measures of competent social behavior.[9]

It stung to see my mother hurting and our family struggling as my father's provision vanished. For the first time in almost a decade, my newly made single mother was obligated to return to the labor force to support her two boys. Thankfully, she was able to hastily locate a job. With my mom being at work most of the time, Darius and I were left with less supervision and more time for misconduct. A representative national sample of male and female youth aged 12-17 found that adolescents in mother-only households were more likely than their counterparts in intact families to engage in deviant acts, partly because they tended to make decisions independent of parental input.[9]

I also became the man of the house essentially overnight, accelerating my maturation. Adolescents living in single-parent families acquire specific strengths, notably a sense of responsibility, as a consequence of altered family routines.[9] My mom exemplified fortitude by her ability to keep our family going. After my dad vacated, we needed $700 per month to stay in our home, which was a grave challenge. We strained, but we never faltered or fell into poverty.

Because many women are new labor force entrants or returning to work after being absent for some time, it is difficult for them to find jobs that pay high enough to support a family.[10] This was relevant in our case, thus, my mom sold a variety of clothing items and accessories to contrive our income. One of my AAU basketball coaches was also big into clothing and utilized several inexpensive shopping channels. My mother went to New York with him and my cousin Jamell, and they purchased a bevy of clothing. She then resold these items, to include purses, shoes, boots, hats, and umbrellas, for profit. God blessed my mother to make the requisite $700 each month, sanctioning us to keep our home, an abnormal undertaking after a divorce.

My mother sold clothing for 18 months, perfecting her craft over time. She even acquired her business license and a credit card machine to expand payment options for her customers. Additionally, she hosted several clothing parties. These parties were attended by her female friends and associates. When held at our residence, my mother would have merchandise professionally displayed throughout our home like a boutique. The women would come by to socialize and purchase goods. One month, we were short on income, and the mortgage was due the next day. Therefore, my mother needed to make the $700 expeditiously. She held a party that day and made exactly $700. This was a true blessing and display of God's grace.

To stay above water, the three of us continued to cooperate and put all hands on deck. Darius and I helped more around the house and the yard and prepared our food as much as possible. It was also convenient that our schools were in close proximity, so my mother no longer had to transport us. Darius walked to Whitman by himself, and I rode my bike to Giaudrone.

Adding more fuel to the fire, my mother had gotten sick during her marriage. She'd been having a very hard time breathing. She was also constantly exhausted. After some testing, doctors diagnosed her with sarcoidosis. Sarcoidosis is an inflammatory disease in which granulomas, or clumps of inflammatory cells, form in various organs. This causes organ inflammation. Sarcoidosis may be triggered by your body's immune system responding to foreign substances, such as viruses, bacteria, or chemicals.[11] To treat her condition, doctors prescribed my mother with numerous medications and an oxygen tank to aid her breathing. It was hugely grinding to see my mother suffering through this illness. Moreover, with my father gone, the magnitude of her illness was amplified.

She was sick for seven years and needed her oxygen tank wherever she went. All the while, she remained positive and had faith God would heal her. During her sickness, she was incapable of working a full-time job, so she sold clothes when she was up to it. My dad's child support payment was a massive help and covered some of the bills as well. She prayed daily, claiming health, and soon after the divorce, God healed her of the illness. We were so thankful that our mom overcame her ailment. Following her triumph, she returned to the workforce again.

As a single mother, she still took us on a few small vacations to Ocean Shores, Portland, and even to Detroit one year. She never bought us Jordan's, but she did give us an allowance that we were able to save and combine with birthday money to buy Jordan's and other luxury things we wanted. On the other hand, I was still dealing with the dissolution torment.

We know that children who grow up with absent fathers can suffer lasting damage. They are more likely to end up in poverty or drop out of school, become addicted to drugs, have a child out of wedlock, or end up in prison. I wasn't aware of it at the time, but the odds were stacked against me. Fatherlessness is not the only cause of these things, but our nation must recognize it is an important factor. Although the absence of a father is not an isolated risk factor, it definitely can take a toll on the development of children.

The results of father absence on children are nothing short of disastrous, along with several dimensions, mainly: children's diminished self-concept, and compromised physical and emotional security (children consistently report feeling abandoned when their fathers are not involved in their lives, struggling with their emotions and episodic bouts of self-loathing). The other prime consequence is behavioral problems. Fatherless children have more difficulties with social adjustment, and are more likely to report problems with friendships, and manifest behavior problems; many develop a swaggering, intimidating persona in an attempt to disguise their underlying fears, resentments, anxieties, and unhappiness.[12] I suffered from just about every one of these behavior difficulties, but rage stood out the most.

Others noticed my anger before I did. I found myself lashing out at people and occasionally unable to control myself. The late Phillip White, one of my AAU basketball coaches, warned that I needed anger management because of how mad I used to get playing basketball. I also had a few instances at school where I lost my cool, resulting in "In-School Suspensions (ISS)." ISS was similar to being suspended, except the suspended time was spent in detention at school. With animosity and abandonment in my heart, I found myself hanging out with the wrong crowds as well. I started getting into trouble and hanging with more of my friends who were in gangs. But it didn't take very long for me to realize that this was not the right company to be around.

One day during middle school, the Tacoma Police Department showed up at lunchtime and escorted one of my classmates to the back of their car. He had committed a robbery and would be serving time at the local juvenile detention center. My classmate was another fatherless kid who channeled his anger into a life of crime. In retrospect, I appreciate my ability to learn from others and avoid emulating their mishaps to get the picture. That event hit home for me and temporarily kept me focused on school and sports, until I needed my next reminder. I found myself teetering a thin line over the years. But I also understood I had a little brother to help care for who was watching my every move, so I wanted to ensure I was a good example for him.

In terms of my relationship with my dad, not much had changed. I did not talk to him again for years. It was my mother who encouraged me to forgive him, as she had done, and reach out to him. She emphasized that I needed to forgive him if I wanted God to forgive me of my sins. Matthew 6:14-15 affirms, "For if ye forgive men their trespasses, your Heavenly Father will also forgive you: but if ye forgive not men their trespasses, neither will your Father forgive your trespasses." Deep down inside, I knew I had to forgive him at some point, but I just wasn't ready. Profound wounds take longer to heal, especially for someone who wasn't as spiritually strong as my mom. It took a lot of prayer, and ultimately deliverance, but after a while, I finally reached out to him.

Deliverance is the Christ-centered ministry practice of freeing individuals from spiritual bondage caused by unseen demonic spirits afflicting the mind, will, and emotions. The ministry practice can be initiated by a devout Christian exercising the authority of Jesus Christ who defeated satan through his atoning death on the cross and resurrection. Deliverance includes counseling of the whole person, prayer, and expelling the demons as needed. It is different than exorcism, which relies on formalized rituals and often secretive acts of appointed clergy within high churches.[13]

Over the years, my anger and unforgiveness had made way for the devil to create hatred in my heart and mind. As powerful women of God, my mom and Toni were able to free me from these chains through a four-hour prayer session. The deliverance called for me to be honest with how I felt towards my father, so my mom and aunt knew what to pray for. They were then able to cast the demons of unforgiveness and hate out by name, commanding them to leave. Afterwards, I was the most relieved I'd been since the divorce.

Anyone can be affected by demons. Demons can be assigned against you to disrupt your ministry, family, marriage, possessions, or your job. This battle may likely go largely unseen and unknown. Satan prefers to operate under the radar. He doesn't want us to detect his presence in our lives. The gifts of the Holy Spirit (especially the gift of discernment) are incredibly important to recognize the work of the evil one, to resist him, and to learn how to walk in freedom.[14]

Toni is the best aunt I could ask for. She is a devoted prayer warrior with a lot of experience. Though decidedly stern, she loves hard and wants all her family to live to their fullest potential. Toni has been through a lot and has gained a mass of wisdom that she is able to share with her loved ones. She's always pushed me to be first-rate and provided advice and spiritual stimulation whenever I've needed it. Toni is also one of the best cooks I know, supplying the finest macaroni and cheese, lasagna, and collard greens every holiday. Toni's husband, Chuck, has been a great uncle for me as well. He's always been a car enthusiast, encouraging myself and my cousins to admire them also. He's also a mean chef, military veteran along with Toni, and a huge advocate for our family.

Things between my dad and I were a bit uncanny at first and it took some time for us to re-establish a relationship. The connection was disparate initially, but eventually, our relationship began to flourish into a novel and fruitful one. The forgiveness I'd undergone afforded me the freedom to restore my bond with him. Our relationship took on some turbulence over the years and came with adversity, but it continuously improved over time. Middle school presented affliction of its own.

Giaudrone is where I would first confront racism. For some reason, my seventh-grade teacher, Mrs. Darlin, simply disliked me. Even though I was excellent academically, and my behavior was not a liability in her class, she still gave me the worst seating assignments and treated me awfully. One day, I'd had enough, so I told my mother, and she relayed the information to my grandfather Cordell, who was living with us at the time. They were agitated, so they scheduled a meeting with Mrs. Darlin. Upon arrival at the meeting, Mrs. Darlin failed to even greet us; she just kept her attention focused on her computer. This pushed Cordell, and my mother over the top, and they strongly expressed their feelings to the teacher. Needless to say, the meeting was a success, and I had no more trouble out of her for the remainder of the school year. Next year, eighth grade was smooth sailing as I eagerly awaited high school.

Directly before high school, in 2005, my mother met a man named Artie Clark at church. Art was thoroughly interested in her, and they began getting to know each other. Art seemed like a cool guy, but I was still guarded, especially when it came to my mother. I did not want her to get mistreated again, and I definitely didn't like the idea of a random guy trying to pursue her. Originally, I was against the connection, but then Art grew on me. I saw how happy my mom was again and how genuine he seemed. He didn't have any kids, so he treated us like his own. He was also an enormous help economically. Art was already financially stable with a solid job in construction. In time, my mom and Art ended up getting engaged and married. Art had won us over, but I kept a close eye on him.

Art was very supportive of my sports involvement. He played basketball with my brother and me and attended as many of my games as he could. He took pride in seeing his stepson excel in competition and bragged to all his family and friends. Generally speaking, Art was a good stepfather. He was a good example, he encouraged us, and he loved us. But since he did not have kids of his own, this was his first hands-on experience with children. So, Art left the authority with my mother. This was fine at the time because no kid likes to be disciplined, but it was ultimately detrimental to our development. The power of a father figure's direction and tough love is monumental, which he simply did not provide. He also didn't teach us much about manhood. In my important teenage years, that's what I needed because there is only so much a woman can teach a young man.

My mother did the best she could as a single mother, but teenage boys need a fatherly figure. Elphin Smith, in his doctoral dissertation, said that without a father or positive male role model, young men will miss out on learning the role of a man. While it is not impossible for young single African American mothers to raise their sons to be good citizens on their own, the help of a positive well-adjusted African American male role model could make a big difference. Male role models could help and increase these mothers' chances for success. In addition, African American men could help with some unique challenges that only African American men in the United States have faced.[15]

Every young man needs an older man to prepare him for and launch him on the journey to manhood. For whatever reason, teenage boys require a catalyst to lead them out of their childhood and into the next stage of maturation.[16] Suffice to say, I did not have a single positive male role model in my life as a teenager. When growing up, boys require a father figure in their life as this has been found to contribute positively to the child's academic and social development. Strong male role models are essential for men as they help to share their emotional maturity, which, unlike puberty, does not happen automatically.[17]

A positive African American role model can provide young men with a very powerful example of life outside of the walls to which they have become accustomed. Once this example is set before them, they will understand the world differently. They will also be able to envision themselves away from their negative environments and become a productive citizen and a positive role model for someone else. There must be a guide in the life of a child if the child is going to have a chance for success and for gaining confidence toward becoming a man.[18] Conversely, boys who become men without positive male role models are often more likely to end up in a life of crime, in jail, or as addicts and participating in risk-taking behavior.[17]

Accordingly, as I set out to begin high school, once again, the chips were stacked against me.

I experienced some of the best years of my life in high school. I pushed myself academically, enrolling in several International Baccalaureate (IB) courses along the way. Henry Foss High School's IB program offers internationally recognized college-level coursework. It is an academically challenging and balanced program of education that prepares students, 16 to 19, for success at university and beyond.[19] I did not participate in the full program, which includes exams at the end of its curriculum due to my involvement with sports, but the few courses I took were extremely beneficial. I maintained a 3.6 GPA throughout high school while achieving accolades in basketball and football. One of my main motivations for performing well in the classroom was my observation of talented high school athletes missing out on college opportunities due to substandard grades. Yet again, I was able to learn from other's errors. I knew I wanted to play college ball, and I needed to earn an athletic scholarship; my family did not have the finances to send me to college, so a scholarship was the only option.

CHAPTER THREE

BORN TO BALL

S ports have been a part of my life for as long as I can remember. I first played basketball soon after I started walking at nine months old, another testament to my acumen. I fell in love with my Fisher-Price basketball hoop, playing on it all the time. The toddler-sized goal was a great way to indoctrinate me into the game of basketball. Home footage of me playing as an infant shows just how joyful it was for me. As I grew older, I started to play on our full-sized, 10-foot basketball hoop in our backyard, propelling me to develop talent at a particularly young age. My dream was to become a professional athlete.

Growing up with four male cousins who were all older than I was also improved my ability. Javenceio, the eldest, is nine years older than I am; Jamell is seven years older; Nicholas is four, and Antonio is two. Vence, who was 5'10" in the fifth grade, never grew another inch. He was a good shooter, with a fine post-game and defense. Vence is a highly intellectual person who has always been into knowledge attainment. Vence is now married with three kids. Mell was on the heavier side but extremely agile for his size. He could also shoot and loved to attempt intricate shots. He was a hard-nosed kid who was viewed as our bodyguard; we never had any conflict with others in the streets when we were with him. He stumbled into some trouble during his youth but was able to get things turned around as an adult. He's since become a minister, a great husband to his lovely wife Lauren, an incredible father of five kids, a successful business owner, and a strong man of God.

Nick was the quickest. He too could shoot well, but his primary skills were his crossover and ability to finish around the rim. Off the court, Nick has always been stylish and into fashion. Nick has two kids of his own. Antonio was a streaky shooter. There were times when he struggled to make a shot, and then there were others when he couldn't miss. He just had his first child a few months ago.

I was the closest with Antonio. Growing up, we were almost like brothers. We jibed so well because we both had similar aggression, attitudes, and interests. We were also the closest in age. Darius focused on shooting because he was the smallest. Every now and then he would score a tough bucket in the paint as well. I had a decent shot but could drive and play defense even better. We played basketball together on our hoop at home, the park, the gym, and backyard football games in the street and local football fields. My cousins had no mercy on my brother and I although we were several years younger. They were tough on us, but it only improved our ability. So, when it came time to play against people our age, we were well prepared. I appreciate their ruggedness because that demeanor has remained with me throughout my sporting career, and it has certainly contributed to my athletic success.

At six years old, I played on my first organized team at Eastside Boys and Girls Club. The Eastside is one of Tacoma's roughest areas, so playing basketball there was intense, even at such a young age. The kids were talented and aggressive. The parents were loud and rowdy and would even get into fights; playing there felt like Rucker Park. I loved the ferocity, and I was still dominant in the league alongside my sidekick, Joshua Lord. Josh was a bit shorter than I was but could shoot exceptionally well and was super quick. Josh and I won a lot of games together and became great friends. We would end up facing each other as high school rivals years later. Concurrently, I played basketball for Whitman. Public school basketball was a lot easier than the league I played in, so I thrived right away.

While playing for Whitman, I was coached by PE teacher Mrs. Mace. She was strikingly energetic and the one teacher who believed in me the most. She detected rarity in my character from day one and constantly encouraged me. She also communicated how bright of a future she believed I would have. These promising words afforded stimulus for me in my elementary years. After elementary, Mrs. Mace continued to follow my athletic course all the way through college, serving as one of my biggest supports.

After a year of dominance in an inferior league at a local community center, I decided to take Josh's suggestion and try football. I started playing tackle football at eight years old. My mother took me to a couple of Boys and Girls Clubs before finding the right one. I was only at Eastside Boys and Girls Club for a couple of days before my mom removed me because she detested the foul language the coaches used with such young kids. She also wasn't fond of how harshly they yelled. Next, we went to Southend. There was still shouting, but the coaches weren't as vulgar. My mom talked with the coach, signed me up, and paid the fee. And that was the start of my football career.

I was a natural. Having played on organized basketball teams for several years on top of countless backyard football games with family and friends, I had already developed a great deal of athleticism. The coaches moved me all around the field from running back to linebacker. I even played lineman at one point with my frail frame. Ultimately, my landing point was at wide receiver on offense and safety on defense, positions I would hold for most of my career. Things were going great at Southend, and then they took a painful turn.

One day after practice, my mom and I were playing catch on the practice field. She overthrew a pass, so I wanted to flaunt and dive for it. Unfortunately, I felt a thunderous crack in my left hand as soon as I impacted the ground, cutting our game short. In the car, my hand began to throb, change to a purple hue, and swell appreciably. I soon realized this was much more than just the average finger jam and expressed my sentiment to my mom, but she assumed I was exaggerating. Once I showed her how severe it had gotten, she instantly grew concerned and rushed me to the emergency room. After waiting, I was given an X-ray and diagnosed with a fractured hand. Next, I was given a cast to be worn for several months. I hated missing time due to injury, a theme that would become all too familiar.

Overall, I had a great four years playing for Southend. My coaches were awesome, and we even made it to the championship one year. Regrettably, we lost the game, and my second quarter fumble contributed to the loss. However, that mistake taught me resilience as a juvenile. I didn't quit or give up, but I practiced to improve my skills for the next opportunity. I didn't know it at the time, but as I grew older, I learned various life lessons from football. So many of the things I absorbed on the field were applicable to other areas of my life, such as leadership, teamwork, comradery, discipline, respect, resilience, hard work, dedication, and composure under pressure.

UNFORGETTABLE MOMENTS

One of the most unforgettable moments of my life took place during summer practice at Southend. In the middle of a fiery tackle drill, we heard the rumble of police cars and helicopters spread across the sky. We could also hear the police over their megaphones directing residents to get inside. Therefore, we immediately evacuated the football field and took shelter inside the Boys and Girls Club. Police had received a tip about a pair of suspects in the area and locked the area down to contain them. There were K-9s, SWAT teams, and helicopter spotlights everywhere. We were amid a bona fide dragnet. Law enforcement scoured the area for hours on the manhunt. While remaining in shelter throughout the juncture, all we could do was hope and pray the search came to an end soon. Even with all the manpower, the Tacoma Police Department was unsuccessful as the suspects managed to escape. We were then released and allowed to go home.

The pair of criminals who became the infamous "D.C. Snipers," had committed their first homicide a few months prior and were on the run in the area. There have been numerous movies made about the D.C. Snipers. John Allen Muhammad and Lee Boyd Malvo took the life of 21-year-old Keenya Cook on February 16, 2002, on Tacoma's Eastside.[20] The D.C. Snipers went on to terrorize the country over the next few years, killing over 20 people and rising to America's Most Wanted List.

I made many friends while playing for Southend, principally Julian Cruell. Julian and his father, Waymon Cruell, introduced me to Amateur Athletic Union (AAU) basketball and the Dynasty basketball team. Coach Cruell was a middle school teacher and the coach of Dynasty, who I started playing for in fourth grade. He was a great coach who had an illustrious coaching career in Tacoma. He not only coached us in basketball but taught us about life off the court. He also preached the power of academics and required each of us to maintain a B average in school. His assistant, Coach White, was also quite knowledgeable.

AAU is where the most elite adolescents across the country compete against each other. Unlike Community Center and Boys and Girls Club basketball, this league was year-around, and I was no longer the most talented. I wasn't even the best player on my team. That would be Shey Patton, AKA "Baby Shaq," who was unstoppable at our age. Shey was blessed with God-given size, built like a young Shaquille O'Neal, tall, strong, and stout. Although I wasn't the best on the team, I would soon find my key starting role as a defender, hustler, and effective scorer, fitting right in.

The bond that developed between my Dynasty teammates separated us from other teams. The great friendships we made off the court are what cultivated our success on it. We are arguably one of the best AAU teams to come out of Washington. Oftentimes, we would play up a grade level because the competition at our age was simply not good enough. Yet, even at higher grade levels, we still thrived. We also did it to challenge ourselves and prepare for nationals. Furthermore, Coach Cruell would have us scrimmage some of his former students who were in high school as an additional challenge. We were clearly unable to outplay them, but the experience was advantageous and strengthened us.

Although we had only been together for a year, we'd had so much success and won so many games that we were eligible for nationals. Throughout our tenure together, we won hundreds of games and tournaments. In 2003, we played in what's called a qualifying tournament. The teams who place in the top spots earn an invitation to play in either the Division I or II national tournaments. We fought our way through the Seattle-based tournament, making it to the championship. In the title game, we faced Rotary Style, the hometown favorite and one of Seattle's finest teams. The environment was just about as hostile as you can get at that level. The turbulent crowd was full of Rotary fans, with our Tacoma supporters only taking up a trivial section. The road game felt like the NBA playoffs. We scrapped the entire game and gave it our all, coming up short by only three points. While we did not win, we surely earned the respect of Seattle. Furthermore, Rotary became our sister city rival for years to come.

The game was lost primarily due to phenom Tony Wroten. He was freakishly athletic and one of the best AAU players in the country for our age. He would go on to play at the University of Washington and in the NBA for several years. That was not uncommon as we played amongst several kids who would go on to play professionally. One of them, Xavier Cooper, was on our team. He went on to play in the NFL after a very successful career at defensive end for Washington State University. Xavier was drafted in the third round, 96th overall, in 2015 by the Cleveland Browns. He played two years for the Browns before being moved over to the New York Jets for his final season in the NFL.

Even though we lost, our second-place finish landed us a bid at the Division II national championship in New Orleans, LA. Once we accepted the invitation to New Orleans, we started fundraising to sponsor our trip. We held car washes, sold Krispy Kreme donuts, and received numerous donations, allowing us to eventually raise enough money for our excursion.

Nationals was an experience I'll never forget. I shared a room with Imar White, Coach White's son and a good friend of mine. He was our shooter who had an uncanny ability to knock down threes. As far as the city itself went, New Orleans was vastly different from Tacoma. There were countless restaurants and a massive amount of culture everywhere. In addition, there was an innumerable amount of Black people who possessed tons of homeland pride and hospitality. Besides basketball, the main enhancement to the visit was our daytime tour of Bourbon Street, showcasing the strong heritage of New Orleans.

On the other hand, our trip to New Orleans was full of adversity. Prior to leaving for nationals, Coach White had suffered a heart attack, so he was unable to join us. This was demoralizing, particularly for his son Imar. But we did not allow that to affect our play; we all knew we had a job to do and were motivated to play for him while he had open-heart surgery. The other downside to the trip was that a hurricane transpired during our tournament. In fact, we were in the eye of the storm at one point. The wind was blowing so vigorously that we could hardly open our hotel room doors. In addition, the rain caused flooding a few inches high. It was a new experience for us, being from Tacoma, where there are no hurricanes. Nonetheless, our eyes remained focused on the prize, and the tournament carried on with the hurricane's peak only lasting a few hours.

Frankly, arriving at the Alario Center was a bit intimidating. This was the biggest stage any of us had ever been on, and we were one of the smallest teams there. After watching a few teams play, we weren't even the most talented. Amongst the players in attendance, were would-be pro athletes CJ McCullum, New Orleans Pelicans' All-Star guard, Tobias Harris of the Philadelphia Sixers, and

Le'Veon Bell, who finished in the top five for rushing yards in 2016 and 2017 with the Pittsburgh Steelers. Talk about talent! Nonetheless, what we lacked in size we made up for with our toughness, cohesion, and heart. We were a close-knit group who had hit our fair share of hardship in our short stint together. This adversity made us stronger and brought us closer together, and our play showed it.

After losing a four-point game in pool play, we didn't lose another one the rest of the tournament. There were 32 teams from all over the country in the double-elimination contest. Our games were against the New Jersey Hurricanes, Maryland Hoopstars, Camp Curtain YMCA Tigers, Ozark Redbirds, and the Charlotte Flames. The Charlotte Flames were our championship adversary, and stiffest opponent. The game was highly competitive, but we hounded them with our relentless defense, great shooting, and fast-paced offense. We were clicking on all cylinders and pushed ourselves ahead for the win after many lead changes. The feeling of winning a national championship was invigorating. We were each awarded gold medals, and the team received a towering trophy. The top four teams in the tournament also received automatic bids to the following years' Division I and Division II national championships.

As a result of our national championship victory, we were invited to meet the Governor of Washington State, Gary Locke, on December 1, 2003. This was yet another humbling experience, highlighting the reward for hard work and dedication. The Governor was a very nice gentleman and shared some nice words with us. He also shook all of our hands and took a photo with the team that I still cherish today.

The next year, we accepted the invitation to Division I nationals in Virginia Beach, VA, along with Rotary. The competition was much stiffer at this level and there we now 134 teams. We held our own in pool play, finishing 2-1. But the tournament was disparate, as we lost our first game 39-63 to Virginia Pride, one of the best teams in the country at the time. Rotary won their first game then lost to Virginia Pride as well, by six. We never caught our stride in the tournament and dropped our next game by one point on a buzzard beater, eliminating us from the tournament. Although we lost the game, we bounced back and played much better. Rotary lost their next game as well. This tournament included Harrison Barnes of the Sacramento Kings, Dion Waiters—eight-year NBA veteran, Jared Sullinger—four-year NBA veteran, Tobias Harris, CJ McCollum, and

Le'Veon Bell again. Overall, the tournament was a great experience, and we did a solid job of representing Washington. We also learned how much we needed to improve to compete at the Division I level.

By the time I reached Giaudrone middle school, my schedule was hectic. Between AAU basketball, Boys and Girls Club football, as well as basketball, flag football, and track for my school, I was playing sports all year long. My mother was running me all over the city for different sporting events, which didn't go unnoticed. I admire my mother's sacrifices for my sporting career, especially during middle school when she became a single mother while working full time. She was my number one fan; she attended every game possible and made sure to let everyone know she was in the stands with her assertive energy. It made me feel good for her to be there throughout my journey.

Darius would also play basketball and flag football for Giaudrone with future NFL lineman, Zach Banner, as they were in the same grade. They had a great deal of success and became close friends. I was two grades older than Zach, but we also got along quite well, growing into great comrades. As a sixth-grader, Zach was already one of the biggest kids at school at six feet tall. Zach continued to grow and topped out at 6'9." A benefit of only being two years older than my brother was I could look out for him while attending the same school. Darius never had an issue with bullying or anyone trying to pick on him because I'd earned a reputation as a tenacious kid, and everyone knew I was his big brother. By the time we reached high school I was well known throughout the city so things for him were smooth sailing. I encountered my fair share of haters, which came with the territory, but I was able to hold my own, primarily with my play on the field and the court.

My climb to Tacoma's pinnacle was different than most Tacoma natives. Most people from Tacoma have local lineage and household names that have been built over generations and are well known throughout the community. With my dad moving there within the decade, I was a first-generation Tacoma resident. Thus, I had no reputation initially. That was until I made a name for myself and my family by way of my athletic performance. By the time I left Tacoma, my name rang as many bells as some of those who were heralded in what is known as "The Town."

I stacked several trophies in my youth, from team MVPs and best player awards to championships. My football career at Southend ended once I got to eighth grade. I decided to take a year off from tackle football to give my body a break. I still played flag football and basketball for my school, and my new AAU team, Armed Forces. My former team, Dynasty, had split due to differences in opinion between the coaches a few months prior. The players remained friends, but some of us went on to join Coach White and Imar on Armed Forces. We didn't reach nationals with Armed Forces, but we were still very successful. We won numerous tournaments and competed at a high level. That sustained level of AAU basketball adequately prepared me for high school basketball.

I chose to attend Foss High School because it was a notorious basketball school, which was my favorite sport at the time. Lincoln, my assigned high school, was out of the question because Nick and Antonio went there and advised me against it because the basketball coach was incompetent. Furthermore, Lincoln was academically inferior and contained more student misconduct. Foss is no academic juggernaut itself, currently ranked 421st out of 455 Washington high schools. To attend Foss, I needed to submit a waiver since it was outside of my assigned school district. My waiver was approved, and in September of 2006, I became one of the newest Foss Falcons. My first day on campus was thrilling. Reuniting with my friends from elementary and middle school for a whole new experience was highly anticipated. The campus seemed enormous compared to middle school, and so were sports. Going from the top of the mountain back to the bottom of the totem pole as a high school freshman was hard-hitting though. I experienced my portion of freshman hazing which only made the transition more demanding, but it didn't take long for me to gain the respect of the upperclassmen.

HIGH SCHOOL GRIDIRON

Although our varsity football team wasn't good, we did not lack talent. Our dreadful record was more a combination of bad coaching and poor synergy between players on the field. Consequently, it took a year before I saw any varsity playing time. My entire freshman year was spent on junior varsity. I was extremely dominant on defense causing turnovers and on offense scoring touchdowns in almost every game, by way of my quarterback DaVante Peterson. DaVante was a lanky kid with a big arm who I connected with on the field all through high school. While I was thriving on JV, I was still disappointed because I wasn't being given an opportunity on varsity, even with their 1-9 record.

I prospered enough to warrant the 2006 JV football "Most Improved Skill Player of the Year." Consequently, not playing varsity for a lousy team only fueled my fire and made me work harder. My sophomore year, I earned the varsity slot receiver role, serving as the fourth option. I finished the season with only four catches, 55 yards, and a touchdown in our last game of the season. I can blame all-star receivers Nicholas Edwards and Te'Aire Bell for my little involvement in the offense. Quarterback Andy Hunthausen loved his All-League receivers, notably Nick. Nick was seemingly unstoppable in high school, compiling huge numbers, including 213 yards against our cross-town rival Lincoln. Nick went on to have a tremendous career for Eastern Washington University along with fellow Tacoma stars Allen Brown and Greg Herd, and elite NFL receiver Cooper Kupp.

Nick's NFL ambitions were sadly cut short, in my opinion, because he was overlooked by going to a Division I-AA school. Nick also wasn't the fastest receiver, but his talent overshadowed that. Moreover, he should have received scholarship offers from more prominent colleges, but as I'll cover later in this chapter, playing football for Foss impaired recruiting. Regardless, Nick championed his football talent into becoming an elite coach. After successful stints with multiple college teams, Nick has recently elevated to an offensive assistant of the Atlanta Falcons.

We finished my sophomore season 3-7, a slight improvement over the previous year, yet still substandard. I also chartered my first varsity involvement on the defensive end as the nickel safety. The nickel package exchanges a linebacker for a safety to help against the pass. We implemented the nickel package to combat Lakes, one of the state's best passing attacks. Our execution was horrendous. We got shredded with a final score of 49-6. The one bright spot for me was I snagged my first varsity action on defense, providing invaluable experience, along with an interception on a two-point conversion. Unquestionably, several players from their team went on to play Division I.

Along my way through the 2007 season, there were a few important lessons I digested from spending most of my time on the bench. The first was that we had poor leadership from the team's upperclassmen. It seemed like they were all in it for themselves and less concerned with winning. This taught me that lousy player leadership is an ingredient to an inferior team. I also noticed that our coaches, aside from Coach Franklin, did a poor job of preparing us for our opponents and promoting college prospects for recruitment. As a result, a lot of networking had to be done by the players themselves, which is uncommon at more renowned football schools.

The last thing I understood was we did not have the best play calling or execution. Our offense and defense were extremely predictable, but even when in the right call, our ability to execute was often absent. Thus, the advantage of standing on the sidelines was the number of observations I made and took forward with me.

Off the field, my grades and behavior were worthy enough for my parents to buy me my first car. With moderate income, my mom and stepdad did the best they could with a $2,500 1989 Nissan Maxima. Though a humble beginning, I was thrilled to have my first set of wheels. The car ran well and allowed me to freely traverse on my own. The dealership was also kind enough to throw in a set of 12-inch subwoofers, making my car sound like a concert every time I played music.

By applying what I discerned from the foregoing year, the summer going into my junior year, along with the actual season, were vastly different. By now, most of our big names had graduated, so I knew it was my time to shine. And I did so vehemently. I led by example on and off the field and provided much-needed leadership to my teammates. The 2008 football season was centered around me, Julian, DaVante, Allen, and Scott Crichton.

Just before the season, we were fortunate enough to attend a team football camp at Oregon State. This camp catapulted my confidence through the roof, and I did not look back. We put on an absolute clinic in front of college coaches against some of the best talent in the Pacific Northwest. So much so, that some of us were frustrated we didn't receive a scholarship offer on the spot. I would later learn why, but at the time, I didn't understand it one bit.

That exasperation was taken out on each one of my opponents. I finished the year with 25 catches for 439 yards and five touchdowns. My work ethic that summer had definitely shown during the season. I've always been self-motivated simply because I've constantly had to prove myself. To do so, I knew I needed to work hard to enhance my natural talent. That chip on my shoulder has stayed with me throughout my athletic career, so, I've never needed external motivation. Any other inspiration has just served as extra catalyst.

My stats weren't outrageous because we had so many weapons, but they were good enough to earn First Team All-League honors and nomination to Tacoma Weekly's 2008 All-City Team. Receiver was my primary position up to that point, so my production was expected, but the biggest surprise of my junior season was how effective I was on defense. I intercepted four passes from my free safety position, one for a touchdown, and recorded 25 solo tackles. Allen, Julian, and Scott all had breakout years as well. Allen was our quick and shifty receiver and killer cornerback. Julian was an explosive running back who could sprint with the best of them. He was also our other shutdown corner, opposite Allen. Scott was an absolute beast on the defensive end too. He bullied offenses as a defensive lineman and received All-League honors along with Julian and Allen.

Allen was an undersized, yet tenacious ball player. He went on to have a solid career playing safety at Eastern Washington University. He played the game without fear, and now expects his players to do the same as he is having an even better coaching career, currently with the University of California, Berkeley. Scott was the first to receive a scholarship offer. This was great news but also disappointing at the same time because I still did not have one myself. Scott would eventually attend Oregon State and play in the NFL for the Minnesota Vikings. Scott was a force at the pro level as well but was plagued by injuries, requiring multiple surgeries. This would be the cause of his short stint in the NFL.

As a result of our improved leadership and widespread production, we went 5-5 and missed the playoffs by just one game, which we had in the books. Julian was normally our sure-handed running back. But for some reason, it was not his night as he fumbled three times, ultimately too many for us to overcome. It was a heartbreaking loss because we held the lead late in the game and lost on a walk-off touchdown. However, after only missing the playoffs by one game, we were even more motivated for the following year.

All in all, once you're as productive as we were, colleges start to notice. I was beginning to receive letters from all over the country. Mail was pouring in for me at school and home almost every day. I received letters from local Division II schools to big-name colleges, such as Michigan, Penn State, and USC. As I would soon find out though, letters meant nothing if a school wasn't willing to offer a scholarship. With my name now out on the high school football landscape and no offer on the table, I was even more inspired for my senior year. With so many weapons on the offensive side of the ball and my production from the previous season, I decided to focus on defense, which paid huge dividends. I worked tirelessly during the offseason so I could take the next step and earn a scholarship offer. I also took time to enjoy one of Tacoma's best festivities off the field.

At the Taste of Tacoma in 2009, I crossed paths with someone who would become immensely special to me. The Emerald Queen Casino's Taste of Tacoma at Point Defiance Park is the "Ultimate Summer Get Together," featuring over 40 restaurants and vendors, local restaurant showcases, craft and commercial goods vendors, and live music on four stages, live cooking demonstrations and cook-offs.[21] I frequented the Taste every year in high school. The Taste takes place at the end of June every summer. People from all over the region visit for a bite of the different cuisines. It is also the place where all of Tacoma's urban youth go to socialize.

While there with my brother in 2009, he stopped to speak to his friend Detra. We exchanged greetings, and I was introduced to her friend, Shaianne Patrick. Shaianne was a beautiful girl who I had never seen before. After interacting with them for a few minutes we parted ways, but I could not get over how gorgeous Shaianne was. I communicated my thinking to Darius and told him to put a word in for me to Detra. Darius worked things on his end, and I was soon connected with Shaianne. We hit things off promptly as we acquainted ourselves with each other and began to chat more. In a short time, we started talking on the phone and hanging out. Shaianne and I shared a unique bond that I had not experienced with anyone else before. We got along exceptionally well, had fun together, possessed similar interests, and developed a great friendship. After the event, my focus shifted back to football.

Due to my receiving production the year before, I garnered much more attention and was often double-teamed. Nevertheless, my receiving numbers were still productive with 16 catches for 271 yards and four touchdowns, comparable to my brother's, who had a fine football career at Foss. His senior year stats at receiver were even better than mine as he reeled in over 30 catches for 350 receiving yards and five touchdowns. He also had over 1,000 all-purpose yards and received first-team All-League honors for returner and second-team All-League for receiver. Darius did not generate much interest from colleges due to his size and speed, but he was still a gifted high school player, putting up reputable numbers.

On the defensive end, I picked off a staggering 10 passes and logged 38 tackles in just seven games. The 10 interceptions were amongst the most in the country. My best game came against White River, where I snagged three interceptions, one for a touchdown, and a receiving touchdown. I was reading their quarterback like an English professor

Regrettably, I was bitten by the injury bug and missed a game and a half with a sprained knee. As always, it killed me not to be on the field. I also missed a game and a half due to an in-game clash. We were in a heated contest at Olympia High School which included a lot of trash talking. After a goal-line play, a player from Olympia struck my helmet, resulting in a double ejection and suspension for the next game. It was infuriating to be wrongfully suspended because I did not retaliate or throw a punch. My coaches appealed the decision, but the ruling was upheld. This unfair judgment caused me to miss my senior season's last game and a half. It also cost us the Olympia game as I had been playing well with three catches for 24 yards in the first half. We went on to lose 17-7. It spurned our playoff hopes as well. We finished the season 5-5, narrowly missing the playoffs by a single game again.

I was distraught, but all was not lost. My astounding free safety numbers garnered a lot of notoriety, as well as increased attention from colleges around the nation. I received first-team All-State honors along with Scott, on top of first-team All-League and All-Area. I was also named Tacoma Weekly's Defensive Player of the Year and invited to play in the All-State game with the best players in the state. Disappointingly, I was unable to play in the game due to an incident the following winter. However, these were huge accomplishments I was extremely proud of.

BALLIN' ON THE COURT

My basketball career at Foss followed an inferior trajectory to football. Upon deciding to attend a well-known basketball school in 2006, I knew I would not play right away because Foss's teams were always stacked. But I did not expect it would take as long as it did, especially with my successful background on the court. The most memorable part about playing JV my freshman year was that we earned the best JV record in school history. We went 20-0, destroying every other team in the area. We were often the reason that the varsity coach lost his temper at practice or just ended practice early altogether. We were a talented squad who didn't fear anyone, and we pushed the varsity to their limit just about every practice. My coach, Mike Cocke, loved every minute of it. On the other hand, the varsity didn't seem to like me, probably because of my cold temperament. Mike and I would have our differences at times, mainly because of my defiance. Once we worked past that issue, we settled on common ground and developed a great relationship, which still lasts today.

On January 4, 2007, the day before our away game at Stadium, an unforeseen incident occurred. It was the morning after returning from winter break, so the hallways were buzzing with students rejoining their friends. I was in the cafeteria with my teammates when the late Damari Lewis, a big-time jokester, frantically broke the news, "Someone just got shot by the classrooms!" Because of Damari's history, we all thought this was just another one of his pranks. But then we noticed waves of students hastily walking in the opposite direction of the classrooms. We soon realized he was not joking, and a shooting had in fact happened. By this time, everyone was racing down the hallways to get out of the building. Once I made it outside, I could feel my heart pounding through my chest. I didn't know if we were in an active shooter situation and there were more assailants or what was going on. I cautiously scanned my surroundings until school staff escorted all the students into the auditorium and placed the school on lockdown. Everyone was hysterically calling their family members, disclosing what happened. Rumors started to circulate, then witnesses of the gunfire revealed the details. Douglas Chanthabouly had killed Samnang Kok at point-blank range. I was in a cooking class with Samnang, so the news was chilling. To make matters worse, Samnang was the parent of an 18-month-old son, Makhai Kok, with his girlfriend, Tiari Johnson, 16.[22]

As the story developed, I later learned that Chanthabouly pointed a handgun at Kok, said, "What's up?" and fired a shot into his face. The shooter stood over the body and fired twice more, hitting him in the lower left side and left buttock, the statement said.[23] Officers had a suspect in mind, but they hadn't detained him before releasing students to go home. The parking lot was full of panicky parents and guardians picking up their children, and it seemed like forever before my mother navigated the congestion. She was so glad to see me and happy to know I was safe. At home, we watched the news and saw the suspect arrested live on television a couple of hours later as the incident made national headlines. Chanthabouly was convicted of second-degree murder in 2009, and a judge sentenced him to more than 23 years in prison.

Students returned to school the next day by order of the superintendent, Charlie Milligan, over the objections of some teachers who said the school needed time to heal. Instead, the blood was quickly washed away, and a locker door with a bullet hole in it was replaced.[24] The first thing I noticed upon returning was the immense police presence around the school. The hallways were also extremely quiet for the next few days. The shooting had long-lasting effects which denied Foss from ever being the same again.

By the start of my senior year, we were provided with a full-time police officer to patrol our school, along with the four other public high schools in Tacoma. Prior to the shooting, Foss was usually home to between 1,700 and 1,900 students per year. Since the shooting, the enrollment has dropped every year to the lowest it's ever been in 2021, 605 students.[25] The class of 2006, the last graduating class before the shooting, was 400 people. My graduating class in 2010 was only 250. Back on the court, it was time for my sophomore year to begin.

Since my sophomore season was split between JV and varsity, I only played a half with JV and then went on to suit up with varsity. I did not see any varsity playing time my sophomore season, which was maddening because I knew I was better than some of the guys who were playing. But as with football, I waited my turn, and used the delay to power my motivation. Despite the fact I was not given an opportunity on the court, I was invited to suit up full-time for varsity once the JV season was over. This was considered a reward for my commitment throughout the season. It also proved to be valuable as I witnessed a contending team compete in the region firsthand. We finished second in the highly contested Narrows League and earned a trip to the state tournament through our playoff play.

Our first game was a two-point, nail-biting victory over Prairie. We lost our next game to Bellarmine Prep. Bellarmine is Tacoma's only preparatory high school, located less than a mile away from Foss. Bellarmine turned out to have two of the best players in the state: Avery Bradley and Abdul Gaddy. We had already lost to them twice during the regular season, so we knew the challenge that lay ahead. Avery became one of the best players in the country and took his talents to the University of Texas. There he thrived and was drafted 19th overall in the 2010 NBA draft by the Boston Celtics. He had a great career with the Celtics, teaming up with our hometown comrade Isaiah Thomas for a few years. Avery quickly gained a reputation as one of the NBA's best defensive guards. After leaving Boston, he bounced around the NBA but ultimately landed with the Los Angeles Lakers. He played a big part with them during the 2019-2020 NBA season in combination with LeBron James and Anthony Davis. Avery improved his three-point jumper and continued to hackle opponents on defense. This earned him a starting job with the Lakers and a very important role.

In 2020, Avery would help the Lakers win the NBA Championship during the COVID-19 pandemic. He did not attend the postseason bubble due to personal matters, but was a vital reason the Lakers made it. I was proud to have played against Avery and see one of Tacoma's own win an NBA Championship. In my opinion, Abdul should have also made it to the NBA, but his cards played out differently. Abdul could handle and shoot the ball with ease. He would go on to the University of Washington and end up in one of the most competitive overseas basketball leagues after several attempts at the NBA.

Avery and Abdul, also known as the "Fire and Ice" duo because of their complementary styles, were especially difficult to stop in the state tournament. We couldn't negate their impression on the game, but we did reduce it. We had a real opportunity to win at the end of the game, but one of our team leaders was unable to convert his game-winning free throws. Thus, we suffered a crushing defeat by one point. We never recovered from that loss in the tournament and lost our next game, resulting in our elimination from the tournament.

The following season, I finally reached varsity full time, but I still didn't play as much as I'd hoped. There was a coaching change prior to my junior year, and Mike became the varsity coach. I was thrilled with the transition because I assumed it would result in more playing time. This only came into fruition during summer league, but the regular season was not as fruitful. Summer league had gone really well, and I was playing a sufficient number of minutes because our whole team wasn't present. That summer, we faced Bellarmine again. They were without several players, aside from Avery, who was available to put his stamp on the game. Even though he managed 45 points, we still pulled out the win.

During the regular season there were some nights I didn't play at all which was vexing. However, I knew for a fact I could go out there and contribute. To make matters worse, most of the guys who I played AAU with were playing for their respective teams well before me, and I knew I was better than they were. Therefore, I contemplated quitting at one point. But I weathered the storm and was rewarded for it in the end. I kept my frustrations to myself for the most part, aside from confessing to my mom. She did not take too kindly to her talented son riding the bench and let Mike know about it. It was embarrassing to have my mother intervene on my behalf, but I knew she meant no harm; she was simply tired of my lack of minutes.

There was an unwritten rule by this stage that you don't get your parents involved and handle things internally. Nonetheless, my mother's discussion paid off, and I started seeing more playing time. I did not let my coach down; I became a solid contributor to an excellent team. I scored valuable points and was able to have a significant impact with my elite defense. Most of our scoring came by way of league MVP, LaQuam Thompson. Quam was a crafty guard with a keen ability to put the ball in the rim from anywhere on the floor. He would lead our team on to become the Narrows League Champions, a significant achievement and the first time Foss had held that title in over a decade.

We made a good run in the playoffs and made it to the state tournament for the second year in a row. We hit the ground running, winning our first two games, one of them against Curtis High School. Curtis is a local school with players we had grown up playing against, primarily talented brothers Dominique and Darnell Williams. It was a hugely competitive game, but we were able to pull out the seven-point victory. However, we would meet our match in the third round against Garfield. Garfield has been one of Seattle's best high school basketball programs for the last few decades, and it showed. We were overmatched and unable to stop Tony Wroten, the same kid I'd faced in AAU. He led them to a 23-point blowout that left us jumbled. Garfield would go on to lose in the Championship and finish second in the state. We lost our next game to Kentridge and UCLA's 6'10" recruit, Josh Smith. We were able to challenge their guards with our athleticism but were short-handed against Josh in the paint. We lost the contest by seven and finished seventh in the state.

Off the court, my attitude still hadn't improved. I continued to have a poor attitude and wore my anger on my sleeve. I also despised authority. This led to conflict with my mother because I would always talk back or have something to say, resulting in constant punishment. I was never disrespectful, but I simply didn't know how to shut up. My mother did not tolerate this conduct. Her preference was to take my phone, which typically served as a temporary fix. That was until she took my car keys for being disobedient. This sanction hit me hard and required me to take the city bus for an entire summer. Waiting for buses while possessing a vehicle and having to ask for rides was embarrassing. Accordingly, my mother did not have any more trouble out of me again. I finally learned my lesson, although the hard way, and my mom achieved breakthrough in my behavior.

The following summer, most of my time was spent preparing for my senior football season. But with so many graduating seniors on the basketball team, I sensed it was finally my time to take over. As with Foss every year, we had ambitions of returning to the state tournament. We also had an electric freshman, Marcus Chambers, coming in, and one of my old AAU rivals we'd just faced in the state tournament, Dontae Davis, transferring from Curtis. With the abundance of talent we were going to have, we believed we could do something special.

I had a great exhibition, projecting a statement season, and that's exactly what manifested. In our first regular-season game against Bethel High School, I finished with 24 points and 10 rebounds, easily scoring from all over the floor. We blew them out by 27 points, and I instantly put the league on notice that I'd arrived. The rest of the season proved to be much of the same. My best performances were back-to-back 30-point games on the road against rival conference opponents. I thrived against rival schools and made a concerted effort to showcase for those games as the gyms were usually packed with jubilant fans. I averaged 17 points and six rebounds for the season and was named first-team All-League. Many presumed I should have received the league MVP, but other voters thought differently. In fact, Mike believed I could have been an even better than I was and played basketball in college if I devoted more time to it. But football had become my bread and butter. Despite my individual accomplishments, our season was up and down.

Throughout my senior year, a good amount of my attention was still on football; it had to be. With my final football season in the books, the recruiting process was fully underway. I had created a highlight film of my top plays and sent it to every school I was interested in. Recruiting was a stressful period, but it did have its perks. One advantage was the ability to visit prospective schools. As a result of colleges showing interest in recruits, they invite prospects to their games and campuses, covering all expenses. These official visits typically include several tickets to one of their biggest games, sideline passes, tours of their facilities, and a meeting with the head coach. I was fortunate enough to visit several Pac 12 schools: Oregon State, Oregon, Washington, and Washington State, all schools I drew interest from.

I received my first scholarship offer midway through my senior basketball season. It was from West Point (Army), and I was enraptured. I remember receiving the phone call from offensive coordinator Ian Shields and just being grateful for the opportunity. I recognized at that point I would certainly be playing college football on a scholarship, barring any major setbacks.

As with most college recruits, I did not commit right away in hopes of amassing better offers. Yet, it was a sigh of relief to finally receive my first one. After that, the offers seemed to be reeling in. I would receive scholarship offers from Eastern Washington University, Portland State University, Central Washington University, and the United States Air Force Academy (USAFA). I did not receive offers from any of my desired Pac 12 schools I'd visited, but I was elated by the one from Air Force.

Prior to receiving my offer from Air Force, I hadn't heard much about them aside from catching a glimpse of their bowl game victory over 25th ranked Houston in the 2009 Armed Forces Bowl. With this win, I noticed how good of a team they were. I recall nervously accepting the buzz from Anthony Sampson like it was yesterday. I was filled with so much joy. Anthony was the recruiting coordinator responsible for the Pacific Northwest Region. A few days after presenting me with the offer, Anthony flew down to Tacoma from Colorado Springs, CO, to visit me in my home. The in-house visit served as a formal introduction and evidence of Air Force's sincerity in recruiting me. The following weekend on January 29, 2010, I would take my last official visit to USAFA.

I was blown away on my trip to the Air Force Academy. Unlike the rest of the schools I'd visited, Air Force offered things they couldn't: a world-class education, a monthly stipend, and a guaranteed job upon graduation. Of course, my chances of playing professional football would be higher at those other schools, but if that didn't work out, Air Force's educational prestige would set me up for the brightest professional future. Air Force's facilities weren't as elite as some of the Pac 12 schools either, yet they were still impressive. Their campus offered a brilliant weight room, a 92,000 square foot indoor athletic training facility (Holiday Athletic Center) that would be completed the following fall, a vast locker room, and a stadium that held over 50,000 fans, just to name a few features.

While on the tour, we dined at some delightful restaurants, met numerous coaches, namely head coach Troy Calhoun, and spent time with active players. The players functioned as our hosts and took us downtown after one of our meals and then to a get-together. The party was a lot of fun and was intended to show us that there was entertainment outside of USAFA's gates. Most of the players were forthright with their answers to our questions about the Academy's rigidity, but others dodged them altogether. This gave us recruits the impression that we weren't being told the whole story.

On the second day of my visit, I met with defensive back coach Charlton Warren. Coach Warren reviewed my highlight film with me and pointed out things he admired about my ability, serving as the reason for them offering me a scholarship. He then went on to discuss how my gifts were exactly what they were looking for and could enable me to compete for a starting job as a freshman. This depiction was music to my ears. As a former Air Force Academy football player and graduate, Coach Warren was very well-spoken, convincing me to commit right on the spot. I gave him a verbal commitment that I would accept their scholarship offer and shook his hand with a feeling of mutual satisfaction.

After the meeting, I found my mom in the hallway with the rest of the parents and shared the news with her. She was thrilled that her eldest son would be attending one of the most illustrious universities in the nation. My dad was also euphoric when I broke the news. I soon found out that a couple of other prospects had committed that day as well. One of them was Justin DeCoud, the first person I met on my visit. Justin was a fellow west coast native from Riverside, CA. He, too, played defensive back, and we hit it off right away. Justin and I would remain in communication until we arrived for basic training the following summer and developed a friendship for years to come. With the recruiting process all but over, it felt like a weight had been lifted off my shoulders. Back home, things weren't going as smoothly.

With my visit at the apex of basketball season, I was forced to miss an important game against Gig Harbor. They were led by future NFL tight end Austin Seferian-Jenkins. Austin was a freight at 6'5", 250 pounds, and hard to deal with in the paint. We had already defeated them once earlier in the season in a close game, so I knew it'd be tough for my team to pull off without me. Assuredly, Foss was edged by nine points.

Upon returning to Tacoma on January 31st, I informed my teammates of my Academy commitment. The commemoration was short-lived, and then it was back to business. Five games were remaining, and we still had one goal in mind: playoffs. I continued to communicate with other schools in the event that a better opportunity presented itself, but nothing came about. I did draw serious interest from Oregon and Oregon State, but they wanted me to walk on without a scholarship and then earn one, which I couldn't financially afford to do, plus it involved more risk. If I were to get hurt, their proposal could likely be off the table.

The Wednesday after my last visit, February 3, 2010, was national signing day. National signing day is the deadline for all high school and junior college football recruits to sign to the college of their choice, based on the scholarships they receive. Signing day is a crucial day that takes place every year on the first Wednesday of February. Across the country, high school student-athletes' lives are changed forever, and verbal commitments evolve into signed letters of intent. TV press conferences are often held for top prospects, while some make small announcements at home. With five Foss football players accepting offers, we assembled an integrated signing day event at school. This was one of the best days of my life with family, friends, coaches, and news reporters in attendance. Customarily, each signee wears a hat for the school they choose to sign with. I wore a white and blue Air Force hat, and each of my teammates displayed their selections as well.

With celebrations finished, it was time for one of our four remaining basketball games against Shelton that evening. We overwhelmed them with a convincing win. However, we still weren't receiving enough production from some of our main players that late in the season, which greatly hurt our chances. Yet, we were still in a position to make the playoffs. That was, until I faced what would become a life-threatening injury.

I was an awfully tough kid who did everything I could to fight through injuries or play while hurt. Effectively, this was one of the times it bit me. I had suffered a thigh contusion, an injury I'd experienced many times before. But this time was different. As a precautionary measure, I sat out the second half of the Shelton game after sustaining the bruise. That night, I went home and iced my thigh, sensing it was cured afterwards. I practiced the following day and even played the day after that in a devastating loss to Wilson.

Unfortunately, that would be the game where I aggravated my contusion. After the game, I tried to ice my thigh again to reduce the swelling, but that was to no avail. I then took an ice bath which was also insignificant. The pain and the swelling escalated to the point where I could no longer take it. I emphatically banged on my mother's door and insisted that she take me to the emergency room. Disoriented and frantic, she jolted out of bed and rushed to the car. By that time, the pain was unbearable, and tears were flowing down my face. I felt like I wanted to die rather than endure the agonizing pain. My mom sped down I-5 like Jeff Gordon to arrive at the emergency room as fast as possible.

After what seemed like an eternity, we finally made it to Madigan Hospital at Fort Lewis Army Base. Upon arrival, I was placed in a wheelchair, only to wait for a couple of hours. Ultimately, I was seen and given all sorts of tests after my initial inspection, including blood tests, an X-Ray, and an MRI. While awaiting the results, I was given morphine to help subdue the pain. The morphine gave me a euphoric sentiment and was monumental in subduing my affliction. After a while, the doctor made his diagnosis and informed me that I'd suffered an intramuscular hematoma. Hematoma results from a traumatic injury to your skin or the tissues underneath your skin. When blood vessels under your skin are damaged and leak, the blood pools, and results in a bruise. A hematoma forms as your blood clots, resulting in swelling and pain.[26] The doctors also notified me that I caught the hematoma just in time because if left untreated, I could have passed away. I was alarmed by the finding, yet relieved at the same time because it was discovered early enough. I thanked God over and over for his grace even during my injury.

The perfect scripture to describe this principle is 2 Corinthians 12:9, "And he said unto me, My grace is sufficient for thee: for my strength is made perfect in weakness. Most gladly therefore will I rather glory in my infirmities, that the power of Christ may rest upon me." In other words, when we are sick, aching, or discouraged, that's when God's strength emerges, which is a display of grace, or unmerited favor.

By this point, my leg was the size of a watermelon, and due to the severity, the only way to treat it was by draining it with a surgical needle. The doctor numbed my leg before the procedure, but it was still hard to watch the six-inch-long needle pierce my thigh. After successfully completing the drainage, I remained under care for a few hours to ensure there were no further complications. My leg felt slightly better, but it would be a long healing process, and I would not return to the basketball court again my senior year.

With two games left and without their star player, my team needed to win both games to make the playoffs. They won the first by a landslide. The second was against Gig Harbor, the same team we'd already played twice and split wins with. Once again, my team had no answer for Seferian-Jenkins as he led his squad to a 17-point victory, ending our postseason hopes. I was at home during the game recovering from my wound and was highly disappointed to hear the game's result. All our hard work and dedication left us empty-handed.

Conversely, in combination with my stellar football season, I had done enough in my condensed basketball season to warrant "Athlete of the Year" honors. The News Tribune hands out this prestigious award to the best athlete in Pierce County over the course of the school year. The News Tribune is Pierce County's most renowned newspaper. Hence, I was delighted to receive this award. I'd had such an arduous journey to attain my achievements, making it invaluable. I conducted numerous interviews with local newspapers and reporters, generating a surreal feeling. It seemed as if I was on track with my goal of playing in the NFL. Next, I just needed to get healthy.

The recovery from my hematoma was widely extensive. In concert with USAFA's extensive admissions process, the remainder of my last high school semester was exceptionally demanding. MRIs were conducted on my leg every month to ensure I was on schedule and wasn't regressing. While I had signed my letter of intent with Air Force, that didn't mean I'd been accepted into the Academy, as signing was only the first hurdle. Unlike most schools, USAFA requires their recruited athletes to be amongst the top of their classes academically. Therefore, I still needed to go through the admissions process. USAFA's admission rate is only 11.4%, so out of the 10,000 candidates that apply every year, only 1,500 are appointed, and about 1,200 accept the offer of admission.[27] The average high school GPA of students who are accepted to USAFA is 3.87, and the average combined Math and Reading SAT score is 1,320, with the minimum being 1,200 out of the new total of 1,600.[28] The national average is 1,060.[29] In 2016, the SAT changed drastically from the old one, going from three 800 point sections each for math, reading, and writing for a total of 2,400, to two 800 point sections for a total of 1,600, combining reading and writing into one.[30]

USAFA's admissions process takes many months and includes numerous factors; final decisions are based on scores calculated as a weighted combination of three elements:

- 60 percent academic composite—includes SAT/ACT score and prior academic ranking (PAR: class rank, GPA, transcript, the strength of high school, rigor of curriculum).
- 20 percent leadership composite—also called extra-curricular composite; includes activities, leadership, and résumé.
- 20 percent selection panel score—selection panel's evaluation of the candidate, which includes a review of admissions liaison officer (ALO) evaluations, writing samples, teacher evaluations, recommendations, and the candidate fitness assessment.[27]

The computed total score, called the selection composite score, is used to rank-order candidates. Admissions are determined from that score.[27] In addition to the scores above, USAFA requires a congressional nomination and, most importantly, in my case, a favorable medical status. To be accepted into the Air Force Academy, I was given until July 1, 2010, to be completely healthy and cleared from my injury. This made my resurgence quite stressful. Thankfully, my 3.6 GPA and SAT score alleviated some of that pressure. I'd proactively taken my SAT the preceding summer, receiving a score of 1,580 in 2010, equivalent to 1,040 under the new scoring format. Regarding the congressional nomination, each United States senator and representative has an allotted number of nominations he or she can use to nominate individuals to USAFA.[27]

Over the next few months, I actively completed my admissions packet. I submitted transcripts, a writing sample, received letters of recommendations from teachers, coaches, and mentors, as well as my congressional nomination by way of a letter to the senator, and met with my liaison officer. The only thing pending was my medical clearance. I continued to lift weights with my upper body as my leg healed and kept my future coaches apprised of my progress. It was a long, tedious process while the July 1st deadline loomed in the background. As time drew closer, I grew more and more anxious.

After several MRIs and follow-up appointments, my final appointment prior to the deadline arrived. It was the day before, June 30th, and my anxiety had reached its summit. The doctor reviewed my swelling, range of motion, and balance. After noting his disposition, he informed me that I had completely regained my strength and passed the exam with flying colors. All I could say was thank God. The chances of getting cleared one day before the cutoff could not have been anything else but God, and I knew it right away. Instances like this are what strengthened my faith in God and certified how real he is.

With medical clearance from my primary care physician, I could finally take the Academy's candidate fitness test and obtain medical clearance from them as well. Both were a walk in the park; however, those were only a couple of the obstacles I had to overcome. I now had to wait for my acceptance decision from USAFA. Ultimately, my SAT score would be too low for direct admittance to the Academy. I was heartbroken as I suspected this was the end of an opportunity, but there was still hope. My situation was not abnormal for recruited athletes, hence the reason for the United States Air Force Academy Preparatory School (USAFAPS).

USAFA's admissions team recognizes how strenuous their requirements are and established the Prep School in 1961. Any applicant who applies for but does not receive an appointment to the Academy is automatically considered for a Prep School appointment.[31] The Prep School is a 10-month rigorous program designed to prepare Academy candidates academically and athletically, build character and militarily to succeed and lead at the Academy.[32] This dynamic applied in my case, which presented a new avenue to consider. The biggest wrench in the situation is that I would not be playing football for the Air Force Falcons right away, but instead for the Prep School's own junior college level Huskies. I discussed the matter with my Academy coaches, and they assured me the Prep School would only benefit me in the long run and that a number of the best players to come out of Air Force started at the Prep School. My mother echoed their sentiment. I didn't have many other options on the table now that signing day had passed, so I took their advice and accepted my appointment to the USAFA Prep School.

CONCRETE JUNGLE

Now that I had my college destination secured, it was time to walk across the stage. On June 14, 2010, I was elated to receive my diploma and close the high school chapter of my life. Sadly though, graduating from high school in Tacoma wasn't an easy task. In 2010, just more than half of Tacoma students (55%) were graduating, and only 33% enrolled in college. USA Today featured Tacoma schools under the shameful headline, "Dropout Factories." Unfortunately, nearly two-thirds of our students were living in poverty, with children of color being twice as likely to be living in poverty than those that were White.[33] Living in poverty adds to this risk by disrupting parent-adolescent relationships, increasing exposure to stress, and increasing the risk of trauma or violence in childhood. Combined, these experiences negatively affect health and well-being into adulthood. Tacoma's South, South End, and Eastside neighborhoods have higher concentrations of families in poverty than other areas of the city.[34] These neighborhoods constitute the "hoods" of Tacoma.

Black people were concentrated in those sectors after World War II through redlining. Redlining is a discriminatory practice that takes place when a lender refuses to make loans secured by property in a certain neighborhood because of the racial or ethnic composition of the neighborhood.[35] The community makeups have since improved but still exhibit repercussions from prejudiced implementation.

From the time I was two years old, I grew up in the hood in South End of Tacoma, on the border of the Eastside, also known as the Lincoln District. I witnessed poverty and the income gap firsthand. Correspondingly, there were three murders within one block of my house. The first took place right across the street. We weren't given many details; we just saw the caution tape around the home and forensics removing a body. The second homicide occurred when I was in high school. There had been a barbeque in a quadplex across the street. An argument ensued, leading to gunfire, and a man was killed at point-blank range. I remember riding my bike home from my aunt Toni's house and having to go around the caution tape to get to my house. The last murder was vehicular. A couple of women had gotten into a quarrel. The victim then stormed off, and the suspect ran her over in the middle of the street. These types of incidents are a direct result of reduced income levels.

Furthermore, Tacoma has had one of the highest property crime rates in the country for the last few decades. For a city with only 200,000 people, there is an abundance of crime. In 2010, the rate was 6,348 per 100,000 people, compared to 3,699 for the state, and 2,946 for the U.S.[36] Property crime includes the offenses of burglary, larceny-theft, motor vehicle theft, and arson.[37] Crime rates are calculated by dividing the number of reported crimes by the total population. The result is then multiplied by 100,000.[38] The chances of becoming a property crime victim in Tacoma are now 1 in 18.[39] I witnessed a car being stolen in front of my home. My parent's car was also stolen and so was my uncle Chuck's. Our house was even shot at before. Almost everyone I know from Tacoma has had their car broken into or stolen at some point.

Tacoma's violent crime isn't much better. Tacoma averages approximately 18 homicides per year, and with a city that size, makes Tacoma more dangerous than most cities. Violent crime in Tacoma is 117% higher than the national average.[39] Tacoma is now one of the most dangerous cities in America. So, in an environment that treacherous, it's conceivable why graduating in Tacoma was such a big deal.

Tacoma students did not have access to the resources to be successful. But how could they? The median household income in Tacoma was $43,715, 15% lower than the state average.[34] According to 2010 census data, just 26% of Tacoma adults held a college degree.[33] A greater portion of Tacoma students reported drug use than their peers statewide in the Health Youth Survey.[34] Early drug use represents multiple dimensions of risk to youth. Exposure to alcohol and drugs interferes with memory, positive emotional and social development and low school performance and academic disengagement. I can call to mind seeing drugs being sold right across the street from my house. In fact, multiple meth labs would neighbor us over the years. They were only discovered because one of them was dismantled during a big drug bust, and the other exploded. Early drug use is also an indicator of vulnerability to gang activity. Gang activity is something I would become all too familiar with in Tacoma, and almost succumb to.

I was heavily familiar with gangs by the time I left elementary school. As a Christian, my parents did their best to keep us grounded in church and sports, and away from our environment. Although we attended church twice a week and had recurring sports practices over the years, the streets still tugged on me. My mother prayed a great deal too, and I know that covered us from a lot of danger. Nonetheless, my parents could not be there with us every minute of the day, especially at school. Whitman was two blocks away from my childhood home, and we could walk there in four minutes. Yet, my mother walked us to school every day until we were old enough to walk on our own when I was in the third grade. Whitman is an inner-city public elementary school housing 400 students a year. It is in the bottom 50% for elementary schools in the state of Washington.[40]

Whitman was also one of the most diverse schools around, with 70% of its students being minorities. Therefore, two of my early best friends were a couple of Samoan brothers. We all shared the same class and played together at recess. They were great kids and fun to play with. Their dad was a member of the Eastside Bloods, and they followed suit. They continuously wore red and showed me all the handshakes. At the time, I wasn't fully aware of all the aspects that came with being in a gang, so I thought their demonstrations were cool since I only saw what they showed me at school.

One day after basketball practice, their dad asked me if I wanted to join the blood gang with his sons. I thought about it, but I refused the offer; my intuition told me it wasn't a good idea. While I'd declined the offer and wasn't formally initiated, I remained good friends with them. Due to our constant contact, I was affiliated with the bloods. I didn't hang with the brothers much after elementary as we parted ways to different middle schools, but my blood association was renewed by way of my other Eastside friends I grew up with. Charlie and Jakob weren't the only gang members at Whitman. In fact, they were only a couple out of many. But they were the minority, as there were many more crips, a popular theme in Tacoma.

Most of Tacoma's crips hail from the infamous Hilltop. The first residential neighborhood to develop in Tacoma outside of the downtown core, the Hilltop community encompasses the upper part of the slope rising from Tacoma's city center along Commencement Bay, as well as the plateau which extends westward from the crest of the slope. The residents of the Hilltop during its initial phases of development were almost all immigrants to Tacoma. Whether from other countries around the world or other states in the union. A person walking down a typical block of the Hilltop on a warm summer night in 1910 would have heard families conversing in a half-dozen different languages. Hilltop residents helped build the city's businesses and industries and helped found the neighborhood's institutions such as churches, schools, and civic organizations.[41]

Over time, Hilltop became home to the Hilltop Crips, Washington's most notorious gang. Tacoma was the state's ground zero for gang activity after California crip and blood members sought new gang recruitment and drug dealing markets. Tacoma's Hilltop was considered the Wild West of gang shootings, street dealers openly peddling crack on street corners, and graffiti that Tacoma's understaffed, and outgunned police department battled to contain.[42] Tacoma's first gang homicide took place on 23rd Street and Sheridan Avenue on August 28, 1988. On that day, Hilltop Crip member Bernard "Clown" Houston was shot in the head and killed on the corner of 23rd and Sheridan. When police arrived, they found the 17-year-old laying on the ground in front of a silver Jeep Cherokee. "He was found unconscious and bleeding heavily, a six-shooter clutched in his right hand with five live rounds in the cylinder," read a wire report published in a local newspaper two days after the shooting. Another man, 18-year-old Michael Jeter, was with Houston at the time and was shot in the right thigh. He hid behind a nearby storefront until police arrived to take his statement. Police said, "Houston and Jeter were standing with three other people at a street corner when a brown-and-white Oldsmobile Cutlass and another car pulled up shortly before midnight Sunday." Witnesses said gunshots were fired after a passenger in the Oldsmobile said, "What up, blood?" Police believed that the murder was gang-related and retaliation for a drive-by shooting that happened in blood territory on the Eastside days earlier. The Houston homicide was the first of many such crimes that plagued the Hilltop in the days, weeks, and years that followed.[43]

In 1989, one of Tacoma's most notable gang incidents took place. Sgt. Bill Foulk, a former Army Ranger at Fort Lewis, purchased a house on Hilltop as an investment. Foulk grew concerned that a house on Ash Street, his block, was being used to deal crack cocaine. He purchased his own house for $10,000 ($20,875 in 2019 dollars) with the idea that property values would rise. He was set on ensuring the "drug-ridden" neighborhood would become safe from gangs and drug dealers - sooner rather than later. He began to videotape the people who visited the suspected drug house. He wasn't wrong. The occupants were members of the crips, the violent street gang spreading from California to Washington, searching for new markets for drugs. Foulk told The Associated Press that gang members began to threaten him when they noticed he was filming their movements. When he feared that the gang was about to take action against him, he called friends from the 2nd Ranger Battalion to his house to have a "party" and be present in case the house was attacked. Again, he wasn't wrong.

Just after the Rangers arrived on September 23, 1989, some 15 to 20 gang members began to shoot up the 32-year-old's house while his buddies were inside. But the Rangers had brought their personal weapons to the party. The crips were probably surprised when their would-be victim's house began to return fire. For an estimated 10 to 30 minutes, the two groups exchanged intense fire in a "gun battle" on the streets of residential Tacoma. Witnesses said, "Hundreds of rounds from handguns, shotguns, and semiautomatic weapons were fired." Somehow, no one was hurt during the "Ash Street Shootout." The police arrived on the scene, and the shooting stopped. All but two members of the gang fled. Those two were arrested, but only one was actually charged. Authorities confiscated the Rangers' weapons, but the Army considered the event necessary for their self-defense. The incident was a turning point for the city of Tacoma. It brought national attention to the gang issues in city streets and prompted residents to take a more active role in policing their neighborhoods.[44]

In elementary, I was good friends with Damari and his brother, Jamell, both members of Hilltop Crips. We got along just fine even though they were crips. Sadly, Damari was tragically shot and killed on February 11, 2018, at a concert in Seattle. When I heard the news, I was in utter disbelief. Damari was one of the most genuine and authentic people I knew, so I was hurt to learn that he had passed away. I lost several friends over the years to jail and gang violence; some are still imprisoned today. As I grew older, I realized the gravity of gangs and did my best to stay out of them, but it wasn't always easy.

Gangs were everywhere in Tacoma: on my basketball and football teams, at school, at the mall, you name it. In fact, almost everyone I knew was affiliated with a gang in one way or another. In my opinion, gangs were a part of Tacoma's culture. If you weren't directly involved, then someone in your family or friends in your circle were, so you were automatically associated with them. However, it wasn't always by choice. It was more of a flight or fight situation. Either you were ambushed and had to run or defend yourself alone, or you joined a group for protection.

It always felt like I was being yanked by the streets when I tried to turn away from them. Thankfully, I never let them get a firm grip on me; sports kept me out of much strife. I was always so busy that I barely had time to get in too much trouble, while I did get into my fair share of it. I'd felt like I was on borrowed time by the time I graduated with all of my near-death experiences; one of them was too close for comfort.

One night on the Eastside with Antonio and my friends from Foss, we were waiting outside of a birthday party for some of our other companions to come out before leaving. We then received a warning to vacate the area because something was about to go down. Before I knew it, a dark gray, four-door sedan leisurely pulled up, and the barrel of a pistol was pointed at me out of the car's sunroof. I immediately bolted to my car in the adjacent parking lot. Shots started ringing out, and I could hear bullets hissing past my head as I darted. Gratefully, I made it to my car and quickly started the ignition. Julian and Antonio were right behind me, so they jumped in, and we sped out of the parking lot.

Once out of the lot, we then had to navigate the collection of cars that had jammed up in everyone's attempt to leave the area. While backed up, I noticed one more firearm emerge in the car to my left through my peripheral vision. The trigger was pulled and fired at another vehicle to its left, and they peeled off. I quickly followed suit as the traffic in front of me had finally cleared. Although I'd observed numerous shootings in the past, I was left disoriented because this was the first time I'd seen someone get shot. My heart was racing in the car, but this was not the first time God had shielded me from death. I'd had guns pulled on me before and witnessed countless shootings that were all too common in Tacoma.

My first experience was when my cousins and I were enjoying our food in a Taco Bell parking lot on the Eastside. Out of nowhere, a random guy pulled up and told us to leave. We rejected, triggering his anger, and causing him to exit his vehicle shouting, "Get out of here!" Again, we declined, claiming, "No! We live in this neighborhood too!" He then punched one of my cousin's friends and returned to his car, retrieving his firearm. As soon as he raised it, Antonio and I peeled off, racing out of harm's way. The man proceeded to chase after my cousin's friends in his truck, shooting at them while speeding down neighborhood streets.

Another time, I was leaving downtown Seattle with Julian and Allen. As we were heading out, we noticed a drunk man physically abusing a helpless woman. Allen quickly intervened, and Julian and I followed right behind. We managed to free the woman from his strangle, but now the fellow wanted to fight us. Once he saw there were three of us, he rushed to his vehicle, returning with a pistol. Allen, Julian, and I turned into an Olympic track team as we flew to safety behind a building. These incidents were certainly alarming but being shot at was different as I saw my life flash before my eyes. In fact, when I was in high school, shootings took place just about every weekend at functions all around the city.

Growing up in Tacoma was rough, to say the least. On November 26, 2009, three days after his release from prison, a man named Maurice Clemmons celebrated Thanksgiving with family and friends in the small town of Pacific, WA. Clemmons was a career criminal with a troubled past. A relative said Clemmons told the gathering that he planned to kill children, cops, and as many people as he could at an intersection.

Three days later, on Sunday morning, Clemmons walked into a Lakewood coffee shop neighboring Tacoma near his home. He approached the counter and, without saying a word, flashed a gun. Next, he turned and began shooting at four Lakewood police officers drinking coffee and working on their laptops. One officer managed to return fire, wounding Clemmons. All four officers were killed.[45]

The shooting instantly became national headlines and rapidly spread around the area. This shooting in Lakewood and the killing of Seattle Officer Timothy Brenton a month earlier revealed the deep divide between law enforcement and communities of color years before the emergence of the Black Lives Matter movement. In November 2009, Western Washington was a hostile place for stocky black men for two days. Clemmons had run from the coffee shop, a gunshot wound in his abdomen, and disappeared. He was quickly identified by coffee shop employees, and a massive manhunt ensued. Police stopped anyone who even resembled him. As a senior in high school, I possessed a vehicle; thus, I was active on the road. I had a skinnier build, but the tension with law enforcement and current situation made me fearful of driving and being pulled over.

The search for Clemmons ended early on December 1st, as Seattle Police Officer Benjamin Kelly was investigating an abandoned car in a south Seattle neighborhood. While he was in his patrol vehicle, writing a report, he saw a man in a hooded sweatshirt coming up from behind him. Kelly recognized Clemmons, got out of the vehicle, and ordered him to show his hands. Clemmons instead moved around the car and reached for his waistband, and Kelly opened fire. Police say Clemmons had a handgun taken from one of the slain Lakewood officers in his pocket. Clemmons was killed during the early morning confrontation with Kelly two days after the murders.[46]

After the manhunt, the strain between police officers and people of color only intensified. Law enforcement, namely the Tacoma Police Department and State Patrol, were justly upset that four of their own were ambushed. Nevertheless, the way they channeled their anger was amiss; it seemed as if they wanted revenge. I recall several people I know being pulled over and harassed for no reason at all, including myself.

In early 2010, the day after my mom and Art had financed a 2007 Pontiac Grand Prix for me, I was pulled over. I was driving down South Tacoma Way, one of Tacoma's main streets, and saw red and blue lights flaring behind me. I hauled over and anxiously waited for the officer. I made sure to keep both hands visible as this was not my first time being pulled over. When the officer approached, he asked me if the car was stolen and who it belonged to. I told him it was mine and my parents had just bought it for me. I forked over my driver's license, insurance, and registration, which denied his suspicion and gave him no cause to proceed any further. Thankfully, he returned with my documents and let me go.

Another time, I was driving on Orchard Street with my brother and some friends. We hadn't committed any violations, so we were surprised when a cop flashed his lights behind us. As soon as the officer reached my vehicle, he asked us where the drugs were. I informed him that we were high school athletes and didn't partake in any drug use. He peeked into the backseat and reluctantly shook his head as he walked away. We were all perplexed by the interaction, which only increased our distrust of the police further. Sadly, this type of association was not a rarity in Tacoma. In my teenage ignorance, I was unaware of my rights, so I did not file charges or tell anyone about the incidents. Nevertheless, maintaining a clean record, yet being treated like a felon was puzzling.

My cousin Antonio wasn't so lucky with his clashes. He was battered by police on several occasions and proceeded to press charges against the officers. I quickly learned the dangers of driving as a young Black man in America. As I grew older, my mindset continued to harden as I witnessed perpetual police brutality against minorities. I learned that it was a culmination of a flawed system, mass incarceration, lack of interaction, and increased racial tensions.

The origins of America's unjust racial order lie in the most brutal institution of enslavement that human beings have ever concocted. More than 12 million Africans of all ages, shackled in the bottom of ships, were sold into a lifetime of forced labor defined by nonstop violence and strategic dehumanization. All were cataloged methodically in sales receipts and ledgers. Around that "peculiar institution," the thinkers of the time crafted an equally inhumane ideology to justify their brutality, using religious rhetoric in tandem with pseudoscience to rationalize treating humans as chattel. After the Civil War, the arrangements of legal slavery were replaced with those of organized, if not strictly legal, terror. Lynchings, disenfranchisement, and indentured servitude all reinforced racial hierarchy from the period of Reconstruction through Jim Crow segregation and on until the movement for civil rights in the middle of the 20th century.[47]

Today, the American criminal justice system is still riddled with biases. As the Washington Post's Radley Balko cataloged, we know that Black people are nearly twice as likely to be pulled over and more likely to be searched once they're stopped even though they're less likely to have contraband; and that unarmed Black people are more than three times as likely to be shot by police as unarmed Whites.[48]

The three main flaws of the criminal justice system are: unconstitutional overcriminalization, point-and-convict adjudication, and near-zero accountability for police and prosecutors.[49] Like the criminal legal system itself, plea bargaining has many shortcomings and serious critics. Some observers say it reinforces unjust outcomes, including supporting bias in our criminal justice system and enabling mass incarceration. Critics also express concern about extreme power imbalances and the trial penalty, which is the fact that defendants often get significantly more prison time at trial if they reject a plea deal. All these factors contribute to pressuring innocent defendants to plead guilty.[50]

Overcriminalization is a dangerous trend that is battled daily. With over 4,450 crimes scattered throughout the federal criminal code, and untold numbers of federal regulatory criminal provisions, our nation's addiction to criminalization backlogs our judiciary, overflows our prisons, and forces innocent individuals to plead guilty not because they actually are, but because exercising their constitutional right to a trial is prohibitively expensive and too much of a risk.

Simply put, mass incarceration is shorthand for the fact that the U.S. incarcerates more people than any nation in the world, including China. And the U.S. is also the leader in the prison population rate. America's approach to punishment often lacks a public safety rationale, disproportionately affects minorities, and inflicts overly harsh sentences.[51]

I actually had a good experience with several officers growing up, primarily the ones assigned to Foss after the shooting. Chief of them were officers Dakarai and Hankins, both Black. Dakarai was the father of a friend, and a huge supporter of my athletic career. He looked out for me during my time at Foss. Hankins was one of my football coaches. Both worked for the Tacoma Police Department and were examples of great police officers.

Even with all of Tacoma's downsides, I would not want to be from anywhere else. It helped make me the man I am today. I'm proud of emerging from the struggle. Being overlooked coming out of Tacoma bestowed a chip on my shoulder every time I lined up against an opponent. Growing up in the hood taught me a great deal and made me resilient. There's a mantra that one of my good friends, Brandon Jimenez, and I say: "If you can make it out of Tacoma, then you can make it through anything." That quote has kept me going at times when I've wanted to give up or been faced with a challenge. "You've been through worse than this in Tacoma," is what I would tell myself.

CHAPTER FOUR

FLY, FIGHT, AND WIN

B asic Military Training (BMT) at USAFA's Prep School is a 2.5-week program with a demanding 24/7 schedule. The USAFA Reporting Instructions state that "BMT will prepare you with the fundamentals of the Air Force life through a transformational process with a deliberate and objective-based training such as behavioral skills development, military skills development, drill and ceremony, military courtesies, and life management skills."[52] Similarly to active duty life and the Cadet Wing at the Academy, candidates are organized into squadrons – three in the case of the Prep School.

Each squadron has a field grade officer who acts as the Air Officer Commanding (AOC) and two non-commissioned officers (NCOs), known as Academy Military Trainers (AMTs). AOCs and AMTs, also known as permanent party, set high standards for the new candidates, and throughout the academic year, they are expected to uphold and exceed those expectations. AOCs and AMTs are invaluable to the Preparatory School experience and provide examples of what it is to be a good, enlisted Airman and officer. The three squadrons, composed of about 80 people each, are Alpha, Bravo, and Charlie; I was placed into Bravo.

The premise of BMT is to indoctrinate you into the military by breaking you down through mental resilience and pushing you past your ceiling, and then building you back up. This could not be closer to the truth; my limits were pushed every day. In fact, I felt like I had been pushed beyond my ceiling, leading me to initiate my discharge paperwork on multiple occasions. At the Prep School, we were allowed to leave under our own free will at any time. After only a week in, I had gotten to the point where I couldn't take the Prep School anymore and didn't think the military was for me. I expressed my displeasure to my mother, but she was adamant that I stay put. She highlighted the opportunity I had in front of me, emphasizing it would all pay off in the end. She demanded, "You better stay your butt at the Prep School!" After careful consideration, I decided to take heed and endure my situation, but not without dismay.

"Basics, welcome to your first full day of basic training. To gauge your physical fitness, we need you to change into Physical Training (PT) gear for your first PT test," ordered one of the training instructors, or cadre. PT tests are the Air Force's way of assessing each Airmen's level of physical fitness. It involved pushups, sit-ups, pull-ups, a long jump, and a 1.5-mile run. There were passing repetition and time requirements for each of the different portions of the test. To pass the PT test, a satisfactory score had to be achieved in each area.

My first PT test as a new member of the military was abysmal. With USAFA's Prep School being in Colorado Springs, the elevation is 6,879 feet above sea level, well over a mile high, hence the reason it was highly suggested that we arrive in peak physical condition. That altitude made it extremely difficult to breathe. I performed satisfactorily on most of the test, but my body was not inhaling enough oxygen to run well. I hit a wall about halfway through the run and started walking to catch my breath. I alternated between walking and running for the remainder of the test. As a result, I failed and was forced to retake it a few weeks later. That worked out great because by then I had gotten more accustomed to the elevation; I passed the test easily my second time around. Overall, it took me a couple of months to fully acclimate to the altitude.

After arrival to BMT, we were loaded onto a bus, and at that moment I knew I was in for a rude awakening. We were commanded to sit up straight with our eyes forward and mouths shut. We were yelled at while descending the bus like a house was on fire; it was unreal. We were then lined up, examined like specimens, and drilled on the seven basic responses allowed by trainees during BMT, which are: "Yes sir/ma'am, no sir/ma'am, no excuse, may I ask a question, may I make a statement, I do not understand, and I do now know." I was immediately overwhelmed. Next, they made us drop and pick up our bags with a sense of urgency and continued to criticize every fault.

One of the first things we did after showing up was take the Oath of Enlistment. Essentially this oath acknowledged that we were "all in," at which point we became members of the Air Force, as enlisted members and placed on active duty for training.[52] There was also a significant emphasis on the Air Force's three core values:

integrity first, service before self, and excellence in all we do. These core values were constantly ingrained in us. The Air Force's mission to fly, fight, and win was also reinforced.

Next, we got haircuts. Logically, I knew this was coming, so I cut my braids off at home two weeks before, rather than being harassed to cut my long hair on the spot. It was extremely difficult letting go of the braids I'd enjoyed for the past 10 years, but I had no choice. The haircut I received at the Prep School was horrible. I almost didn't recognize myself when I looked in the mirror, especially with my clean-shaven face. While I didn't have much facial hair, I looked like a shaved duck without it. Due to my coily hair texture, I soon suffered from ingrown hairs. Shaving became a nuisance for me, causing numerous bumps and scars. Before long, I required a shaving waiver that I would maintain at the Prep School.

Next, we were given uniforms which prescribed eight total hours of standing. I felt like I was in-processing into prison. After that, we were taught how to march. We were taught different marching commands and how to remain in step. There were also times when we ran in formation. Any running during basic training was brutal because running in boots at altitude was demanding. It was even worse when we had to run with our M-14s—I hated that. Marching was emphasized because we were graded on our movements during marching competitions. Marching competitions showcased our ability to follow commands, synchronize our steps, and display which flights could perform the best maneuvers.

In addition to marching were open ranks inspections (ORIs) and rifle counts. ORIs involved lining up in marching formation and being inspected on our uniforms and grooming. In terms of grooming, our hair had to be below an inch and a quarter and could not touch our ears. Our faces had to be clean-shaven unless we had a shaving waiver. For our uniform, all loose threads on our blouses, trousers, and boots had to be removed. If any of these requirements were violated, points were deducted from our flight's final score. Rifle counts consisted of several different rifle motions and positions at the command of our cadre.

We were given countless briefings about honor and the way of the Air Force, but these were sighs of relief because we were able to get off our feet, away from the heat, and even sneak naps at times. Another thing to look forward to was the mandatory sporting activities. As a football player, I couldn't wait to participate in these.

But as soon as practice ended, it was back to reality. I had difficulty sleeping during BMT because I consistently anticipated the abhorrent morning wake-up throughout the night, consisting of thunderous banging and hollering. Without clocks or watches, there was no way to tell the time or when we would be woken up. In addition, we were not allowed to sit in our rooms during basic training. If caught sitting, which happened to a few of my classmates, we were punished as a group and forced to do PT. Additionally, we were taught how to salute with our right hands along with the specifics on how salutes should be rendered.

Room inspections were very thorough. Our dorm rooms included a twin-size bunk bed, a wall locker, and a desk for each of the two occupants. There was a proper location for everything we were allowed to have in our rooms, and we were expected to keep our rooms in perfect order.[51] Our desks had to be categorically organized and could only hold a set number of items. Our beds had to have crisp, 45-degree angle hospital corners, and the fold had to be six inches long, twelve inches from the head of the bed. I never got the hang of hospital corners, so I'd have my prior-enlisted classmate assist me. Prior-enlisted Airmen are individuals who have already served time in the military as an enlisted Airman but decide to attend the USAFA Prep School in hopes of commissioning. Lastly, we were required to stand at attention during room inspections.

The position of attention is assumed by bringing one's heels together smartly and in line with one another. The heels are then placed as near each other as the confirmation of the body permits, and ensure the feet are turned out equally, forming a 45-degree angle. The legs are kept straight without stiffening or locking the knees. The body is erect with hips level, chest lifted, back arched, and shoulders square and even. Arms hang straight down alongside the body without stiffness, and the wrists are straight with the forearms. You place your thumbs, which are resting along the first joint of the forefinger, along with the seams of the trousers or sides of the skirt. The head is kept erect and held straight to the front with the chin drawn in sightly, so the axis of the head and neck is vertical; your eyes are to the front, with the line of sight parallel to the ground. The body's weight rests equally on the heels and balls of both feet, and silence and immobility are required.[53]

One of my favorite parts of basic training was the shooting range. I'd shot plenty of pistols in the past, but this was my first time shooting a rifle. The M-14 was exceptionally fun to shoot. We shot from the kneeling, prone, and standing positions, and wore a gas mask for one of the standing shots. Overall, we were given 50 shots on target from 25 meters away. We needed 25 shots to qualify; I barely qualified with 26 out of 50 shots on target. Granted I didn't perform as well as I'd liked, I was still pleased to qualify.

In terms of physical training, we were beaten all the time. A beating is another name for physical training during BMT. I was under the impression I arrived at BMT in very good shape, but I would soon find out how wrong I was. Everyone had a physical breaking point where they just could not do anymore push-ups or sit-ups. With the cadre being able to rotate out and perform the training, it was impossible to outlast them. I found myself breaking numerous times during BMT. No matter how strong you think you are, muscle fatigue cannot always be overcome. The cadre knew this, and it was all a part of the basic training mind game.

I would say 80% of basic training is mental. A good chunk of it may feel physical, but it's meant to stress your mental fortitude. I had been given this insight by several individuals prior to BMT, but it took me a while to internalize. In addition to being culture shocked, I would often find myself frustrated and upset during BMT. The main factor I took issue with was group punishment for one person's failure. Having to pay for someone else's mistake was a matter I truly struggled with in the military until I gained more self-control. I still had a poor attitude and hated authority, which makes joining the military ironic.

There was one notable incident that took place BMT where I flat out lost my composure. We were standing in formation after having our hour of phone privileges taken because one our classmates had gotten caught sleeping in his desk chair during the day, which was prohibited, so I was already agitated. Then, one of my peers began talking in formation, but I was singled out for it. This pushed me past my boiling point, and I lost it. I cursed out all the cadre, delivering a piece of my mind. The cadre were all appalled by the episode, to the point where they just sent me to my dorm rather than punishing me. They then pulled Bobby Watkins, BWatt for short, aside and told him to check on me because I seemed overly distressed. His consultation went over much better now that I'd cooled down, plus the cadre apologized for the mishap. The cadre also relayed to BWatt that my behavior would not be tolerated again.

One of the first things I did after BMT was meet my sponsor family. The cadet candidate sponsor program offers cadet candidates a home-away-from-home during their 10-month journey at the Prep School. Sponsors act as positive adult role models and provide cadet candidates with a local support system, as many do not have family in the local area. Many sponsors either serve on active duty, in the Air Force Reserve, or are retired military; however, this is not a requirement to become a sponsor.[54] My sponsors were the Burrells. They were the greatest sponsor family I could have asked for and were there for me during my Prep School tenure. In fact, the Burrells became the sponsor family for several of my teammates. Mr. and Mrs. Burrell allowed us to come over whenever we pleased and treated us like kids of their own. They also had two children, Bria and Austin, who became like sisters to us.

Shortly after basic training was the much-anticipated Parents' Weekend. Parents' Weekend takes place over Labor Day weekend. It includes a number of scheduled events such as an academic overview, a commander's welcome briefing, squadron open houses, a parade, and a home football game.[52] Parents' Weekend was one of my favorite times at the Prep School because it allowed for time away from campus, and I was able to spend time with my family. I was so happy to see them after my dreadful BMT experience. My mom and stepdad were able to make the three-hour flight from Tacoma. At the end of the USAFA football game that Saturday, we were permitted to leave campus for the first time since arriving; it was gratifying to calmly sit down and eat at a restaurant without being reprimanded.

Meals were some of the worst stretches of BMT. We had to eat at the position of attention and could not look around or speak without permission. Bringing food to our mouths required a robotic 90-degree motion, and we could only take small bites. We were forced to sit on the front third of our chairs and could not move our heads. Because of all the rules, it was impossible to remember each one and we were constantly grilled, making meals seem like torture.

After marching into formation, parades, including the Parents' Weekend one, almost became a display of attrition. Anytime a parade was on the horizon, we were instructed to hydrate as much as possible because standing at attention in the sun with service dress on, in addition to dehydration, increases one's chances of fainting. "The low rate of blood return to the heart in these situations results in hypoperfusion of the brain, and at times the fainting spell. Standing at attention, or with one's knees locked, may amplify the process."[55] Thus, after about 10-15 minutes of standing, people would begin to fall out. It happened every parade, without fail. This is not something I ever experienced because I made sure to continually bend my knees.

One of the methods of counteracting the blood-pooling problem is to contract the leg muscles or move about, thus stimulating the blood return to the heart and improving circulation to the brain.[55] The other demanding part of parades were the long salutes. We were required to salute during the entire national anthem. The average time to sing the National Anthem is one minute and 57 seconds.[56] Holding salutes for that amount of time was physically exhausting. It became difficult to bear to such a degree that my arm would begin to shake, and nearly fall.

Although the Prep School was strenuous, it did feel good to be on my own as an adult. My mother ran a vastly tight ship and had a lot of rules. She loves to share the story when I was five years old and I told her and Toni, "I can't wait until I'm grown so people can stop telling me what to do!" Well, I finally got my wish, but now the military was telling me what to do, though in a different aspect. The Prep School possessed plenty of rules as well, but they weren't supervisory. They primarily guided our conduct through military instructions, but our personal life was largely unconfined. On the contrary, the Prep School's onerous studies felt like shackles.

STUDENT ATHLETE

The academic year began in August. The Prep School's academic program is tailored to prepare cadet candidates for the rigorous curriculum they will face, with the ultimate goal of becoming a cadet at the U.S. Air Force Academy.[57] The Prep School academic curriculum is delivered over four academic quarters in a 10-month program and is designed to lay the groundwork for success in required Academy classes, focusing on English, math, and science. Each quarter, cadet candidates are evaluated and placed in academic "tracks" that best fit their developmental requirements.

During the first quarter, cadet candidates take a required course in basic study skills to learn time management and study techniques, facilitating the transition to the demanding requirements of Academy academics. All cadet candidates take four classes per quarter—two math, one science, and one English.[57] The course load was much more difficult than high school, but I was able to handle the demand and performed well, at least initially. My best academic showing at the Prep School came in the first quarter, and then it was downhill from there as classes intensified. I started with a strong 3.04 GPA, including an A-, three Bs, and a B-. I expected the rest of the year to be a breeze based on my solid beginning, but I guessed wrong.

In the second quarter, I was introduced to trigonometry and chemistry, both courses I struggled with. Consequently, my GPA dipped to 2.34. The next quarter was even worse once calculus emerged, on top of another chemistry class. Hence, I managed a 2.00 GPA, hardly avoiding academic probation.

Academic probation is placed on individuals who achieve a GPA lower than 2.00 in a quarter or fail a course. Cadets will be removed from all conditions of academic probation when their quarter, core, and cumulative performance meet the minimum GPA of 2.00 with no "F" grades. The popular phrase at the Prep School is "2.00 and go," denoting you were able to advance as long as you achieved a 2.00 GPA. It was a half cynical expression that developed as a result of the challenging academic curriculum. In my final Prep School quarter, I rebounded by attaining a 2.35 GPA, raising my cumulative to 2.45.

Our schedules were exceedingly structured. A candidate starts the day early with morning formation for accountability. Following accountability, breakfast is served in the Dining Facility, and then it's straight to class until they break for lunch. After lunch, candidates will have one hour each day for military training time. After military training, all members are offered Extra Instruction (EI) before attending the three hours of athletics. Dinner is available in the evening, and then it's time to hit the books for Academic Call to Quarters, or study time. Candidates are required to end each day in their room with TAPS and "lights out" to properly rest for the next day's events.[58] TAPS is the nightly bugle call played on the campus intercom to honor fallen soldiers. Due to the robustness of my schedule, I chose not to obtain much EI. My grades surely could have benefitted from tutoring, but that simply was not my priority. After football season, I either used that time to play basketball, work out, take some much-needed time to myself, or nap.

Athletics are a huge part of the Prep School curriculum. Approximately 40% of the cadet candidates attending each year are recruited athletes for any of the 27 NCAA Division I teams at USAFA.[59] As a recruited athlete, my athletics time was spent at football practice. Football at the Prep School was unquestionably different from my expectations when I signed with Air Force. Expecting to play Division I but having to attend a prep school first forced me to shift my mentality. However, I kept in mind that it was only temporary and would make me a better Academy football player. Besides, this unique situation did have a perk: the year of playing football at the Prep School did not count towards my Division I eligibility, so I gave it my best shot.

There were exceptionally talented players on the team, and everyone was Division I caliber. Everyone's story was different, but all roads led to the Prep School for one reason or another. Each player seemed to be highly motivated and, on that account, fostered a particularly competitive environment. The two safety positions entailed a three-way battle between myself, BWatt, and Jordan Mays, two of my better friends at the Prep School. BWatt was from Dallas, TX and had range all over the field. His dad had played in the NFL, and that athleticism had been passed on to his son. Jordan, from North Carolina, was a hardy football player who could tackle especially well. Hence, Bobby would play free safety, and Mays would be the strong safety. I was a bit of a hybrid, so I split time between both positions. What I liked most about sharing time with BWatt and Mays was that we all wanted to see each other succeed. Of course, we were contending for playing time, yet we were still on the same team and had the same goal. This resulted in everyone improving and our practices being extremely fierce.

In addition to the rest of our defense, our offense was truly gifted. Our running backs were the deepest position group, but in my opinion, the best player on our team was wide receiver, Al Lasker. To this day, he is the most skillful receiver I have defended. He was a 6'3", 215-pound freak of nature, also from the Dallas area. Al's athleticism was out of this world. He could outjump everyone on the team and possessed great speed. Undoubtedly, Al should have made it to the NFL purely off talent alone. But Al had a poor attitude at times and dealt with some off-the-field issues, which kept him from reaching the league.

I relished the chance to guard him at practice. It was definitely a chore, but it paid dividends to my coverage ability. The defensive backs had some great battles with our offense, and the team reaped these benefits. One of my best practices came as a result of punishment. Earlier in the day, Justin and I were in Coach Coleman's math class having a blast. We were making jokes about one of our teammates and could not stop laughing, to the point where we disturbed the class. After class, Coach Coleman scolded us, so I thought that was the end of it. Little did I know, our defensive back coach, Nathan Allen, had caught wind of our theatrics. At practice, we were chastised by having to defend each of the receivers one-by-one, with just us two. This retribution was so grim because we weren't given any breaks. After all, it was only us against the dozen or so receivers on the team. It was exhausting! But it was also hugely rewarding. Though fatigued from all the reps, we held our own and did not allow a single catch from any of the receivers. That practice made me a better player and taught me not to clown around in class anymore.

At the Prep School, we played football against junior college level competition as members of the Kansas Jayhawk Community College Conference (KJCCC). The KJCCC is a national junior college conference with some of the best junior college teams in the country. Throughout the 2010 season, we played three nationally ranked teams: #3 Butler, who would move up to #1 by the end of the season and win the regional championship, #4 Coffeyville, and #8 Hutchinson. Teams in the league possessed extraordinary talent, including players who are still in the NFL today.

Our first game was against New Mexico Prep, who we defeated handily, 49-0. Our next game came against New Mexico Military on Friday, September 3rd, of Parents' Weekend. They were a much bigger team than we were. However, we still got away with a score of 33-28. We were able to feed off the additional home crowd visiting for Parents' Weekend. Our third game was on the road against #8 Hutchinson. Our team grew to dislike away games because the road trips were so brutal. We did not have the luxury of flying to our away games like the Air Force Falcons did, so we took a team bus from Colorado to Kansas each time. The bus rides usually lasted between eight and sixteen hours. Accordingly, we were unprepared for our first road game and lost 45-3.

A big reason for the thumping was Cordarrelle Patterson. Patterson finished the game with 19 rushing yards, 118 receiving yards for one touchdown, and 127 yards on two kick returns. He became a first-team All-American that year and the next, granting him numerous offers from upper-tier Division I programs. As a 5-star prospect and the top junior college player in the country, he committed and became the 29th overall pick of the 2013 NFL draft by the Minnesota Vikings. Patterson, currently with the Atlanta Falcons, has played for a total of six teams and even won a Super Bowl. Hutchinson also had Markus Golden, Arizona Cardinals linebacker and 58th overall pick of the 2015 NFL Draft. Markus finished with ten tackles, a sack, and an interception in our contest. Although we suffered a horrific loss, I played a pretty good game. I closed with four tackles, a fumble recovery, and an interception late in the game. BWatt reeled in an interception as well. We were shocked by the pounding, but it proved to be valuable experience for the rest of our season.

Our next game was at home against #3 Butler. This was a much more contested game that we certainly could have won. Our defense played well, but ultimately, our offense was unable to manufacture many points. We ended up losing 21-7. Butler's quarterback was Zach Mettenberger, former LSU, and three-year NFL quarterback. The bright spots for me in this game were that I picked off two of his passes for a total of ten yards and recorded three solo tackles. Performing this well against major Division I recruits was a huge confidence boost for me.

After two straight losses, we finally got back in the win column in our fifth game against Garden City, defeating them 26-14. The following week we faced #4 Coffeyville in Kansas. We fell behind early and never caught up, falling 32-23. The notable name on their team was Duron Carter, son of hall of fame wide receiver Chris Carter. D. Carter had previously attended Ohio State but was declared academically ineligible, resulting in his departure and enrollment at Coffeyville. Although D. Carter yielded 151 yards, we were able to keep him out of the endzone. After the season, D. Carter went on to attend the University of Alabama. Following that loss, we caught our stride and won our remaining five games, defeating our opponents by an average of 38 points. We concluded the season 7-3, obtaining the best record in Prep School history. That record, still held today, was tied by the following year's class.

With football season over, the bulk of my time was spent working out in preparation for the Academy, and playing basketball. I was one of the best basketball players on the football team. Predictably, Al was also elite, in addition to running back Eugene Glenn. We had some tremendously contentious games. Basketball was good because it allowed us to stay in shape while having fun and playing at a high level. I worked out and played basketball just about every day after class, that was until I encountered yet another frightful injury.

It was Saturday, November 20, 2010. Several of my classmates and I were enjoying a highly cherished weekend hanging out in one of the common areas, known as the dayroom. I was casually speaking with one of my peers with my hand on the wall and one of my squadmates closed the heavy day room door and walked out. My hand that was perched on the wall was in between the door hinge. When the door closed, it crushed my left middle finger, causing excruciating pain. My agony was mounting, and the pain became unbearable, so I forcefully yanked my hand from the door. I was silently suffering from the torment, but also temporarily relieved because my finger was finally removed from the wedge. As I walked out of the dayroom, I was shocked by a bevy of screaming and pointing at my finger. I looked down, and to my surprise, blood was profusely gushing, and my fingertip was missing. The weight of the door, amalgamated with the force created from removing my hand, caused the tip of my finger to sever, partially amputating my finger and exposing the bone.

I had only thought my finger was throbbing from being locked in the hinge, hence I did not feel nor notice the residual effects. With blood all over the floor, one of my colleagues wrapped my finger in dozens of paper towels, and another rushed me to the emergency room. There, a doctor placed a couple of sutures inside of my fingertip to assist the wound with closing. It was then bandaged up, and I received a tetanus shot along with an antibiotic injection until I could see a hand surgeon the following Monday.

My finger was constantly pulsating for the next few weeks and continued to hurt; thus, I was given Percocet to help subdue the pain. Upon my examination with the hand doctor on Monday, a digital block and incision were performed. The sutures were then removed to disconnect the dead tissue from my exposed bone. Finally, the soft tissue was closed using an absorbable suture that would not have to be detached again. Unfortunately, they were not able to reattach the missing portion of my finger because the complexity to fasten such a small part was not worth the procedure.

Due to my injury, I was unable to do upper body weightlifting or run for a while. I was only able to go to class and perform leg workouts. It was frustrating to be going through yet another setback, but I knew I would come out on top. On the other hand, I was unhappy with the way things were going at the Prep School. I disliked the military environment, all the restrictions, and the idea of having to endure inferior circumstances as a freshman at the Academy did not sit well with me. For that reason, like many of my teammates, I decided to make a highlight of my Prep School football film and reach out to other colleges. My efforts did not turn up any kickback. There were several colleges still interested but wanted me to walk on, which was still not in the cards for me. Therefore, I stuck things out and focused on my current situation.

As my finger healed, I was slowly able to increase my physical activity. Sadly, some of the nerves had been damaged by the partial amputation, so it was still very sensitive and painful when touched or impacted. That being so, I had to wrap my finger in gauze and elastic bandage anytime I engaged in exercise. When I finally made my way back onto the football field, I was sure to bandage my finger and wear a glove for protection. Regarding the weight room, I was never able to return to full strength when it came to pull-ups. The pressure exuded from pulling my body up weight made my finger throb to the point where I abandoned pull-ups for the next few months. Subsequently, I would always be deficient when it came to pull-ups due to my injury. Yet, it was still possible for me to graduate from the Prep School.

Completion requirements for the Prep School are that each cadet candidate must demonstrate an aptitude for commissioned service and leadership, exhibit satisfactory conduct and personal integrity, and have successfully met all physical, academic, and military requirements.[59] Successful completion of the 10-month Prep School program is critical but not a guarantee of admission to the Academy. Approximately 75–80 percent of cadet candidates are offered appointments annually. The Prep School Commander recommends deserving cadet candidates for appointment to the

Academy Board, the final authority concerning appointments. Nominations are also required for admission to the Academy.[59] With my up and down academic performance and fingertip amputation, I had my reservations about my Academy appointment, fueling my apprehension. Thus, I was unsure if I would be receiving one.

Thankfully, I achieved every completion requirement and participated in the graduation parade, but this did not mean I had been accepted into the Academy. The graduation parade took place in May in front of family and friends. It was such a proud moment, and I felt so accomplished. Unfortunately, my parents could not make the trip, but I was able to have family friend's Paris, and her mom, Nichelle Ferribee, there to support me. Paris and Nichelle were instrumental to my welfare at the Prep School. When my parents found their way to Israelite during my dad's Colorado tour, they met a multitude of great people and eventually became members. The Hardings, who became my Godparents, were one of them; another was the Ferribees. So, in addition to my sponsor family, I also spent time away from the Prep School with the Hardings, but even more with the Ferribees. Paris and her mother enabled me to come over as I wished and would even make home-cooked meals for me. With Prep School graduation now in the books, I anxiously awaited my Air Force Academy appointment while back in Tacoma. Fortunately, I did not have to wait for long as I was given my appointment shortly after graduation. Consequently, I spent the rest of my eight-week summer preparing for my freshman year at the United States Air Force Academy.

CHAPTER FIVE

THE AIR FORCE ACADEMY

Although I had already completed a basic training and graduated from the Prep School, I still needed to fulfill the Academy's six-week Basic Cadet Training (BCT). While this basic training was over twice as long as the Prep School's, I enjoyed a leg up because I knew all about the mind games, in addition to possessing a stronger mentality. I was also in much better physical shape. USAFA appointees come to the Air Force Academy from all over the United States, bringing very different backgrounds and life experiences. The goal of BCT is to quickly adapt these diverse individuals to a military lifestyle and instill the same set of skills and core values in each of them.[60]

The Air Force Academy's BCT began on June 23, 2011. USAFA characterizes BCT as: "During these first six weeks at the Academy, you will develop into highly disciplined, physically fit fourth-class cadets, ready to be accepted into the Cadet Wing. Taking orders from upper-class cadets who may be your age or sometimes younger, may be difficult at first, but these cadets have the authority and responsibility to train you, as they were trained by those that came before them. They will learn to lead while you learn to follow." Fourth-class cadet is one of the names used to address freshmen, as well as four-degree and "Doolie." At the Air Force Academy, one starts out as a four degree or fourth-class cadet and progresses each year until they become a first-class cadet or "firstie" as a senior.

Each member of the incoming class receives a random assignment into one of the 40 cohorts, or squadrons, with approximately 25 other cadets from their class year. These squadrons are not predicated on a sports team or academic major. Cadets live in these squadrons for their entire first academic year, at which time they are randomly shuffled into a different cohort or squadron. While social groups naturally form based upon various clubs, academic interests, and sports teams, every night cadets return to their dormitory rooms where attendance is taken. These rooms are proximate to other squadron mates, effectively disallowing any socially based groups to persist around the clock. Thus, there are no sports team dorms or fraternities and sororities.[61]

My room arrangement was atrocious as I was one of only three cadets in my squadron to be assigned a room of three, rather than the standard two cadets per room. It made cleaning extremely difficult, and personal space was nonexistent, so was privacy. Because willfully entering the hallway to travel risked running into upperclassmen or making a mistake, one of my roommates did so as infrequently as possible. Therefore, when he had to use the restroom in the middle of the night, he elected to urinate in our bedroom sink. This was a disgusting matter to face, establishing unsanitary conditions. The sequence lasted a few weeks before he was confronted. Over time, I learned other cadets dealt with this problem as well.

Even though I possessed an improved mindset, I struggled with being yelled at by people younger than me. This was possible because many cadets enter USAFA directly after high school, some only 17 years of age. With Prep School attendees going the junior college route for a year, we are sometimes older than direct entry sophomores. I knew this was a reality going in, but I still had a hard time grasping it.

There were three different positions we were sanctioned to be in during BCT: attention, ease, and rest. Most of freshman year was spent at attention. Still, there were times when we were allowed to be at ease or rest, in particular when performing a physical activity or being rewarded. The position of rest was usually granted after the football team beat Army or Navy, our service academy rivals. USAFA takes considerable pride in conquering Army and Navy and makes a big deal of it. Thankfully, we beat both teams my freshman year, so I was able to reap the position of rest benefit both times.

Another difference about this basic training was that it had two portions; the first segment took place in the cadet area, and the latter in Jack's Valley. The first BCT focuses on the transition from civilian to military life. Military customs and courtesies, the cadet Honor Code, Air Force heritage, and room inspections may be new areas of study for most, but all cadets are tested on their knowledge and must demonstrate proficiency in drill, rifle-manual competitions, and parades. In addition, during Field Day, squadrons compete against each other in events to test teamwork, such as distance races, log relays, and tug-of-war. When combined with daily physical conditioning, these activities prepare cadets to tackle the physical and mental demands of the second phase of BCT, the academic year, and ultimately, life in the Air Force.[60]

One more dissimilarity between the Prep School and the Academy I noticed right away was the lack of African Americans. USAFA has about 6% of its students being Black, and 64% are White.[62] This was a towering culture shock to me because the Prep School usually has about 21% African Americans, according to a study done by the MLDC between 2006 and 2009, which was more in line with my childhood.[63] This was over a 71% drop in proportion, and I soon noticed the ramifications.

Albeit most prejudice at the Academy was covert due to USAFA's zero-tolerance policy, I still received and observed my fair share of it. In a 2016 interview with *The Atlantic*, Lieutenant General (Lt Gen) Michelle Johnson, former USAFA Superintendent from 2013-2017, acknowledged, "The absence of overt unrest does not mean the absence of discontent." Her comment hints at the reality that while there were few overt instances of race discrimination, there may yet be relatively hidden problems regarding race that do affect cadets and, ultimately, their decision to stay or leave. In this military setting, many White people want to think of the institution as colorblind and only judge its members on their capabilities and service records.

At the same time, many military members of color, in particular African American cadets, have experiences of exclusion and lack of belonging.[64] In general terms, a sense of belonging denotes a feeling of relatedness or connection to others. Although, specific definitions of a sense of school belonging vary. Most researchers maintain that school belonging refers to a student's "sense of being accepted, valued, included, and encouraged by others in the academic classroom setting and of feeling oneself to be an important part of the life and activity of the class."[65]

Examples of how the Air Force messages who belongs and doesn't belong are: the recruiter who doesn't offer special operations opportunities to Black recruits, assuming they can't swim, sends a message. The military trainer who accuses the Black male trainee of having an attitude when he's been conditioned to respond to strength with strength sends a message. The supervisor who determines the

Black airmen's protective hairstyle to be faddish and makes her take out her cornrows sends a message. The Black Air Force Academy cadets who are required to pay for barber and beauty salon services that they can never use because hairstylists are unfamiliar with their hair, sends a message. The Airman teased about his accent by his supervisor, sends a message. The pictures on the wall send a message. We must understand the direct link between a lack of a sense of belonging to the performance issues, behavioral shifts, and poor choices made by our Airmen that lead to administrative action and, radically, own our role.[66]

The essence of having to pay for barbershop fees was baffling to me. At USAFA, a flat toll is deducted from each cadet's pay to cover haircuts and styling at the campus barbershop. This was bothersome because none of the barbers were Black, nor were they competent in cutting Black cadet's hair. Therefore, to get a decent haircut, we needed to go off base to a civilian barbershop for a trim. Yet, this did not result in a refund of our cadet barbershop bill. We had to bite the bullet and pay the duplicate expense.

Furthermore, I was often singled out for having an attitude because of the way I was taught to react when treated aggressively. I'd improved the way I responded to authority since the Prep School, but I still I only knew how to meet force with force, and there was no mercy for that instilled behavior. I was also called out for my stroll, being told that "I walked with too much swag to be in the military." These were challenging circumstances to navigate, and directly contributed to my unique Academy experience.

In her doctoral dissertation titled *Sense of Belonging and Racial Diversity at the U.S. Service Academies*, Leah Pound, USAFA graduate and Doctor of Philosophy, declared "Anecdotally, I have witnessed incidents during my time as a junior faculty member at one of the service academies that suggest that a lack of sense of belonging can spiral a cadet of color into deciding to leave despite having the formal credentials to graduate." A lack of sense of belonging is associated with negative effects on students who live on campus. Low belonging can undermine academic performance and increase perceptions of campus discrimination in a hostile campus racial climate. Further, having a low sense of belonging has discernable impacts on the mental and emotional well-being of college students. It has been linked with psychological distress, depression, stress, an increase in problem behaviors and a decrease in positive coping skills and levels of belonging can moderate psychological adjustment; i.e., improving or worsening adjustment to college life.

At worst, failure to belong can lead to detriments in mental and physical health, and suicide. Claude Steele, an American social psychologist and Professor of Psychology at Stanford University, argues, "African American college students face doubt about whether they belong or will succeed in rigorous academic environments, given the history of negative stereotypes about the academic abilities of African American students." Supporting Steele, Terrell Strayhorn, Virginia Union University Provost & Senior Vice President, Professor & Director, notes, "African Americans attending Predominantly White Institutions (PWIs) report feeling alienated, marginalized, socially isolated, unsupported, and unwelcomed by their peers and faculty members."

A common theme across the country is also existent at USAFA. Black students recognize that race relations are strained, and White students do not think there is anything wrong. With racial disparity in the Air Force, White male Airmen are placed in a position of plausible deniability while the taxpayers' investment works to stabilize a force built on an increasingly damaged foundation of inequity and inequality.[66] In a 2016 study of 2,635 students from an unspecified service academy, Black students reported a significantly lower sense of belonging and poorer perceptions of the institution's commitment to diversity than did White students. Belonging is typically seen as central to self-esteem and is one of Maslow's basic human needs.[67] Maslow's hierarchy of needs is a motivational theory in psychology comprising a five-tier model of human needs, often depicted as hierarchical levels within a pyramid.

From the bottom of the hierarchy upwards, the needs are physiological, safety, love, esteem, and self-actualization. Needs lower down in the hierarchy must be satisfied before individuals can attend to needs higher up. This five-stage model can be divided into deficiency needs and growth needs. The first four levels are often referred to as deficiency needs. Deficiency needs arise due to deprivation and are said to motivate people when they are unmet. Also, the motivation to fulfill such needs will become stronger the longer the duration they are denied.

Esteem needs are the fifth level in Maslow's hierarchy. Our esteem needs involve the desire to feel good about ourselves. According to Maslow, esteem needs include two components. The first requires feeling self-confidence and feeling good about oneself. The second component involves feeling valued by others; that is, feeling that other people have recognized our achievements and contributions. When people's esteem needs are met, they feel confident and see their contributions and achievements as valuable and essential. However, when their esteem needs are not met, they may experience what psychologist Alfred Adler called "feelings of inferiority."[68]

I experienced this lack of self-confidence early into my academic career at the Academy. The Academy's rigor simply did not assure me of my ability to perform in the classroom, nor did my peers. I was confident going into the school year, considering my academic performance in high school and the Prep School's difficulty. However, I soon learned I was in for a rude awakening. Not receiving a direct appointment to the Academy, in addition to hearing my peer's educational achievements in high school and my premature Academy grades, instantly made me feel inferior. My educational confidence and self-esteem from high school and the Prep School vanished soon after classes started. I doubted I could compete with my classmates, holding true during my cadet career.

Black students are unequally burdened with negative cross-racial interactions and the harm it brings to their psychological well-being. Their White participants reported experiencing less of the negative type of cross-racial interactions as compared to our Black participants. In a military academy, the permanent party members represent the authorities and become embodiments of military policy. Black and White students are generally being told the same diversity messages from the institution and instructors during class. Still, those messages might be interpreted differently, depending on experience, schemas regarding racism, or other memories and mindsets associated with the students' race.

The significant differences found between Black and White students' perceptions of institutional commitment to diversity suggest that it is a racially subjective experience. Black and White students disagreed on their perceptions of the institution's commitment to diversity, with Black students consistently having more negative impressions than White students.[64] This was true in my case. As I previously mentioned, the Academy did not seem diverse at all, especially with my cultural background. The Academy claimed it was diverse, but I saw otherwise anytime I looked around me.

In 2017, a study was conducted by the National Public Radio and the Harvard T.H. Chan School of Public Health on 802 Black adults. Their findings reported the more money Blacks have, the more they report experiencing interpersonal discrimination and differential treatment. This means that Black adults higher in socioeconomic status (SES) face more prejudice. Black students at the U.S. service academies find themselves experiencing this bind of Black success. Attending a service academy is a competitive and elite process. And as Strayhorn and Dr. Royel Johnson, Assistant Professor of Education at Penn State, pointed out, Black students are forced to interact with White students simply because there are so many of them proportionately on a PWI campus.

Black cadets have even less opportunity for complete self-segregation because of mandatory training and living environments. Regardless of their own SES or previous exposure to White people, Black cadets are immersed into a large, novel group of high-status White people. They will routinely interact with upper-income White cadets who potentially have had limited exposure to non-White people. This experience can be described as "the bind of Black success:" not only are Black people higher in the SES in more contact with White people, they also "more acutely experienced the stakes of being in direct competition with them.[64] This phenomenon was precise in my encounter, as I had never interacted with so many White people in my life, let alone high-status ones. Accordingly, I was in unfamiliar territory. It took some getting used to and required a shift in my approach, also known as "playing the game." This included behaving politely, going with the flow, and even going out of my way to appear more invested than I actually was at times.

White faculty tend to explain or rationalize or downplay minority students' experiences because they believe it helps the student move past the damaging experience. However, denying someone's reality and feelings can be damaging. All in all, any one of the single negative impacts of a low sense of belonging mentioned above is enough to impede academic success and decrease a student's motivation to graduate. In 2015, the attrition rate for Black cadets at USAFA was 35.4% for the junior class compared to the attrition rate for White cadets at 21.3%.[64]

A combination of these deficiencies can lead to social identity threats. Social identity threat describes a social psychological process that 'occurs when an individual's self-view is challenged' based on membership in a social group with a negative reputation. It can detrimentally affect performance when an individual's group is of low social status, culturally/structurally marginalized, or in an unfavorable comparative relationship to other groups.

One prominent form is a stereotype threat, the threat of being judged as a member of a negatively stereotyped group, such as African American students, with respect to general academic ability. The consequences of threats, increased vigilance, threat appraisal, and lower performance—are recursive. Increased vigilance can lead to a greater perception of danger, therefore increasing vigilance further. Situational threats lead to poor performance, which begets perceived threats. These social psychological feedback processes may explain some of the negative trajectories that African American and Hispanic students experience in school, especially given that schools are a location where evaluative scenarios are "chronic."[69] This is exactly what I experienced during my time at the Academy; I did not feel like I belonged. I also felt marginalized and expected to perform worse by others because I was Black, impairing my mentality.

One way to combat social identity threat is through self-affirmation. Self-affirmation is asserting personally important values. It is reported to have "behavioral or cognitive effects that bolster the perceived integrity of the self, one's overall self-image as competent, effective, and able to control important outcomes." By affirming personally important values other than school, such as family, religion, or sports, vulnerable students acquire resources that buffer them against the negative consequences of identity threats. For instance, a potentially susceptible student who has reflected on the value of her sports participation may be less likely to interpret negative teacher feedback as a threat to her sense of belonging in the academic domain, therefore heading off a negative performance-evaluation feedback loop.[69] Self-affirmation is the same concept I implemented. Throughout my time as a cadet, I continuously proclaimed how proud my family was of me and that I had to persevere for them. I assured myself that God was with me, and he would not let me down. My merit as a Division I football player was monstrous because it asserted my motive for selecting the Academy. It also served as a stimulus to perform well in the classroom, driving me to circumvent academic probation so I didn't miss time on the field.

From day one, my Academy experience was much different than that of my peers. I was often set aside during training sessions and received extra physical training. I was accused of plagiarism for a well-written paper that was properly cited. Additionally, I was often the only African American in my classes. During their college experience, many minority students face instances of racism, tokenism, stereotyping, lack of college preparedness, and social marginalization. Negative minority student experiences become observable through several indicators, including minority student retention rates and minority student sense of "fit"—a student's feeling of academic and social integration into their institution.[69] Even though I was able to withstand the Academy, many of my colored friends did not. Sadly, more of my companions were dismissed from the Academy than those who survived.

Furthermore, the involvement of minority faculty has a positive impact on the experience of minority students.[70] Throughout my scholastic career at the Academy, I only had one African American professor, which wasn't until a majors course my senior year. A study conducted by the GAO in 1993 determined the following: while minority cadets had comparable physical fitness scores, they had lower academic admissions scores, academic grade point averages, and military performance averages than White cadets. Minorities were also subjected to more academic and honor reviews than Whites. Minority cadets had higher attrition rates, and proportionately fewer minority cadets were either in the top 50% or the top 15% of their graduating classes.[71]

Of the 19 million undergraduate students enrolled in higher education in the United States in 2012, fewer than 5% were African American males.[72] I knew graduating from a university would be a notable achievement because I was the first in my immediate family to attempt the feat, but I was unaware of the extent or statistics behind it. Unlike White students, whose social integration into the college environment may occur primarily with peer interactions, social integration for minority students occurs through more formal associations like involvement in out-of-class organizations. Although there are several types of out-of-class organizations that African American students can be involved with, they often join organizations established to support their particular affinity group. Researchers propose that these "in-group" friendships affect a student's social and academic adjustment to campus.[73] One benefit of the Prep School was that it allowed me to establish some very good friendships, which carried over to the Academy. We were able to lean on each other and provide support when necessary. I also joined the USAFA Way of Life Committee (WLC).

The USAFA WLC is the largest mission/affinity club open to all cadets with over 200 members, like Black Student Unions at other college and university institutions. The WLC is dedicated to promoting and preserving cultural consciousness, excellence, integrity, and service. The WLC sponsors activities open to the entire Cadet Wing to encourage professional, academic, and social engagement throughout the academic year. WLC members also represent USAFA at national professional conferences (engineering, management, and leadership) and local community service activities. The club helps broaden the experiences of all members of the entire Cadet Wing. It increases multicultural awareness through community service, cultural activities, and open discussions on cultural/inclusion issues affecting USAFA, the USAF, and communities throughout the nation/world.

By exposing members to different ideas, cultures, and experiences, cadets are better equipped as leaders to make decisions necessary to improve the social climate and encourage mutual support among the Cadet Wing and organizations they will lead as future officers. The club provides cadets opportunities in leadership, personnel management, logistics, and long-range planning similar to that expected of future officers.[74] The WLC was an enormous benefit to my time as a cadet. Speakers at the meetings frequently provided stimulating words that kept me going. Equally, I met minorities in leadership positions and expanded my network.

Establishing a mentoring relationship with a faculty member can be perceived as one of the most important relationships a student can form in college. Influential faculty mentors provide mentees with knowledge, advice, challenge, and support. Although research suggests that faculty relationships are essential for minority students, they are even more significant for African American students. In a study involving over 1,200 college students, it was found that African American students demonstrated the strongest positive correlation between frequency of out-of-class contact with faculty and GPA.[73]

I received superb mentorship from faculty members while attending the Academy. Chief of them being Lieutenant Colonel (Lt Col Pipes), Lt Col Vanagas, Major Jason Harris, Coach Eldrick Hill, and Sgt Derek Davidson. Their guidance was so instrumental because many of them had played football at the Academy and been in my shoes, so they knew exactly what I was going through. They were also where I wanted to be in life and inspired me to persist. All of them were great role models who wanted to see me succeed, hence they helped in every way possible. I needed this counsel to help me brave the Academy's demands, especially BCT.

BCT days seemed to be eternal. They began every day at 4:30 a.m. and finished around 9:30 p.m. By the time I laid my head down I would be exhausted and fall right asleep. The end of long BCT days was one of my favorite times because we were allowed to read and write letters to friends and family. In those letters, I expressed my strong dislike for BCT, especially inspections.

Room inspections, AMI for morning inspection, and SAMI on Saturdays, were much worse at the Academy than the Prep School. Even after BCT, rooms had to be maintained in inspection order each morning during the school week until noon and on training Saturdays until completion of training.[75] Each room was looked over for roughly two minutes and while the room was being inspected, the cadets were required to stand at attention in the middle of the room. Otherwise, the cadets were allowed to be at ease in their rooms, whether that meant working on homework, talking amongst themselves, or visiting with other cadets in their rooms.

The cadets leading this SAMI had rules and measured bed folds, folded shirts and shorts, and checked for dust in certain areas of the room, as well as the floor for cleanliness.[76] The graders followed strict criteria they used to score our rooms. Our closets had to be aligned in a specific order, along with the display of a specific number of clothing items. Our hats and belts were to be distinctly displayed. The inspectors used white gloves to scan for dust, and any speck of it resulted in a deduction. Our drawers needed to be precisely organized, and any clothing items off by a quarter of an inch or more were docked. We were not permitted to display any civilian clothes in our rooms. Our beds required the same tedious folding as the Prep School. SAMIs were extremely painstaking and took several hours to prepare for, even with our rooms already in decent order.

The first two days of BCT were spent in-processing, including the swearing-in ceremony, uniform and equipment issue, and orientation briefs. The pinnacle of the briefings we received surrounded the Honor Code. The Honor Code is the cornerstone of a cadet's professional training and development - the minimum standard of ethical conduct that cadets expect of themselves and their fellow cadets. The Honor Code was developed and adopted by the class of 1959, the first class to graduate from the Academy, and has been handed down to every subsequent class.

Cadets are considered "guardians and stewards" of the code. Cadet honor representatives are chosen by senior leadership and oversee the honor system by conducting education classes and investigating suspected honor violations. Honor violations occur when a cadet lies, steals, or cheats. Cadets throughout the wing are expected to sit on honor boards as juries that determine whether fellow cadets violated the code. Cadets also recommend sanctions for violations. The presumed sanction for an honor violation is disenrollment but mitigating factors may result in the violator being placed in a probationary status. This "honor probation" is usually only reserved for cadets in their first two years at the Academy to reinforce the importance of honor, character, and integrity to future officers; cadets are given an extensive character and leadership curriculum.[77]

Uniform issue was the worst part of the first two days of BCT and required 10 hours of standing, even worse than the Prep School. Not only that, but all the equipment was placed in a large military duffle bag that we had to carry in our left hands, instead of on our backs. This was a form of hazing which continued throughout freshman year. Left hands were designated so that our right hands could be free in case we had to salute an upperclassman or permanent party.

Our class color, which rotates every year, was gold; hence we were given gold caps as we in-processed. Red, blue, and gold were chosen as the original Academy colors representing the three primary colors in modern architecture. Silver was later added as the fourth and final color to represent stainless steel to mirror aircraft technology. Gold represents the grasses on the plains.[78] The first USAFA class (1959) was a gold class.[79] The residential and educational buildings are gold as well. In addition to our gold caps, we were given class-colored comforters and blue robes with gold trim. The comforters were required to be displayed as part of our bedding.

Our class exemplars were Wilbur and Orville Wright, also known as the Wright Brothers. The cadet exemplar program is both a leadership development and heritage education program. It is designed to provide a role model—in the form of an aerospace leader of the past—for cadets of each class to emulate. It is also meant to instill pride and provide a connection to our nation's Air Force heritage. Each cadet class will form an exemplar committee, nominate and select an exemplar, and then maintain their identity with that exemplar through a class-wide exemplar dinner, an exemplar display case, and other activities throughout the class's tenure at the U.S. Air Force Academy. Since the Class of 2000, each class has chosen someone who "exemplifies" the type of person the class wishes to emulate.[80] Wilbur and Orville Wright were American inventors and pioneers of aviation. In 1903 the Wright brothers achieved the first powered, sustained, and controlled airplane flight; they surpassed their milestone two years later when they built and flew the first fully practical airplane.[81]

Days 3-5 of BCT incorporated administrative requirements such as academic placement tests and medical/dental clearance. Days 6-24 consisted of Physical Fitness Tests (PFTs), military drill movements, military customs and courtesies, inspections, Uniformed Code of Military Justice, Air Force heritage and education, and Air Force capabilities demonstration. The PFT was the same as the Prep School one. Due to my improved physical fitness, I was able to pass initially this time around.

The second BCT expands upon the military and physical preparation of the first BCT, taking cadets to Jacks Valley, a 3,300-acre rural training area on Academy grounds. Cadets march to and from Jacks Valley, where activities push their physical limits to build self-confidence, and teamwork skills. Second, BCT also introduces cadets to small-unit tactics and firearms.[53] Our tent sleeping arrangement in Jacks Valley was dreadful. We slept on cots with about 10 basic cadets per tent. Accordingly, space and privacy were even more limited that the dorms.

We marched everywhere during BCT and a sizable amount the rest of my cadet career. We marched to lunch every day as part of the daily noon meal formation. This formation was usually only canceled during inclement weather. Marching as a group is an effective way to travel from training event to training event during BCT. Most of all, drill is instilling discipline and order in everyone in the flight. You cannot get from A to B without moving together as a team.

First and foremost, the military is a team, and being able to conform to the team's standards is critical to all military members. Drill teaches you not only to perform as a team but helps your flight get ready to look good during the final graduation parade. Somewhere in the middle of basic training, the basics will probably learn some marching "jodies." A jodie is a marching song. These are sung during non-formal marching events, typically done when traveling or running as a group. These songs/cadences are done when you are doing PT and not marching to the beat of the drummer of the band in formal appearances.[82]

I found marching to be futile as I never saw the purpose behind it. At no time did I understand how marching would help me become a better officer, especially when it is not a part of operational Air Force. Days 25-35 encompassed first aid, field living conditions, combat arms, military training courses, and culminated with a capstone field training exercise. The last four days of BCT focused on transitioning to academics.

While in Jacks Valley, there was a cosmic flu outbreak, known as the Norovirus. On July 26, 2011, Air Force Academy officials announced that they were treating basic cadets and active duty service members for cases of gastroenteritis, or the stomach flu. All included, there were about 240 cadets (18%) and active duty personnel receiving treatment. As a result, medical group officials took measures to prevent the virus from spreading. Approximately 180 basic cadets were removed from training in Jacks Valley and bused to Vandenberg Hall, where they were placed in isolation.

Flight surgeon Dr. Ruth German provided his disposition for the outbreak expressing, "Basic cadets are placed under physical and mental stress during BCT, which can compromise their immune systems. In addition, while cadets live in close quarters throughout their four years at the Academy, this is even more true during BCT. The field environment of Jacks Valley makes disease prevention that much more complicated. It's much more difficult to maintain sanitary conditions. When you're camping, your sanitation is not as good as when you're at home."[83] I was one of the cadets that suffered stomach flu symptoms. The vomiting and constant stomach pain made me feel lifeless. Ailing in the infirmary amongst my sick classmates was horrendous and a very unpleasant place to be. But at the same time, it was also a relief to be separated from BCT and resting while I was symptomatic. I was quarantined for a handful of days before I was healthy enough to return to BCT, just in time for one of my favorite activities.

During the Jacks Valley portion of basic training, there was a fervent pugil stick competition. The winner was crowned the "Big Bad Basic." I could not wait for this contest. All my anger and frustration built up from being yelled at and hazed was burning to get out. The weapon of choice was a pugil stick, a four-foot-long pole with padding on both ends and grips in the middle. Cadets are expected to use fighting techniques they learned during field training to make definitive head or body contact with opponents. One solid prod equals one point, three points, or a knockdown for a win. The Big Bad Basic competition is the final test of the freshman's six-week training. It puts freshman cadets in single combat against classmates in a circular sandpit.[84]

My opening fight did not go as expected. First, I gauged my opponent, and then we tapped pugil sticks. The whistle blew, and the fight was on. The first few moments were spent feeling each other out with jabs. Then, I noticed there was a hole in his defense and took advantage of it. With my right hand at the top of the stick, I quickly swung and hammered my opponent with a forcible blow to the head, knocking him to the ground. The fight was over just seconds after it started. The medical team escorted him to the hospital, where he was diagnosed with a concussion. Thankfully, he ended up being alright. But I was thrilled with the results of my first match and assured I could win the tournament.

In my second match, I was up against a much bigger cadet. He had won his previous match by a landslide, so I knew he was a respectable fighter. Keeping this in mind, I tried to use my speed and keep my distance. I then planned to take my shots when I saw an opening. His power was overbearing, though, and eventually, he knocked me out of the ring. I was disappointed by the loss, but still had a great time. All in all, this was one of the better parts of basic training that made for an enjoyable experience.

The very best part of basic training was the beginning of athletic activities. Our first football game was on September 3rd, which meant training camp started on August 1st. With freshman players undergoing BCT, we were still able to attend football practice. This was a huge break from training and refreshing during a strenuous time, albeit football was no easier; it was just more rewarding. Training camp was extremely tough, especially for us freshmen coming to the elevation from sea-level states. It was hot, and the air in Colorado was exceptionally dry, making it that much harder to breathe. I gave it my all during training camp, but I was not fortunate enough to make the Falcons varsity football team. The AFA is one of the few colleges that houses a JV team for freshmen who do not play significant time, on top of being on the scout team. The benefit of this is it allows freshmen to continue developing and gain meaningful experience in games against real opponents. A couple of days after football camp began, I reached another milestone.

On August 3rd, my class was formally accepted into the Cadet Wing during the Acceptance Day Parade. This parade marks the transition into the academic year and the acceptance of new fourth-class cadets into the Cadet Wing.[59] In a ceremony associated with the parade, the newly minted fourth-class cadets culminate the intensive BCT core values, honor, ethics, and human relations training by taking the Academy's Honor Code Oath and pledging to live by its principles. The oath is administered to fourth-class cadets when they are formally accepted into the wing at the conclusion of BCT. The oath has remained unchanged since its adoption in 1984 and consists of a statement of the code, followed by a resolution to live honorably: "We will not lie, steal, or cheat, nor tolerate among us anyone who does. Furthermore, I resolve to do my duty and to live honorably, so help me God."[77]

We were also supplied with copies of Contrails from our legacy class of 1975. Contrails are the Air Force Academy handbook, or "cadet Bible," containing information on the United States Air Force and United States military history; Academy history; notable Academy graduates; aircraft, and munitions in the current U.S. Air Force inventory; transcripts of important national documents such as the Preamble to the U.S. Constitution and the full national anthem; also included are famous quotes, which are usually patriotic, or leadership related. Cadets in the fourth-class year are expected to learn most of the information from Contrails and be able to recite much of it verbatim.[85] Contrails are issued to all cadets entering the USAF Academy. To round off the Acceptance Day Parade, we exchanged our gold baseball caps for Airman Battle Uniform (ABU) caps and joined cadets from the classes of 2012, 2013, and 2014.[86] We were now referred to as cadets and no longer basic cadets.

Many segments of Contrails are recited during PT and exertion. Academy graduate Regan Hefner eloquently describes the freshman year Knowledge Tests: before each test, we are given an outline pertaining to that week's pertinent information required for memorization on that week's Knowledge Test. "Cadets must get above 80% to pass. Quotes are a major part of the Knowledge Tests. Some of the quotes are over 150 words long, and everything must be exactly rewritten on the test as shown in the Contrails, or it is considered incorrect. This means if you do not capitalize a letter, forget punctuation, or write the word two instead of spelling it numerically as 2, you are wrong and will likely fail. As a result, my classmates and I are always kept very busy. Each cadet is expected to know the entire military chain of command, starting with government officials, followed by the Academy military leadership, the Cadet Wing, your group, and finally, all upperclassmen within your squadron. Upperclassmen greetings included an individual's rank, first name, middle initial, and last name, followed by their full job title, and it ended with saying our squadron call sign with pride. In total, this comes to knowing details for approximately 200 people."[85]

This quote rings entirely true. With education and football taking up much of my life, I did not have much time to study Contrails. Time management is crucial at the Academy, and academics hold substantially more weight than Knowledge Tests. I would normally study the outline last minute and hope for the best. I generally passed my Knowledge Tests because the information wasn't too complex, so I was able to grasp it quickly, although I did fail a reasonable amount of them. My sophomore "coach" was a prodigious help as well. Each four-degree is assigned a three-degree coach to assist with fourth-class progress, including Knowledge Tests. Our scores counted towards 25% of their Military Performance Average (MPA), so sophomores had a vested interest in our success. The other key to my prosperity was acquiring help from my classmates and studying with them as a group. Concerted learning was chief because if we collectively did poorly enough, we could be restricted from leaving the premises, which happened on several occasions. Moreover, we were graded on our military performance as well.

Not only were we required to maintain a 2.00 GPA equivalent to the Prep School, but we also had to maintain a 2.00 MPA. An MPA is a rating received by cadets through military performance evaluations at the end of academic semesters and summer leadership programs. The cumulative MPA is the average of

MPAs from previous semesters and summer programs. To get the best possible representation of a cadet's performance, inputs for semester MPAs come from a variety of sources including instructors, coaches, officers in charge, the primary rater, additional rater, leadership attributes survey, and the professional development program. Several factors determine a cadet's MPA. Cadets receive ratings in military bearing, job performance, professional knowledge, personal appearance, initiative, attitude, and leadership ability. In addition, each cadet receives an individual rating from their primary rater—usually a cadet supervisor—and an additional rater, the next ranking member in the cadet's chain of command.

This rating process provides cadets with detailed feedback on their performance and helps to set the standard for future performance. Like GPA, the MPA is also graded on a 4.00 scale. An MPA rating below 2.00 is a deficient evaluation and is subject to review as required by USAFA directives.[87] I managed to keep my MPA above 2.00 throughout my term at the Academy, which was fairly easy. An MPA below 2.00 requires serious misconduct or consistent misbehavior. MPA, along with GPA, and Physical Education Average (PEA) amalgamate to make up a cadet's Overall Performance Average (OPA). GPA is 60%, MPA 30%, and PEA 10%.[88] OPA is what determines one's class rank. PEA, which included football, was by far my best area.

Altogether, playing football at the Air Force Academy was one of the best ordeals of my life; one I will always cherish. It was an experience filled with blood, sweat, and tears. I was able to play in multiple bowl games, visit the White House, start several contests, and travel across the country. I didn't enjoy every minute of it, but it was worthwhile. The downfall of my career was injuries, and that's something I still struggle with today. But generally speaking, I am content with my time on the football field.

What I also appreciate about playing football at the Academy is our resilience. Student athletes at civilian universities aren't burdened with hefty course loads and military training like cadets are. Therefore, they have a lot more time to devote to football. Moreover, Air Force doesn't receive the same caliber of players as most schools and our linemen are often much smaller due to the Academy's weight restrictions. Nevertheless, year after year, aside from irregular down seasons, Air Force manages to not only compete against other teams, but prevail against them as well. This is a testament to the type of intelligent, hardworking, overlooked, and steadfast players who commit to Air Force. It is also a reflection of head coach Troy Calhoun, prior Houston Texas offensive coordinator and Denver Broncos assistant. Coach Calhoun, former Falcons quarterback and 1989 graduate, has been a staple of continuity since taking over the Falcons in 2007 with a record of 114-76 and 11 bowl game appearances. He is a sound coach who focuses on grit and developing well-rounded football players of character, on and off the field.

Based on Coach Warren's assurances during my visit, I walked into training camp highly confident. The main difference I noticed right away between Division I football and high school was just how technical football is. In high school, we played one coverage, and I just roamed the field at free safety. We played some of the same coverages at the Prep School, but they were condensed for simplicity. I was already a serviceable tackler, could defeat blocks, and possessed tremendous ball skills. But at the Division I level, each player has a precise assignment on every play. Alignments in terms of your location on the field are critical to fulfilling your job. Technique, play recognition, formations, and coverages were all paramount additions as well.

Consequently, it took me a while to learn all these new facets. I worked my butt off, but ultimately, I was not ready to assume the starting varsity safety role Coach Warren had presented. I knew I could contribute to the varsity in a useful capacity, so I was thoroughly disappointed I did not see any varsity playing time at all. Coach Warren was a very rugged coach and expected perfection from his players, which I could not provide right away. Since I was on JV with a separate set of coaches, I did not have much interaction with him my freshman year, so most of my observations came from afar. But none of our communication was like it had been on my visit.

I did not play varsity my freshman year thanks to Jon Davis. Davis was an All-Conference safety and one of the team's best players. He was a great leader who I learned a lot from. I was coached by JV defensive back coaches, John Rudzinski, Rud for short, and Reggie Rembert, former Falcon All-American cornerback, and good friend of mine today. Coach Rud recently accepted the defensive coordinator job at the University of Virginia. He may have been more rigid than Coach Warren. He was a foregoing USAFA linebacker and wanted us to play the game savagely. I loved his enthusiasm because he was always full of energy, even if he was a little rough around the edges. Reggie was much more sociable. He, too, expected great things from his players, but he took a lighter approach. Despite their differences, they were both great coaches I enjoyed playing for.

Playing JV was yet another humbling experience I coped with. Nevertheless, I played well in the games and had fun being able to let loose on other teams. My involvement on the scout team was terrible though. We had to follow play cards for the varsity's weekly opponent to the "T." If we ran the play incorrectly, we were rebuked and forced to run it until we got it right. With expectations so high on varsity, they banked on demolishing the scout team.

For this reason, the varsity treated us harshly at practice—hitting us after the whistle, grabbing us, and committing all types of infractions that would be penalties in real games. I did not take too kindly to this with my competitive spirit and pride, so I stood my ground and defended myself when I felt disrespected. This resulted in numerous altercations that I did not mind being a part of.

Regardless of my situation on the football team, it was still a getaway from the cadet area, or the Hill. Treatment on the Hill was gruesome compared to the football field. Life on the Hill was nothing but onerous academics, military training, and deflating freshman year obligations such as PT, running the strips, censure, and greeting upperclassmen. Football was an essential escape from all of that. The adversity on the football field was something I'd faced before, so I knew I'd overcome it. Although it was temporary, I did not share the same sentiment about the depleting cadet area.

While I was only on JV, I earned the respect of the coaches and upperclassmen in a short time; I became known as a gritty football player. The best part about playing JV was executing well against the varsity. There were some practices when I would intercept the starting quarterback, earning recognition from my coaches. What made things harsher was some of my freshman teammates were playing varsity while I was stuck on JV. BWatt, Jordan, Ryan Pollard, and Jon Lee were a few of the ones fortunate enough to play varsity. I wished them the best but nevertheless, I was unhappy with my situation. The varsity finished 7-6 and lost by a single point to Toledo in the Military Bowl. On the bright side, they were victorious in bringing home the Commanders-in-Chief (CIC) trophy, each of the service's academies' most sought-after prize.

The CIC is awarded to the service academy that wins the triple-threat match between the schools. If the competition for that year is tied, the previous year's winner retains it. Since its initiation in 1972, the trophy has been awarded to Air Force 20 times, Navy 16 times, and Army 9 times, with four ties. In addition, the President of the United States often awards the trophy himself at the White House for its presentation. The 2.5-foot-tall, 170-pound trophy is topped with three footballs that rise above figurines of the mascots of the three academies.[89] The Commander-in-Chief's Trophy is one of only two NCAA Division I FBS triangular rivalry trophies awarded annually.[90]

The last game of my freshman season was the JV's rivalry game against the Prep School. There was a lot of trash talk leading up to the highly anticipated game, making it that much more heated. It was an extraordinarily competitive game that we went on to lose. On the last play of the game, I tackled the elusive Jaleel Awini low and immediately felt a pop in my left foot. I could walk off the field after the game, but once we made it to the bus, I knew something was wrong; my foot was pulsating. I immediately went to the training room and let the team doctors know. They examined my foot and conducted some imaging. Days later, I learned I had suffered torn a ligament in my foot, yet another setback. I was situated in a boot and given crutches for several weeks. Commuting on crutches during Colorado's harsh winter between distant facilities made the injury even worse. This was a towering inconvenience, but as always, I made do. I received treatment every day in an attempt to expedite my recovery. It was dreary, but necessary if I wanted to be ready for spring football in March.

Frustratingly, I was forced to miss a portion of offseason workouts. Although I never enjoyed working out, I understood it was necessary to be a sound football player, so I worked hard. I was too motivated to taste varsity action not to persist. That being so, my rehabilitation went well enough for me to return just in time for "Cages." Cages are two days of fierce offseason workouts designed to push players past their limits, develop camaraderie, and determine which players are mentally tough. Cages were undeniably the most tiring workouts I've ever done. The workouts commenced at 5:00 a.m. on school days. There were eight stations set up on the indoor practice field, each with a different drill. The drills were run by position coaches and tailored towards their applicable position group. Each day of Cages only lasted an hour, but it was the most intense hour in all of football training. Each station lasted five minutes, and position groups rotated through each drill until the time expired.

Every football player was compelled to go full speed through every workout and give it their all. The coaches could usually tell when a player was lingering or holding back and went off when it happened. Correction during Cages prescribed players to repeat the drill either until they did it right or the time was up. No matter what shape a player was in leading up to Cages, everyone was pushed beyond their maximum. After a while, one's body can only handle so much until it becomes fatigued.

By the end of the drills, several players were vomiting all over the Holiday Athletic Center, including myself. The final exercise was the tire pull. There were four tires spread across the field, with the offense and defense facing each other along opposite sides of the tire. Coaches would select two players alike in size and weight to battle for the tire. To win, one had to pull the tire five yards in their direction. To make it more interesting, the coaches would tally up the wins and make the losing side of the ball do additional sprints. This was an exceedingly vehement competition that forced us to dig deep because no one wanted to lose or be the reason their squad had to run. I won and lost my fair share of battles, but I always emptied my tank.

Even though we had finalized BCT and were formally accepted into the Cadet Wing, life as a fourth-class cadet was still rocky. There were so many restrictions. We couldn't have a vehicle, nor could we use any elevators on USAFA's campus, just to name a couple. Further, we were not allowed to wear civilian clothes until "Recognition" in March. This meant that we had to always remain in uniform, even while off campus. We could only use the rear stairwells of buildings as the front ones were off-limits to freshmen.

On top of the 5:15 a.m. start to our days, freshmen were required to conduct "Minutes." Minutes entailed waking the upperclassmen up for morning meals or formations by reciting pertinent information for that day every five minutes, such as the meals of the day and Air Force history on that day. We would also be physically trained during this time. Episodes like this were what made the Academy so grueling, in addition to the rest of our exhaustive schedule.

Our schedules were even more demanding than the Prep School. After Minutes, was the mandatory morning formation. This served as roll call for accountability and uniform inspection.

Afterward, mandatory breakfast began at 7:00 a.m., then we were off to classes from 7:30 a.m. to 11:00 a.m. After morning classes was the mandatory noon meal formation at 11:30 a.m., which led to lunch at 11:55 a.m. Afternoon military training started sat 12:30 p.m., when military training and briefings occurred. Afternoon and Physical Education (PE) classes took place between 1:30 p.m. and 3:23 p.m. Also, during the afternoon, clubs and athletics commenced. For football, we started with film at 1:00 p.m. Next would be a team meeting, followed by weightlifting and medical treatment, if necessary, before heading to practice. Practice occurred between 3:30 p.m. and 5:30 p.m., or later.

After practice, we would stretch, visit the training room as needed, and attempt to squeeze in an ice bath. The difficulty with taking an ice bath was that it was a necessary recovery routine for athletes, yet at the same time it left less time to study. After athletics, there was occasionally evening military training which also included briefings and lectures. Dinner at Mitchell Hall occurred between 5:00 p.m. and 7:00 p.m., but there were times when football players would miss dinner altogether because football activities ran late. Nonetheless, Academic Call to Quarters, or mandatory study time occurred from 7:45 p.m. to 11:00 p.m. At 11:00. TAPS was played, signaling optional bedtime.

Undoubtedly, our schedules were exceedingly laborious. Promptly making it to bed was a victory, which rarely happened. Naps were even more prized and difficult to obtain. A little over three hours was not enough time to study for five or six arduous courses, although they were split between alternating days. The Academy's instructors hand out more homework than can be accomplished, and they know this. It's a part of the Academy's time management training. Therefore, prioritization is imperative. My average bedtime was 12:00 a.m., thus 2:00 a.m. and 3:00 a.m. nights were not uncommon. Fatigue from my daily activities made it even more difficult to effectively study during this time, advocating for early sleep. Doing so meant my studies would suffer, so it wasn't an option unless I threw in the towel as I did on some nights. Accordingly, late nights and early mornings became a never-ending cycle that only led to aggregated exhaustion. Extreme sleep deprivation, in combination with the Academy's obligations are what contribute to making the Academy experience so rare and arduous. Cadets and grads have a saying about USAFA, "It's a great place to be from, but a terrible place to be at." This phrase has remained relatively untouched throughout the history of USAFA.[91] While difficult, the cadet area is highly secure.

After BCT, four-degrees were finally allowed to leave campus with a day pass on Blue Weekends. Blue Weekends are non-training weekends where cadets are permitted to leave the Academy if they have liberty to use. The Academy refers to liberties and authorizations as permission for cadets to leave the Academy during off-duty periods. Individual passes on Friday evening, Saturday, and Sunday will depend on your cadet's class and their overall squadron performance. Authorizations and liberties are gradually increased by class in recognition of added maturity and responsibility.[92]

The number of day and overnight passes earned by each cadet is determined by both their performance as well as their squadron's overall performance in all facets of Academy life. AOCs may also grant discretionary passes for business, religious activities, and official social dining events. Silver Weekends are training weekends that generally take place two weekends per month. Silver Weekends are devoted to military training from Friday afternoon through early Saturday afternoon. Activities during this time include room and uniform inspections, parades, marching practice, military briefings, guest speakers, and professional military education and training.[93]

Throughout each cadet's career, we were required to sign out with the location of where we would be traveling. I went to my sponsor family's house the first chance I could. I hadn't seen them in a while, so it was great to reconnect and get a break from the Academy going into the school year. Although we were not permitted to stay out overnight as freshmen, I cherished being able to get away.

Though not very appreciated as a cadet, USAFA's campus is strikingly beautiful. USAFA sits on about thirty square miles of forested land at the north end of Colorado Springs. Although like other public and private universities, it is very unique because every aspect of education and training and life is contained within a small campus.[91] Cadets are not allowed to live off campus at any point. Numerous have secretly tried to in the past and been expelled. USAFA also has a feature famously known as the Terrazzo, T-Zo for short. The name stems from the walkway's terrazzo tiles that are set among a checkerboard of marble strips.[94] The T-Zo is an open space enclosed by four buildings that form the core of daily cadet life and is used for daily musters of the entire Cadet Wing.[95]

As four degrees, we were only allowed to travel by running on the marble strips while on the expansive T-Zo. We were only permitted to walk when there was inclement weather. If caught walking in the absence of poor conditions, we were scolded and sometimes even punished. During harsh weather, the T-Zo strips were hazardous because the marble became extremely slippery under moisture. Therefore, fourth-class cadets were authorized to walk next to the strips when coming and going. In the center of the cadet area is a hill known as "Spirit Hill," nicknamed "The Hill," which suffices as the central grassy area of the T-Zo. At the east end of the T-Zo are the "Air Gardens," 700-feet of lighted pools, lowered grass sections, and maze-like walkways.[94]

The central quad area also lends itself to the frequently used phrase, "the T-Zo gap," to characterize the perceived chasm between intercollegiate (IC) athletes and non-ICs in terms of treatment, expectations, priorities, and performance. But as a military institution, the USAFA also strives for a measure of standardization and equality to bolster requisite morale and discipline among its students or cadets. As a result, the institution undertakes deliberate efforts to bridge the natural divide between ICs and non-ICs that can occur. The Cadet Sight Picture (CSP) defines two initiatives, representativeness, and integration, as central to the goal of enhancing learning outcomes for student-athletes. Representativeness measures how similar the academic, community, and campus experiences are for IC and non-IC athletes. Integration addresses the efforts of athletic departments and coaches in aligning athletic programs with the educational mission of the institution.

Similarly to its nonmilitary peer schools, many (approximately 25%) of cadets are IC athletes. Another way that ICs and non-ICs share similar experiences is via promotion. Although it is conceivable that a freshman athlete competing at the highest levels could receive favorable treatment in some college settings, all USAFA freshman cadets undergo a fourth-class system. This system ensures all first-year cadets remain subordinate to all upper-class cadets until a time-based promotion to upper-class status occurs. Further military "promotions" occur each successive year, for ICs and non-ICs alike.

ICs and non-ICs at USAFA also experience a remarkably similar academic program. While there are 32 academic majors, most cadets do not select a major until partway through their sophomore year. As a result, almost the entire first and second years are similar for most cadets. These two years consist primarily of a relatively common battery of "core" or general courses that all cadets must take. In total, there are approximately 96 hours of these core courses, and by completing them, every cadet graduates with a Bachelor of Science degree, whether it is in English or electrical engineering. This relative standardization of core courses, which occurs every year of a cadet's career, is the primary way to compare academic performance in a consistent manner. All cadets graduate in four years—a few minor exceptions notwithstanding—with an approximately equal total load of 147 academic credit hours. These academic requirements translate to semester course loads between five and seven academic courses for ICs and non-ICs.

According to a study by the University of Nebraska, non-ICs are predicted to perform better academically than the ICs. In their study, they found that in a common set of academic classes, represented by the "core GPA," ICs perform as expected overall based on the previously described academic composite score. Examining the results for cumulative GPA across the entire sample shows that ICs and non-ICs do not have systematically different GPAs after controlling for predicted performance. This result supports the CSP supposition that integration and representativeness could reduce athletes' underperformance. Significantly, this finding holds across all GPA measures, even the cumulative and majors GPAs, which could be noisy since they encompass all cadets' academic performance in their common core courses as well as (i.e., potentially uncommon) majors courses. Finally, although cadets do have a measure of control over which courses they take based on the selection of their academic major, randomness permeates much of their coursework. Specifically, cadets do not make decisions about their class schedules (e.g., morning or afternoon section) or faculty members (e.g., Professor Smith) who teach their courses. Instead, these are random assignments. This dynamic leads to sections that routinely have a representative sample of ICs and non-ICs, particularly in core courses, and further enhances the representative experience for athletes.[61]

An Academy education is valued at more than $416,000, and its difficulty is otherworldly. USAFA's rigorous academic program balances Science, Technology, Engineering, and Mathematics

(STEM) with the arts and humanities. The robust core curriculum places cadets at the intersection of these disciplines, generating opportunities to cultivate and apply creative and complex problem-solving abilities. The Academy holds reputable rankings to include: the #1 funded undergraduate research university, #3 U.S. News top public school, and the #6 school on Forbes' list of top 25 STEM colleges.[96] Due to the educational strain at the Academy, many of the courses are graded on a curve. Withal, many courses at the Academy have historical averages that are expected to be abided by. Grading curves proved to be colossal in my academic career as a cadet and at times, were even my saving grace.

Jamie Callahan, a professor at the Newcastle Business School, conducted a study in 2009 that explored the role of training practices at USAFA. In her study, Callahan suggests that adversative education, exercised by USAFA and other service academies, traumatizes both women and men and leads to dysfunctional reactionary behavior. She states that problems experienced at USAFA originate in cadet training practices that deprive individuals of personal control. "That sense of personal empowerment is the ability to engage successfully as a functioning adult within any given social system." Cadets subsequently seek avenues in which they perceive they can exert control when the institution deprives them of power and control.[91] Adversative education, or doubting, model of education, features physical rigor, mental stress, absence of privacy, minute regulation of behavior, and indoctrination in desirable values.[97] I can attest that receiving an education while undergoing this type of training made it immensely challenging to succeed, not to mention our course load.

I was given five classes for 14.5 semester hours amid my freshman football season. The minimum course load for all cadets is five academic courses (must be a minimum of 15.5 semester hours).[98] Due to the wonderful work of my academic advisor, Paula Britton (Mrs. B), my schedule was orchestrated in a way that allowed me to undertake less than the minimum course load during the fall of my four-degree year with the arrangement to take two summer courses during my cadet career. This was monumental in my success as a cadet. Academic advising is a very common collegiate experience. The positive effects of academic advising on college student retention and overall success in the research are clear. In addition, students who participate in academic advising are more likely to graduate.[72] Mrs. B's tailored advisory put me on a lucrative trajectory to do just that.

Going into the Academy, I loved computers, so I planned on majoring in computer science. That would soon change after my experience in USAFA's core computing class, Computer Science 110. This class, along with Calculus I, on top of football season, was vastly difficult; hence I struggled throughout the semester. I would conclude my first semester at the Academy with a 2.56 GPA, earning a C+ in Computer Science and a C in Calculus. Initially, I was distraught that I was unable to extend the academic success I'd enjoyed leading up to the Academy. Still, over time I accepted the fact that my best would not always lead to my desired outcomes.

I would become very familiar with Cs at USAFA, unwittingly adopting the popular mindset that "Cs get degrees." Evident by my GPA, I did not finish with all Cs my first semester. I made a B in Behavioral Science and a B- in French, my two best grades of the term. My GPA was nowhere near what I was used to, but considering the instructional complexity in conjunction with football and military training, I settled. Especially after comparing my grades with some of my teammates, I was doing fairly well. Although I was in the middle of the pack amongst my teammates, I was towards the bottom on the Hill. So, when it came to scholastic matters on the football team, I felt valued because I was viewed as one of the smarter players. On the Hill, I did not feel appreciated as my efforts were not recognized.

A few of my teammates were placed on academic probation because of their struggles in the classroom. Fortunately, I was only stuck on academic probation for half a semester and never faced a dreaded Academic Review Committee (ARC). ARCs are designed for cadets who have been placed on academic probation and represent each of the four cadet classes. Each ARC evaluates cadets deficient in academic performance and forwards recommendations regarding retention or disenrollment to the Superintendent or their designated representative.[99]

One of my most valued four-degree commodities was borrowing vehicles from upperclassmen. Since we were not allowed to have vehicles until our junior year, the next best thing was to use other cadet's cars. Oftentimes, there would be upperclassmen who were either studying over the weekend or carpooling, so they didn't need their vehicles. I had several reliable upperclassmen who granted me permission to use their car anytime. Joey Okai, CeCe Carter, and

Wale Lawal were the ones I could count on the most. I can't thank them enough. Their generosity allowed me to frequent restaurants off-campus, go to church, and get away when I needed to.

A favorable part of being an intercollegiate athlete at the AFA was that we automatically received an A for our semester's athletic grade while in season. It is mandatory for all cadets to participate in the school's athletic program. PE is an integral part of the Academy's core curriculum.[100] Consequently, we received a grade for athletics each semester. This automatic A-grade wasn't a tremendous help to my GPA, but it did give it a slight boost every semester. Outside of academics, there were a lot of extracurricular activities taking place amongst cadets. One of them was a party that would be of epic proportions.

On December 2, 2011, several of my teammates and I enjoyed one of our Blue Weekends at the Burrells. We had been talking about the party and making plans to attend. When it came time to leave for the function, everyone secured a ride in the cold, inclement weather except Jordan and me. We spent several hours trying to find one, even after the party had been going on for a couple of hours but were unsuccessful. Although we were disappointed at the time, this turned out to be a blessing in disguise, and we would soon learn why.

Agents of the Office of Special Investigations (OSI) at the Academy were told about a party where cadet-athletes used spice, a synthetic marijuana, and allegedly engaged in gang rape. It was the most stunning set of allegations after nearly two years of investigations into off-campus parties, drug use, and athletes' conduct. The blowout was held in the woods west of Colorado Springs on December 2, 2011, a week after the football team ended its regular season with a 45-21 thumping of Colorado State. "The girls' drink, or Captain Morgan with the blue lid, was only for girls to drink," OSI confidential informant cadet Eric Thomas told investigators in a written statement obtained by The Gazette. The blue-capped bottle, he explained, was laced with "roofies," a street term for flunitrazepam, a powerful sedative known as a date-rape drug. Thomas told investigators that "four or five females did not recall what occurred the following day after the party." In one bedroom during the party, "multiple male cadets had sexual intercourse with other unknown females," Thomas alleged. Acting on that and other tips, OSI ran a dragnet that probed the activities of 32 cadets, including 16 football players and several other athletes.

According to Commandant of Cadets, Lt Gen Michelle Johnson, three of the 32 cadets were court-martialed, sentenced, and discharged - two football players and a women's basketball player. Five more cadets received administrative punishment that resulted in their dismissal - three basketball players and two football players. Another half-dozen cadets resigned. Three more cadets were kicked out for unrelated misconduct. Of the 16 football players investigated, seven made it through to graduation. Officials say while OSI, which does not fall under Academy commanders, kept quiet about its investigation, so did the partygoers.

A month after the party, some female revelers were told by cadets to "keep their mouths shut or they won't like what will happen," Thomas told the OSI. The Academy's leaders began to learn of the investigation in January, which led to a wider probe dubbed "Operation Gridiron." OSI special agent Brandon Enos, who worked on the investigation at the Academy, describes the operation on his LinkedIn page: "Case agent and responsible for Operation Gridiron at the United States Air Force Academy. This operation identified and proactively removed approximately 18 starting division one football players and 20 other collegiate athletes from the Air Force Academy for controlled substance use and distribution and sexual assaults. This was the largest and most successful operation in the history of the Air Force OSI Region 8 and the United States Air Force Academy."

There were no charges brought from alleged activities at the December 2, 2011, party, but other allegations of misconduct sent athletes to court. Linebacker Devin Journer was convicted of abusive sexual contact after a woman said Journer sexually assaulted her. He was sentenced to the five months he'd already spent in pretrial confinement and discharged. Wide receiver Charles Mack was convicted in March 2013 of attempted sodomy after two women testified about alleged sexual assaults. He was sentenced to eight months behind bars. Recruited athlete Carlos Foster was convicted of wrongful sexual contact in June 2012 after women testified that he groped them. Foster got six months and a discharge.[101]

In total, there would be 51 reports of sexual assault my freshman year, mainly due to the December party. I found this number startling since we attended a military institution and received mandatory sexual assault training. There was also a zero-tolerance policy in place. I am aware that not every report resulted in a conviction, but the perception was still there. I never directly encountered sexual assault at the Academy, but I was called as a witness in a case. J. Lee was accused of sexual assault by one of our peers years after the instance took place our freshman year. Immediately after the alleged incident, J. Lee informed me that everything was consensual; thus, I was already knowledgeable that no illicit activity took place.

It wouldn't be until our senior year that the accuser made her report, although she'd already withdrawn from the Academy. I was disturbed by this gesture after so much time had passed and we were on the cusp of graduating. Consequently, numerous interviews with OSI ensued, including one with myself. I gave an honest testimony and incorporated the conversation J. Lee and I had freshman year. I left the interrogation confident that Lee would be acquitted. At the same time, I was still nervous because I'd heard of these types of cases resulting in negative outcomes simply based on proofless false accusations. It was discouraging to see Lee so stressed out with his future on the line. Ultimately, Lee would be found innocent. Everyone was ecstatic he could put this behind him and move on with his life. I was also proud that my testimony was able to play a part in rightfully clearing his name.

After the party, Jordan and I became aware of a portion of the function's happenings by way of our friends who went, but we were shocked when the whole story was revealed. I knew God was looking out for us because several of my friends who attended the party were dismissed as a result. Genesis 28:15 confirms this, "And, behold, I *am* with thee, and will keep thee in all places whither thou goest, and will bring thee again into this land; for I will not leave thee, until I have done *that* which I have spoken to thee of."

Acey Palmer, Ryan Pollard, and BWatt, had not participated in any of the malevolent acts, but were not supposed to be interacting with upperclassmen in a social environment in what is known as fraternization. Fraternization prohibits Airmen from developing relationships that involve or give the appearance of partiality, preferential treatment, or improper use of rank or position. For these reasons, unprofessional relationships, including dating between cadets and officers, enlisted personnel, or USAFA Prep School cadets and between cadets in each other's chain of command (those holding leadership positions within the squadron, group, or Wing) is prohibited.

Additionally, fourth-class cadets are not permitted to date or become too familiar with upper-class cadets.[54] Acey, Ryan, and BWatt would all go on to withdraw from the Academy for one reason or another, in connection with their party attendance. Sadly, attrition was an occurrence I became all too familiar with at the Academy. It was exceptionally demanding to see so many of my good friends leave over the years. Honestly, it was draining. Several of my friends didn't even make it to the Academy from the Prep School. My Prep School roommate, Al Lasker, Eugene Glenn, and FeDale Hall being the closest of them. BWatt was one of my best friends at USAFA, so his departure was harrowing. Frederick Blow was another tough loss. Fortunately, though, most of them were able to land on their feet and ended up playing football at other Division I schools. I was happy to see them go on and do great things. Meanwhile, I remained in communication and am still good friends with some of them today.

On December 13th, the Cadet Wing gained more bad news. One of our football managers, Stephen Williams, was killed in a single-car accident on the Academy campus. His death surely impacted the football team and was a tragic loss. These two incidents gave the Academy a bizarre feeling and were the talk of the town for a while. But that didn't stop time from moving on and us freshmen advancing one step closer to being recognized.

Recognition takes place for freshmen every year in March. Recognition is a three-day event where fourth-class cadets are "recognized" in the Cadet Wing as upper-class cadets. Upon completing Recognition, fourth-class cadets earn the right to wear the Prop and Wings crest on their flight caps and are given more privileges and responsibilities at the Academy. The Prop and Wings (propeller and wings) is a military insignia used to identify various aviation-related units in the United States military.[102] Other privileges earned are being able to wear civilian clothing and getting to walk across the T-Zo instead of running on the marble strips.

This Recognition is a vital and traditional step in the United States Air Force Academy experience. It is a ceremonial acknowledgement that the fourth-class cadet has successfully met military training requirements and is prepared to continue the rigorous and rewarding Academy journey.[103] Recognition is an intensive military training assessment that includes a variety of physical, mental, and emotional challenges to measure how well the cadets have performed as individuals and team members since arriving for BCT at the Academy in June. "Recognition is not something you are given, it's something that is earned, and that's really special because it means they have worked hard for it," said cadet first-class Madison Froebe, former cadet officer-in-charge of Recognition. Froebe said the event mimics the high-stress service environment cadets will face as future Air Force officers while developing resiliency and agility.[104]

I was brimming with angst as Recognition drew closer. I'd heard stories from previous classes about how harrowing the event was, so I dreaded the day it would come. In the days leading up to Recognition, there was a 40-day countdown when things began to ramp up. We now had to include upperclassmen's hometowns and majors in their greetings, making it impossible to remember each person's information. Upperclassmen were also giving us the silent treatment ahead of Recognition which made the lead up that much more concerning.

The event commenced on Thursday, March 15, 2012, at the end of the final class period. All athletic activities were axed for the three-day event so sadly, we didn't have football practice. However, most football players still went to the locker room after our last class until the mandatory formation that afternoon. We were all expressing our fear of what was to come and how bad each of us would have it. Because football players often miss out on numerous training sessions throughout the year due to practices and games, we all thought we would have it the worst. Upperclassmen couldn't train us as much as they'd liked, so this was their chance to make up for it.

The Academy is typically composed of 70% men and 30% women, but a small percentage of upper-class women in training environments appeared more vicious. In my opinion, these women raved at being able to use the power of their rank to pulverize fourth-class males because this is the most authority they'd ever had over a man. Thus, this fragment of women was feared by freshmen football players because they were relentless, and there was nothing we could do about it. Moreover, there was no guarantee we would pass Recognition; we had to perform well enough to receive that passage. There had even been cases where Recognition was abandoned in its entirety due to insubordination by entire freshman classes.

Once I made my way into formation, my stomach was in knots; the time had finally come. Whistles chimed all around the T-Zo and the announcement of Recognition 2012 was made. Suddenly, things took a wild turn right after it started. One of my fellow teammates, Aaron Oats, had led a powerful charge to the Hill. The rest of my class followed suit and stormed the Hill. This was significant because it was a slap in the face to the upperclassmen, displaying that we were unafraid of them. Recognition is already hard enough, hence, in my mind it did not make sense to show the upperclassmen up and make it any worse. This charade landed our class in deep mud. Accordingly, the upperclassmen vowed to give us "the hardest Recognition we could ask for," and immediately started training us right there on the Hill. It was chaotic. The upper classes delivered on their promise and gave us three of the most intense days of our lives.

Recognition made BCT look like a walk in the park. The entire first evening of Recognition was filled with incessant PT sessions which left me doubtful of my ability to make it through the next two days. We were subjected to countless push-ups, sit-ups, burpees, jumping jacks, sprints, and flutter kicks. I didn't feel like I could go on any longer, but I dug deep and persevered.

The next morning, I woke up feeling like I'd been hit by a truck. Friday was filled with more of the same in addition to the infamous assault course. The assault course is a physically and mentally strenuous course where cadets are put through combat-like situations with simulated small arms fire, artillery explosions, and obstacles.[105] This course is also a part of BCT, but it seemed augmented during recognition. It felt like we were amid a warzone as I struggled through the circuit.

On Saturday morning, the upperclassmen conducted our most meticulous SAMI yet. They were tremendously thorough and charged us to iteratively fix corrections they made to pass. Recognition terminated with a five-mile run to Cathedral Rock, known as the Run to the Rock. After the run, we changed into service dress and conducted the final Recognition ceremony. This ceremony was performed by each squadron and officially announced the Recognition passage or failure for each freshman. Cadets who aren't recognized are given another chance during the make-up Recognition.

I was quite nervous leading up to the ceremony, but altogether I had a good inclination I would pass. The announcements were made in alphabetical order. Everyone ahead of me was successfully recognized, but that still did not eliminate my apprehension. It seemed like forever before my name was called as I restlessly waited in the dark hallway. As soon my name was announced, I nervously strolled into the middle of the hallway to the tune that I had passed Recognition. I then made my way down the hall lined with upperclassmen, each rendering a salute. I was gratified after enduring such a demanding experience. Everyone in my squadron passed Recognition, and our teamwork played a giant part in our success. Recognition brought us four-degrees closer than ever as we had just surmounted an exceedingly important milestone together. After Recognition, I repeatedly listened to "Never Would Have Made It," by Marvin Sapp over the next several days. I recognized that God was the reason I made it through, and I couldn't have done it without him.

When I was a part of Recognition as an upperclassman, I made sure to provide purposeful training. I did not yell at cadets without a valid reason, but only to correct deficiencies. I wanted to supply freshmen with a rewarding experience they could learn from. I looked out for underclassmen as well. When presented with the opportunity, I furnished them with advice, saved them from unnecessary training, and encouraged them. I especially helped younger IC athletes, regardless of their sport. I did this because I understood their struggle and how IC athletes at the Academy are often frowned upon by Non-Athletic Regular People (NARP). NARP is used to label any cadet who is not an intercollegiate athlete, although cadets hold differing opinions about its definition.[91] I persisted in helping freshmen in general each year I rose through the cadet ranks. I supported them and paid the usage of my vehicle forward to them as well.

Aside from Recognition, academically, the second semester was more of the same as I finished with a 2.55 GPA. I performed well in my most challenging classes, earning a B- in Chemistry 100 and Calculus II, improving on my foregoing Calculus I grade. Unfortunately, a fraction of my classmates weren't so fortunate in Calculus II. There was an enormous cheating scandal during one of our arduous online Calculus II exams, known at the Academy as Graded Reviews (GRs). About 650 cadets took the test in late April of 2012. Most were freshmen, but some were sophomores. Of the 650 cadets that took the exam, 78 cadets were caught cheating and consequently placed on honor probation. Most cadets took responsibility for their actions and partook in a six-month remediation program.

Honor probation is a remediation program that includes reflection, marching in service dress, writing in journals, and mentoring with senior officers and other cadets. The focus is "what you did and why you did it and how to learn from your mistake," Lt Col John Bryan, an Academy spokesman at the time, said.[106] The mantra at the AFA is that you will make mistakes, but if you do, then own up to them. If you make a mistake and lie about it, then that gives you the potential of being expelled. The cheating took place during the exam through a website called Wolfram Alfa. Through this webpage, one was able to input a calculus equation and the site provided the solution. While the page was acceptable for checking homework answers, it was not allowed during closed-book exams. Lt Col Bryan said that the cadets acted individually, and there was no evidence of collusion.[106]

Astonishingly, the best grade I earned that semester was a B in Engineering 101 - Intro to Air Force Engineering. I did not have an engineering background whatsoever, but I'd always been good with numbers, so I was able to leverage that skill. Furthermore, I was heavily assisted by the grading curve.

I was also introduced to the Air Force Academy PE program my second semester. The USAFA PE program is designed to expose cadets to a wide variety of physical skills, promote a positive, self-confident attitude, and contribute to cadet development of the USAFA institutional outcomes of Warrior Ethos as Airmen and citizens and leadership, teamwork, and organizational management. The objectives and assessment criteria of PE at the Air Force Academy are:

- Provide every cadet with situations and experience that will help develop such leadership attributes as self-confidence, emotional control, persistence, courage, discipline, and teamwork.
- Provide every cadet with the opportunity for maximum development of physical strength, stamina, flexibility, and motor performance. The USAFA athletic department assesses the development of each cadet by using physical fitness and aerobic tests and graded evaluations in each PE

course. Students must pass all core and elective courses to meet USAFA graduation requirements.

- Cultivate in every cadet a keen interest in, and the ability to perform, a number of physical skills to enable them to participate in vigorous activity throughout their lifetime.
- Each cadet is required to satisfactorily complete the core PE curriculum. Through core and core elective courses, cadets are taught basic lifetime fitness principles that will allow them to meet and exceed USAF fitness standards. In addition, they will learn specific skills in sports which can be used throughout a career of service to the nation.

In order to graduate, cadets must pass Basic PT during BCT, participate in a competitive experience (intramurals, clubs, or intercollegiate athletics) every semester, and pass a minimum of 10 PE courses, each worth 0.5 semester hours of course credit. With few exceptions, cadets take PE courses each of their eight semesters. Classes are 75-minutes long and meet every other day for eight lessons (10 contact hours, 0.5 semester hours). The only exception is Basic Swimming, which is a 16-lesson block. Two PE courses will be taken freshman and sophomore years. Three PE courses will be taken junior and senior years.[107]

The first PE course I took was boxing. "Boxing enhances cadets' educational opportunities," voiced Lt Gen Michelle Johnson. They learn to overcome adversity, develop resiliency, act with ethical decision making and maintain composure under pressure. This is all part of something bigger – the Warrior Ethos, a mindset all of us in the profession of arms must maintain every day we serve.[108] The Academy doesn't necessarily expect all of its graduates to find themselves in hand-to-hand combat, but they could well encounter high-stress situations under fire or in other circumstances. Boxing helps prepare you for that. "You can train your neurotransmitters, so they respond in a certain way and communicate more clearly," said Air Force boxing coach Black Baldi, who instructs the classes. "That's really what we're trying to do. The first time they get in there, everything can get a little messy; just very nervous and anxious and not thinking clearly. The more time they spend in those highly anxious moments, the more comfortable and confident they become in themselves."[109]

When cadets step into the boxing ring here, they don't senselessly knock each other around; they hone their defense drills, their guard position and footwork, so when they think they can't go the distance, they find a way to survive and win. Lt Col Matthew Glover, interim head boxing coach at the Air Force Academy in 2015, said the skills cadets learn from boxing, and combative courses at the Academy are relevant for the modern warfighter. "Courage under fire and grace under pressure translates directly from the boxing ring to combat," he said. "It's better to start here, where there are no real bullets. Some cadets have never been in a fight or had to take a punch. This course familiarizes them with physical stress in a controlled environment, with the best safety equipment available. A West Point study concluded, without real or perceived danger, courage cannot be measured."[110]

Growing up in the inner city, I had gotten into a decent number of fights, from heated exchanges on the football field to defending myself in the streets. I grew up to be a particularly tough and vigorous kid who loved to roughhouse, hence the reason I enjoyed football so much. I was thrilled once I discovered boxing was a core PE course. Mind you, I had never taken an official boxing class, so I learned a lot of skills and techniques that I was able to combine with my previous experience.

The first few lessons were tailored around the two main boxing stances: orthodox and southpaw. I favored the southpaw stance simply because that had been my posture growing up, and it was most comfortable. We also learned about the three primary punches—the jab, hook, and uppercut. Furthermore, we learned how to counter, defend ourselves, and ultimately how exhausting boxing was. I had a great time during the course. Once we completed the initial training lessons, we were able to spar with our classmates using headgear, which was required anytime we sparred or had an exam.

The rearmost phase of the course encompassed graded exams against comparable classmates chosen by the instructor. The class consisted of two of these. My best one was against one of my squad mates, Jeff Jacobs. Jeff played on the water polo team and was a great kid, but boxing was not his strong suit. After we touched gloves, I instantly penetrated his frail defense. I connected with a solid three-hit combo, showcasing his vulnerability. I chased him with a jab and then received a jab in return, creating space for Jeff. I regathered myself and went on the attack again, delivering a large blow to the face. I followed that up with a mean left hook, forcing him to retreat. He threw another couple of jabs in an attempt to keep me away, but they were ineffective. I went on my final pursuit, landing a massive right hook to the head that jolted his whole body. The instructor immediately stopped the match after 21 seconds because of the force behind my hits, and my opponent was not doing a good enough job of protecting himself. With headgear on, this signified a knockout. It felt good to exhibit my boxing ability in front of all my classmates and thrive in such a visible setting. I finished the class with a solid B.

During the spring of my four-degree year, I sat down with Mrs. B to discuss what my major would be. All cadets must declare a major, and like core courses, must earn a minimum 2.00 major's GPA in that major. The major's GPA includes grades for courses designated by the Department Head responsible for that major, regardless of whether the course is being used to satisfy a major's requirement. Inevitably, I took an exhaustive look at my grades up to that point, my workload, educational interests, what I wanted to do after graduation, and my time allocation. That, in combination with prayer and much deliberation amongst graduates, upperclassmen, and football alumni steered me to my decision.

Based upon my analysis, I went to the management department after class one afternoon and declared. One of the instructors customarily rang a bell and the rest of them thunderously applauded. I signed a form confirming my declaration and was on my way. I was very uplifted by the ordeal and felt like I'd made the right decision.

The management major prepares cadets for management and leadership roles in today's technologically complex, global Air Force. The curriculum is designed to develop cadets who can understand, analyze, and improve organizations through the efficient and effective use of systems. The courses in the major help students develop adaptive capacity and the organizational knowledge and skills vital for Air Force officers as well as future national leaders. The management major ranks among the most prestigious undergraduate management and business degrees in the nation. The management major produces critical thinkers who will lead organizations to quickly adapt and succeed in rapidly changing, highly technical, global environments.

Management majors study traditional managerial and business topics such as organizational perspectives and theories, global organizations, complex human systems, financial and managerial accounting, finance, human resource management, marketing, production, and operations management, information systems, and strategic management.[111] Management is thought to be one of the "easier" majors at the Academy, though none are undemanding, compared to the technical ones such as engineering, chemistry, and astronomy.

The time commitment required for science majors was much too extensive with football. I hardly had enough time to study for my core classes as it was, and even those were a burden. I knew there was no way I'd be able to put in the requisite time to take on computer science and play football concurrently; one would have to give. Not only was time a factor, but the complexity of the technical courses was above my comfort level; the highest grade I'd received up to that point from those classes was a B-. Moreover, I had always been interested in business and management which aligned with acquisitions, my preferred Air Force Specialty Code (AFSC), or Air Force job. Across the board, management endorsed my goals and allotted me the most time to study and still play football. Foreseeably, I was one of many football players to declare management as their major. With my field of study secured and freshman year behind me, I was ready for my first summer at USAFA.

Summer breaks at the AFA are nine weeks long, broken down into three, three-week increments. My first summer break was split between Expeditionary, Survival, and Evasion Training (ESET) during the first period, leave during the second, and summer school last. During the third-class year, training begins in the summer with ESET, where cadets learn how to set up modular facilities and contingency utilities, passive defense, force protection, secure individual and team movement, and survival and evasion skills.

Cadets begin taking on additional responsibilities and develop interpersonal leadership competencies as supervisors of fourth-class cadets.[112] The focus is not on the evasion portion or combat skills portion, but rather a combination of both. Cadets are training for a deployment."[113] The worst part of the 10-day graduation requirement was the survival training. Intended to emulate real-world survival on a deployment, we were planted in the woods for three days.

The program is run by senior cadet leadership, but is overseen by Survival, Evasion, Resistance, and Escape (SERE) trainers. SERE specialists are remarkably fierce people. These experts know how to survive in the most remote and hostile environments on the planet. It's up to them to make sure that when a mission doesn't go as planned, the Airmen involved are ready for anything and can return with honor.[114] The survival training we took was not even a fraction of their operational training, but they were there to provide us with an idea of what real survival training was like.

The first day of ESET was just a series of in-class briefings that covered several training techniques. The next few days were spent applying what the SERE trainers taught us regarding land navigation, tactical movements, and firearm proficiency. Finally, we were sent into the woods for three days and two nights for the ghastly survival training. We were not allowed to bring phones, snacks, or any additional necessities besides our uniform and a utility pack which included a poncho, flashlight, and bandages.

Our ponchos were used on the first night as a rainstorm pounded us. It was not very helpful, seeing that we still got drenched, making for a grisly first night. The daytime was spent traveling and navigating to different coordinates. We were obligated to make it to specific destinations by certain deadlines to pass the training. We also had to steer clear of other cadet leadership who were to be treated as hostiles. Once we made it to the journey's end on the last day, we were finally given an unpleasant meal composed of random foods thrown together. It was a disgusting mixture, but it did the trick after not eating for three days.

Meals at the Academy in general were not much better. The Mitchell Hall cooks certainly labored to prepare food for 4,000+ cadets at each meal, but mass producing that amount of food was unsavory. Although there were some meals that were surprisingly good, more often, the food lacked flavor or had a poor taste. Moreover, foods like powdered eggs often led to unbearable stomach aches. After reporting for mandatory meals, there were times I departed Mitchell Hall after the food was served because I was turned off by the meal, or it wouldn't sit well with my stomach. This resulted in a consistent dose of peanut butter and jelly sandwiches, snack bars, and instant noodles.

After ESET, the next three weeks of my summer were spent on leave in Tacoma. It was great to be back with my family and friends and away from the Academy. It was especially good to see Shaianne. Between my departure to college and different life events, our communication had been on and off over the years. But one thing remained the same: our connection when we ran into each other. Whenever I came home and we crossed paths, it was like nothing had ever changed; we didn't miss a beat. We always shared the same initial bond.

At the end of summer leave periods back home, I would have going away BBQs before returning to the Academy. Shaianne made it a point to show up and support me each time, continuing to display her fondness for me. Shaianne had her first child, Derek Holliday II, also known as June, on July 30, 2013. After his birth, she soon left the child's father. I disqualified Shaianne as companion prospect after this event because I'd never considered dating a woman with a child. I had seen some of my friends and family deal with drama pertaining to biological parents and wanted to avoid that dilemma. I was also in college, and in no place to take care of an adolescent. Moreover, the Academy forbids cadets from having dependents, so we remained friends.

One huge difference I noticed about being home was while I had been 1,000 miles away working towards my future, a lot of my old friends were back home doing the same things they were before I left. Some of them hadn't done much since we graduated high school, which was disheartening. Several people had even plummeted into poverty, drugs, and prison. Witnessing this forced me tighten up my circle because I could no longer afford to be associated with people who didn't have the same dreams and ambitions as I did. I enjoyed being home, but I remained committed to the upcoming football season by working out five days a week. All in all, my time at home felt short-lived, and the three weeks flew by. Before I knew it, I was back in the classroom.

Chemistry 200 is one of USAFA's hardest sophomore classes, so Mrs. B used her expertise and registered many football players to take it during the summer. Even though the semester-long course was condensed into a three-week period, it was decidedly beneficial for us to take in the summer. One major advantage was that it gave us the ability to retain more information since the material was fresh in our minds. It also allowed us to focus on one course as opposed to five or six simultaneously during the school year. Furthermore, it qualified the teacher to provide more intimate instruction as they were only responsible for a single class. Finally, due to the course being compressed into a few weeks, the class was held for eight hours a day.

This permitted us to complete our homework in class. With these factors synthesized, I finished Chemistry 200 with a B-, a grade I would gladly accept in any core class at USAFA, especially a scientific one. I was thrilled because I knew my grade would have been much worse had I taken Chemistry during the academic year.

I went into the 2012 school year thinking my classes couldn't be any more challenging, and I couldn't have been more wrong. Fall semester of my third-class year would be the worst of my entire cadet career. I consummated with a 2.01 GPA, hardly circumventing academic probation. I simply had a hard time staying above water. As Dr. James Joon Woo Do describes in his doctoral dissertation *Crossing Into the Blue: Cadet Culture and Officer Development at the U.S. Air Force Academy*, I, too, arrived at USAFA with lofty goals and aspirations for myself. He further describes his experience by asserting, "While progressing toward graduation and commissioning into the Air Force, I became disenchanted with USAFA and easily slipped into a routine of mediocrity and even underachievement. The institutional values of duty, honor, and country gave way to cynicism, non-compliance, and the pursuit of occupational benefits. These attitudes and behaviors, where the ends justify the means, were not uncommon among past and current cadets. Years of informal observation and participation within the institution interested me in the processes by which cadets become disenchanted with USAFA." This pronouncement resonates well with me because I encountered the same feelings. My skepticism went through the roof, and I lowered my standards, accepting mediocrity. I even refrained from giving my all at times because I knew my best effort would still fall short.

Woo Do's research also revealed that many cadets drift through USAFA with an occupational mindset, focused on enduring four years of the Academy experience, and committed to escaping the institution to obtain monetary incentives, a guaranteed job, and free university education. They set their time at USAFA as a means to an end. Others, however, prioritize their commitment to the institution and the values of patriotism and duty. It emerged from my interviews that the commitment to an individual pursuit, almost always occupational in nature, overrides the greater institutional good at USAFA. The cadets are in college and want to live that college lifestyle, but USAFA is also a military academy with rules and regulations governing their daily lives.[91]

Personally, I believe this clash results from a lack of explanation and reasoning. Often, we were just commanded to do things because they were the rules. But we were left in the dark as to why the rule was valid or how it would make us better officers. If there had been more clarification, then that would have driven commitment. With my academic performance suffering, I adapted the operational mindset. I shifted my focus to football and graduation and the fact that the struggle would be worth it in the end, using those to preserve my ambition.

My sophomore year on the field was surprising as well. The most noteworthy opponent of the season was #19 ranked Michigan. Playing in the "Big House" in front of 110,000 fans was surreal. The crowd was so loud that it was difficult to hear my teammates standing next to me. The Big House was by far the loudest stadium I played in. We were overmatched and undersized, but that did not impact our resolve. We fought hard and kept the score close the entire game, but they pulled away at the end, 31-25. Michigan was not prepared for our triple-option offense. The game was a lot closer than many expected as the Wolverines were favored by 21 points, thanks to Heisman hopeful Denard Robinson and receiver Devin Funchess.[115] Robinson carved our defense on the ground and through the air with 426 yards and four touchdowns. He was an All-American quarterback who was also dubbed the most electric man in college football during the 2012-2013 season. Funchess logged four catches for 106 yards and a touchdown. Both players would go on to play in the NFL. Funchess, now a free agent, was the 41st pick of the 2015 NFL draft by the Carolina Panthers.

I finally made varsity, but I did not see many snaps on defense my sophomore year as the backup to Brian Lindsey, thus, most of my time was spent on special teams. Although not ideal, I was thankful I to see the field. Finally playing in Division I football games was intoxicating and felt surreal every time. Especially home games with our smoky tunnel entrance, the energy was second to none; I exploded from the tunnel on fire every game. I also took pleasure hearing how excited my family and friends were to see me on television, even if it was only for a few plays a game.

Although I played in a limited capacity, experiencing the luxury of a Division I football player was exclusive. We only traveled private via commercial aircraft, directly on the runway. Every home game, the team had Carrabba's catered. Carrabba's is a fine Italian grill with delicious pasta, sauces, and steaks. After every home game, our team provided Chick-Fil-A, and each player would have two sandwiches waiting in their locker. Equipment wise, we received unlimited gear as well as all the in-game accessories we desired. Our hotels only consisted of the best accommodations. On gameday, we were escorted by a police convoy to our games. The football team staff was incredible from top to bottom, providing extraordinary treatment, and making for an alluring experience.

I believe some of my minute playing time stemmed from politics and my poor relationship with Coach Warren. I was a strong-minded player who had no trouble speaking my mind, a trait that did not sit well with some of the coaches. The two special teams I started on were kickoff return and punt. I played in all ten games, recording a mere six tackles, four of them coming at Fresno State. I saw the most playing time against Fresno on defense because of their prolific scoring attack. Fresno was a spread offense who aired the ball out, so we implemented a dime package to try and combat it. The dime package exchanges two linebackers for defensive backs, providing more speed and better coverage against the pass.

This was the first time we had used our dime package against an opponent, and it was a disaster. We failed profusely, largely due to Davante Adams and Derek Carr, both stars in the NFL today. We went on to lose 48-15 and allowed huge numbers. Derek Carr went 28-32 for 452 yards and four touchdowns. Davante Adams reeled in 9 of those passes for 141 yards and 2 of the touchdowns.[116] Both players being NFL starters today makes the loss a bit more tolerable, but at the time, it was appalling. Adams, the better of the two, is now known as one of the best receivers in the NFL. He was taken 53rd overall in the 2014 NFL Draft by the Green Bay Packers but has since been traded to the Raiders in a blockbuster trade, reuniting with his college quarterback.[117] Derek Carr posted one of the most productive rookie seasons in NFL history after being drafted 36th in the same draft.[118] Carr's had an up and down career since then, but recently had one of his best years in 2020. Although we were hammered by Fresno, it felt good to gather meaningful defensive reps on varsity.

We finalized the season at 6-6, good enough for an invitation to the 2012 Armed Forces Bowl against Rice in Fort Worth, TX. This was my first bowl game experience, and I enjoyed every minute of it. As a reward for the team's performance that season, the NCAA not only honors them with a bowl game but also gifts from the bowl game.

Every year, a list is produced that exhibits what gifts each bowl donates that year. The NCAA allows each bowl to award up to $550 worth of gifts to 125 participants per school. Schools can, and almost always do, buy additional packages to distribute to participants beyond that 125 limit. In addition, participants can receive awards worth up to $400 from the school and up to $400 from the conference for postseason play, covering both conference title games and any bowl game.[119] The Armed Forces bowl, sponsored by Bell, provided us with a Sony gift suite, Fossil watch, Dakine backpack, and a Big Game football, all items I cherish today. We didn't play well, losing the game 33-14, but it was still a great episode overall.

Two months into my sophomore year, there was another death at the AFA; death seemed to occur every year I was a cadet. On September 28, 2012, senior Matthew Patrick was found unconscious and later pronounced dead at the hospital. Cadets learned of the incident at lunch that day; his death would be ruled a suicide. I did not know Patrick personally, but any death at the Academy was glaring. The most alarming part about this incident was that Patrick was a senior, so he was less than a year away from graduating. Taking his own life so close to graduation was diminishing, mainly because I was only a three-degree and had so much further to go. I cast no judgments on those who take their own life, but I am strongly against the phenomenon. I am of the mindset that suicide is selfish and there are alternatives to going that route. I have struggled with suicidal thoughts in the past, one time with a loaded pistol in my hand. Gratefully, the thought did not turn into action, and I have been able to rectify these negative thoughts with my faith and family. I now thank God for waking me up each day by treasuring life and not taking it for granted.

As a Christian, I believe in God's word that suicide is self-murder and God is the only one who is to decide when and how a person should die (Job 1:21). Ecclesiastes 7:17 says, "Be not over much wicked, neither be foolish: why shouldest thou die before they time?" In Deuteronomy 30:19, God instructs us to choose life: "I call heaven and earth to record this day against you, *that* I have set before you life and death, blessing and cursing: therefore choose life, that both thou and thy seed may live." According to John 10:10, suicidal thoughts come from satan, who "comes to steal, kill, and destroy." Suicide is a serious issue, but it is an erroneous solution. That's why it's imperative to check on loved ones and even associates when dejected behavior is noticed because you never know what someone else is going through. If you or someone you know is contemplating suicide, I would essentially recommend pursuing Jesus. I would also highly encourage seeking help from a loved one, a professional, or reaching out to the National Suicide Prevention Hotline at 800-273-8255. With another regretful incident at the Academy, I still had to try and concentrate on my challenging sophomore studies.

Among the rest of my classes, the two hardest would be EngrMech 220 - Engineering Mechanics and Physics 110 - General Physics I. Amidst football and my four other courses, I purely did not have enough time to dedicate to the two juggernaut courses. Now that I was a Falcons football player and traveling, I was forced to miss class on Fridays for distant away games. When a test took place on those days, it was necessary for me, along with several of my teammates, to study on the plane ride. Moreover, the academic department had a policy where they sent an instructor on trips with IC teams in these situations. Between team meetings in preparation for our games, players who had an exam would study with the professor and take the GR at the hotel.

I finalized Physics 110 with a C and Engineering Mechanics with a D. I was truly pleased with my physics grade, given the difficulty, and having completed it during football season. I began physics with a 30% on my first GR with the expectation that I had failed. To my amazement, the grading distribution showed I wasn't alone, as the ordinarily failing grade resulted in a C. The grading curve undeniably saved me in Physics 110. Regarding Engineering Mechanics, I simply was unable to understand the statics and mechanics of materials that are applied to aerospace systems, hence the reason I struggled. Passing the arduous course was yet a moral victory for me.

The successive spring semester improved academically, as I managed a 2.39 GPA. Amazingly, my best grade of the semester came by way of a B in Physics 215 - General Physics II. Physics 215 was actually easier than Physics 110, in my opinion because I had begun to understand the content better. The rest of my academic classes contained a B-, a C, and three C+s.

Physically, the second semester of my sophomore year was the worst of my cadet life. For my PE class this spring, I was placed into swimming. I had heard rumors from upper-class teammates about how difficult swimming class was. So, in the back of my mind,

I was dreading its genesis. Growing up, I had a horrifying experience in the water. When I was six years old, my frightful encounter took place while swimming in an apartment pool with my uncle and cousins. I was grasping the edge of the pool and making my way around the deep end when my hands slipped off, and I steadily descended to the pool floor. At that moment, I did not completely understand that I was in the process of drowning. I possessed no swimming ability, nor was I holding my breath. I was vulnerable as I ingested heaps of water, struggling for air. I began to panic and instantly realized the danger I was in because I could no longer breathe. Thus, I clumsily tried to paddle my way back up to the top, only to stall. I was ineffectively flapping away at the bottom of the pool, unable to muster any upward velocity. I started to get exhausted and helplessly ceased my toil. I soon noticed I was drifting to sleep. On the surface, my uncle Chuck's friend realized I was drowning and submarined into the pool. She briskly made her way to the base and transported me to safety. After being saved, I was positioned on the ground and revived. I laid there, gasping for air, and coughing up the water I'd guzzled. From then on, I was a lot more cautious around water.

After my near-death experience, I tried learning how to swim several times. My grandfather taught me, I took a swimming class at the YMCA, and a mandatory swimming course during high school, but I never quite got the hang of it. Not only was I uneasy in the water and fearful of drowning, but I also had a very slim build which made me unsuited to stay afloat. With an even more muscular physique in college, it was much easier to sink.

Entry into the USAFA's swimming class is determined by each student's aquatic ability assessment, a 250-yard timed swim, and input from aquatics instructors.[107] 250 yards is equal to 10 laps in the 25-yard-long swim lanes. This initial evaluation had different time limits which determined one's swimming aptitude and a threshold that functioned as the pass or fail boundary. Students who achieved a passing time were admitted into the normal, eight-lesson curriculum. Pupils that fizzled were placed into the remedial, 16-lesson, Basic Swimming class. Going into the test, I knew I would flop because there was no way I would be able to swim fast enough to meet the minimum time. To no surprise, I failed the test miserably. I swam on my back for much of the exam because I did not know how to breathe underwater or generate much speed with my front stroke. I was still also uncomfortable with my swimming proficiency.

The Basic Swimming course is designed for cadets with little exposure to aquatics or those needing work on specific swimming endurance. Both factors applied to me. The first eight lessons focus on technique. The final eight lessons focus on building swimming endurance with continued work on technique. Cadets will be introduced to survival skills in preparation for the 200 level aquatics course. Cadets are encouraged to move on to regular water survival. However, more typically, they move on to Basic Water Survival for their 200-level aquatics.[107]

Basic Swimming was even worse than the initial exam. At the start of each class, our 250-yard swim was timed and recorded to track progress. This undertaking exhausted me for the rest of the period by itself. Over the course of the class, my time and ability both improved. Therefore, I finally started becoming more secure in the water. My most-liked technique was the backstroke because it was the most comfortable and empowered me to relax. My biggest takeaways were controlling my breathing and maintaining my composure underwater. One of the difficulties with swimming class was that I had to go directly to football practice afterward. Thus, there was fine line between conserving myself for what I cared about and doing well enough to pass the class. This was one of the most punishing circumstances I had to maneuver at the Academy. Being compelled to expend bounds of energy and still perform at a high level on the football field was a grave challenge. Moreover, coaches at the college football level have extremely high expectations and are unyielding to excuses, justified or not. I hated this arrangement with a passion, but I had no choice except to cope with my temporary circumstances.

The one bright spot about basic swimming was being in class with some of my teammates. Knowing that I wasn't suffering alone made the experience better. Further, being able to laugh at each other's swimming misfortunes really helped our psyche. At the culmination of basic swimming, we were required to take another timed test to pass and move on to water survival. I was deeply saddened I had not improved enough to top the course and was forced to retake it. This torpedoed me into a low place, to the point where I contemplated quitting USAFA altogether. But I persisted, and my hard work paid off. I continued to improve over the next 16 lessons and was able to succeed my second time around. The next demand ahead was Basic Water Survival.

The Basic Water Survival course continues the development of Basic Swimming and teaches cadets basic aquatic survival skills that last a lifetime. These survival methods serve officers well throughout their careers. The class provides sufficient aerobic and anaerobic activities that challenge cadets to maintain an above-average fitness level while having fun through aquatics. Cadets learn to save their own lives and assist others in a water emergency, survive in the water for an extended period, and build confidence to swim long distances. Moreover, cadets experience situations that develop self-confidence, emotional control, persistence, and courage. Various skills challenge cadets to move beyond their current skills and comfort levels. Cadets are evaluated in each of the skills taught throughout the course.[107]

Basic Water Survival may have been worse than Basic Swimming. I struggled with most of the exercises; the first was treading water. As a lean, 5'11", 205-pound football player, my frame was simply not meant to stay on the surface, so the amount of energy I exuded to stay afloat was too high. One of our tests required us to tread water for five minutes. At first, learning how to tread water was very taxing for me, but I eventually found a technique that worked. The next drill I grappled with was removing and inflating my ABU pants while treading water. This task was extremely complex because we had to tread water while removing, then inflating our pants by blowing into them. This activity emulated a real-world situation of being shot down over water during wartime. The inflation of our uniform operated as a floatation device once aerated. During our first practice round of this drill, I noticed myself starting to sink while removing my pants, so I began to flap wildly and thumped one of my classmates. I observed that Broam was still floating, so I latched onto him for help. He pulled me up and started laughing hysterically. Until this day, this is one of his favorite stories to tell.

The third challenging and most daunting exercise was jumping off the diving board. I am not very fond of heights, so that, combined with water, did not sit well with me. To graduate, it was required that each student jump off the five-meter diving board at a minimum. Most of my classmates jumped from the 10-meter one. I went up to those heights with the encouragement of my classmates and instructor but was never actually able to make the leap. Needless to say, I did eventually jump off a diving board. The instructor was kind enough to waive the five-meter requirement for me to pass the course by leaping off the three-meter diving board instead. Even then, the three meter was still unpleasant for me; I was immensely nervous looking down into the water from the top of the diving board. The height looked much higher than it actually was. After several minutes, I talked myself into making the dive, with my stomach dropping during descent. To make matters worse, I would have to complete the dive once more as part of our final test.

The last and most dreaded activity we had to complete was springing off the diving board and then swimming underneath a bulkhead located 25 meters away, all within a time limit and without coming up for air. This was a vastly complicated test, yet I gave it my all and was able to pass on the first try! I did not want to redo the test, take the class over again, or jump off the diving board another time.

The feeling of finally passing all my swimming courses was incredible. It was one of the most difficult challenges of my life, but I managed to overcome it. When life hits the fan, you truly find out who you are. This victory was a massive boost to my psyche because it gave me the confidence that I could do anything. God gave me the strength to conquer my fear, and I was ever so grateful. Isaiah 41:10 describes this point exquisitely: "Fear thou not, for I *am* with thee: be not dismayed: for I *am* thy God: I will strengthen thee; yea, I will help thee; yea, I will uphold thee with the right hand of my righteousness." After the final lesson, my teammates and I celebrated in the locker room before football practice and afterward with a group dinner.

I went into spring football in February of 2013 completely healthy for the first time in a while. Spring football was much more physical than regular season practice and often where starters were decided for the following season. Therefore, I knew I had to be ready and perform optimally. I had taken every mental repetition I could from the offseason and studied my playbook thoroughly, and it manifested. I found myself in a battle with one of my friends, Dexter Walker, and was able to separate myself. I showed out and had the finest practices of my Academy football career up to that point. Competing so well while enduring the hardships of swimming class was a blessing. It was a testament to God allowing me to prosper and my determination paying dividends.

My victory was short lived when I encountered a reverse of fortune towards the end of spring ball. I went in to deliver a vigorous tackle against one of our tight ends and suffered my first concussion.

Injuries are much more significant in college because the domain is so competitive that players often rush back to avoid losing their spot. This was true for me also. In addition to the healthy ImPACT test I'd previously taken, I was given another one to compare the severity of my symptoms. Healthy ImPACT tests are used as a baseline against tests taken when injured. ImPACT tests are computerized exams that measure the effects of a concussion on the brain. The ImPACT test assesses verbal memory, visual memory, reaction time, and processing ability. ImPACT testing is a tool used to help those involved in concussion management to determine when an athlete is ready to start the return-to-play process.[120] I was not particularly fond of the ImPACT test because I thought it was inconsistent. There were times when I would perform better with a concussion than I had on my baseline exam.

Anytime I was subjected to an injury, I did whatever I could to return rapidly. Thankfully, my first concussion was mild, so I was able to make a swift return. I picked up where I left off before my injury and continued to thrive. I played some inspired football, knew my assignments, and came up big during scrimmages with timely interceptions. This was so satisfying. I had performed well enough to earn the starting job at strong safety and even received my own article the ensuing August in the Colorado Springs Gazette newspaper.

The interview was conducted with sportswriter Brent Briggeman. As a result of the article's content, it was named *Byrd offers high-flying ability in the Air Force secondary*. The article centered around my athleticism and keen ball skills. Coach Warren praised me in the article and even compared me to Jon Davis. He also stated that I maybe had the best spring of any Falcons defender, which meant a lot to me because I had worked so hard. My understanding of the playbook empowered me to execute precisely, allowing me to react to plays quicker without thinking. It also seemed that Coach Warren and I were seeing eye-to-eye.

SILVER LINING

Unfortunately, the spring semester would take in yet another suicide. Freshman James Walsh was found dead on February 9, 2013.

I was starting to get afraid of all the suicides happening at the Academy. This one was striking because Walsh was a four-degree, so he still had the opportunity to leave without penalty. Among the burdensome sophomore year, it was time for a much-needed summer break.

This summer term was far superior to the foregoing one. I was able to go home during the first block of the summer, participate in my operational Air Force assignment, and serve as ESET cadre. Prior to these summer activities was the procurement of my Career Starter Loan.

Once cadets are within one year of graduating, they become eligible for the USAA Career Starter Loan. The USAA Career Starter Loan is offered to cadets, midshipmen, and officer candidates.[121] The loan authorizes cadets to borrow up to $36,000 at a 0.75% interest rate, repaid over 60 months after graduating. This is essentially a free loan because the interest rate is so low. It was very enticing at the time, and most cadets ended up taking the loan. After speaking with a USAA representative, I followed suit.

Beholding $36,000 in my checking account was invigorating. I had never possessed that much money. All in all, I don't think I did a very good job of managing it. I was far too generous and made a lot of unwise purchases. If I were as knowledgeable as I am now, I would have consumed the money much carefully and invested more of it. But not all of my acquisitions were poor. Unlike many of my classmates, I already owned a vehicle, so that was not something I needed to buy. Yet, I did pay off the $10,000 remaining balance on my Grand Prix.

Since I was preparing to ship my Grand Prix to Colorado, I would no longer possess a vehicle when I visited home. Hence, I acquired one of my favorite classic cars: a 1985 Chevrolet Camaro I-Roc Z28. I negotiated the deal for only $3,400. When I bought it, the car was in great shape and ran without any issues. Over the years, I've made numerous modifications to it, turning it into a project car with plans of completely restoring it. That enterprise is still underway today with a swapped LS1 motor and the value now over $15,000. The rest of my funds went to family and various material things I could have done without. Ultimately, my loan was spent over the course of a couple of years, so I did not blow it right away as many of my classmates did.

A couple weeks later, I welcomed the shipment of my Grand Prix. A portion of my loan had gone towards the $600 shipment of my car from Tacoma. It was such a relief to finally have my own car and no longer have to rely on others for rides. I was now capable of coming and going as I pleased. Furthermore, I was able to attend Israelite more frequently as well. This was good for my well-being and edified my spirit each time I went.

Alas, my car was only practicable for three-quarters of the year in Colorado. With my front-wheel drive vehicle having 20-inch rims, it was useless during the snow. Colorado averages 33 inches of snow per year.[122] The worst period is between November 14th and February 21st.[123] One cold winter day, I attempted to drive down to the Field House, USAFA's athletic complex, on the icy pavement. Since the roads were clear of snow, I assumed I would be able to make it. I was halfway there when I lost traction going up a hill and spun into a rocky wall. My tires would only turn in place when I aimed into reverse. Luckily, defensive lineman Nick Fitzgerald was nearby and towed me out of the hazard. I only scratched a small amount of paint off my front bumper in the accident. More importantly, I learned my lesson about testing Colorado's harsh winters on the road.

One of the coldest times I experienced was in December of my senior year, with lows between -10 and -20 degrees amid a windchill of up to -40. The high was a meager six degrees. It was so cold that cadets were recorded throwing pots of boiling water out of their windows and the water freezing before it hit the ground. I was miserable in this chilly weather. Even so, classes still weren't canceled.[124]

In advance of getting my car to Colorado, I often had to walk to practice in the jarring weather. The fifteen-minute stroll was even worse coming back because of the inclined slope. I would be bundled up from head to toe with several layers and still be cold. Colorado's grating weather was just one more hindrance to my Academy experience. After enjoying my three weeks at home, I hopped on a flight to Texas for my operational period.

"The operational Air Force program is used to acquaint scores of Air Force Academy cadets with the operational Air Force. Operations (Ops) Air Force is a two-and-a-half-week summer training program for Academy cadets," said Lt Col Anthony Salvatore, the Cadet Wing's group-one commander. More than 900 upcoming two-degree cadets, visit more than 40 bases to check out career specialties for officers and spend time with Airmen. Ops Air Force is a tremendous opportunity for cadets to experience active duty Air Force operations before receiving their commissions as second lieutenants," Salvatore said. "Our cadets say the program influences their career choices, helps them better understand their career options and education and teaches them how to plan for their eventual duties as company grade officers.[125] Each cadet is randomly assigned a base for their participation in the program. There are a number of bases located in beautiful locations such as Hawaii and Tampa. Lamentably, I was dispatched to dreary Sheppard AFB in Wichita Falls, TX, the middle of nowhere.

Generally speaking, the program was a great experience. But the base itself was secluded and blistering in the middle of Texas summer heat. I was there with 20 other cadets, and we often found the temperature in the triple digits. One of the cadets present was Joseph Champaign, a fellow football player, and friend of mine. Due to the extreme Texas warmth, we were forced to complete our strength and conditioning early in the morning prior to the 8:00 a.m. start of the operational program, and after its 4:00 p.m. conclusion. Champaign and I were both mightily dedicated football players, so we would accomplish our running in the morning while it was the coolest and lift weights in the afternoon.

The program took place Monday-Friday. We were given authorization to shadow and learn about different functions at Sheppard Air Force Base. One of the most interesting days was spent with the Security Forces. As the largest career field in the Air Force, it's the job of Security Forces to protect, defend and fight. They are responsible for missile security, defending air bases around the globe, law enforcement on those bases, combat arms, and handling military working dogs.[126] As a part of the experience, they offered each cadet the opportunity to be tased. The occurrence was conducted using taser prongs. Four prongs were placed onto the cadet, and then a trigger was pulled that released the charge. There were Airmen on both sides of each cadet to catch them and brace their fall.

After watching a couple of my classmates undergo the tasing, I decided I would not subject myself to the voluntary pain. But once my turn came around and I relayed my choice, everyone in the class ridiculed me. So, I ended up giving in to the peer pressure and engaged in the electric shock. The Special Forces lead counted down from three to one, and then the prongs jolted my entire body. I was unable to move for the few seconds the power was surging. The current prompted my frame to go limp and the Airmen slowly guided me to the ground as I endured the agonizing pain in what felt like an eternity. Once the energy terminated, I regained control of my body and rose to my feet. I knew from this exposure that I never wanted to be confronted with a taser in a real-world situation.

The absolute best day of the program encompassed a ride in a T-38C jet trainer. The T-38C Talon is a twin-engine, high-altitude, supersonic jet trainer used in a variety of roles because of its design, economy of operations, ease of maintenance, high performance, and exceptional safety record.[127] The top speed is 842 miles per hour.[128] Having the ability to ride in this aircraft was an unforgettable, once-in-a-lifetime opportunity. Before the trip, we were given a briefing on safety and aircraft features, fitted into G-suits, and taught various durability tactics.

Resilience was emphasized because the T-38 can pull more than 7 "G's," or seven times the force of gravity.[128] The techniques were necessary because the added gravitational forces can prompt one's body to lose consciousness at elevated levels. As a result, your body crunches up, and you start seeing tunnel vision.[129] G-suits are pants with air bladders in them. As we enter a turn, the bladders inflate, squeezing our legs and preventing blood from rushing towards our feet. To increase endurance, we have pressure-breathing, which forces air into our lungs during high-G's. Instead of struggling for a breath, with what feels like an elephant on our chest, we can take a small sip of air and rely on the pressure-breathing to fill our lungs.[130] G-suits are also thought to provide about 2-G protection.[131]

The pressurized cabin helps with breathing, but we also needed to apply several strategies. One of them was to tense our muscles to keep our blood pumping while the G-forces pushed down and pooled our blood in the abdomen and legs. The other was to inhale, hold for several seconds, and then powerfully exhale, which allowed blood to flow into our hearts and chest.[132] In my case, I could feel my body losing awareness and my eyes starting to close, making my perception appear as I were looking out of a peephole. Therefore, I applied the techniques and managed to stay alert the entire flight. The pilot pulled off numerous exhilarating maneuvers, making a roller coaster feel pedestrian. We even flew inverted for short bursts. The tandem-cockpit jet also possessed a steering wheel with limited capabilities in the rear cabin. During the flight, the pilot gave me permission to take the wheel and fly the jet. I was extremely nervous for the segment, so I kept the jet steady, turning slightly at most. I should have done more because I had nothing to fear with the pilot capable of taking control of the plane at any time. Nevertheless, being able to guide a jet was unimaginable.

The last summer period was spent as ESET cadre, which was much more enjoyable than participating in the program. As different third-class cadet groups went through ESET, my job was to act as the adversary during their survival training. This involved being dropped off at various places in the woods and attempting to ambush them while they were on their routes. Sadly, due to being nested in the woods for extended periods of time, I would be subjected to more bacteria than normal. Accordingly, I contracted gastroenteritis again, which is an inflammation of the lining of the intestines caused by a virus, bacteria, or parasites.[133] This time was worse; my main symptom was abdominal pain, which I bore every day for months. The pain was so severe that I underwent testing to discover if I had something worse. Doctors suspected I may have had an ulcer, but further examination proved that to be negative. Regardless, gastroenteritis created an uncommonly difficult spell for me, especially while training for football.

Every day after executing ESET cadre, I would still have team workouts. However, ESET would often extend beyond normal hours, causing myself and several of my teammates to miss scheduled workout times. Consequently, strength and conditioning coach Matt McGettigan would stay late and offer us an auxiliary session. Coach McGettigan is one of the most intense people I've ever met. He is no-nonsense, exceptionally serious, thorough, and knowledgeable. He propels every player to be their best in the weight room. He's also widely considered one of the best strength and conditioning coaches in the country. Since his arrival in 2006, the Falcons have won over 70 percent of their games over the second half of the season. In addition to being in better physical shape, the Falcons have seen fewer significant injuries.[134] Working out with gastroenteritis was unusually disturbing, but I toughed it out and withstood the affliction. This resilience led me right into my critical junior year.

Any time before a cadet's junior year, they can leave without penalty. Freshmen and sophomore cadets are ordinarily relieved from all military duty, active, or reserve commitment, but may still be required to reimburse the government if they are disenrolled for serious misconduct. But once a cadet reports to class on the first day of their junior academic year, they have pledged their commitment. Accordingly, it is advised that cadets ensure they've thought long and hard about the obligation because there is no turning back. The day before school starts, the celebratory Commitment Dinner is held. Once the cadets return to the Air Force Academy for their second-class year, they incur the financial or active duty "commitment" for their education if they depart the Air Force Academy prior to graduation. The Class Spirit Committee works with the Cadet Wing to give each cadet a coin to honor the event.[135]

This was one of the preeminent decisions of my life, necessitating a good deal of thinking, praying, and consulting. Although things weren't going as planned on the football field, I'd made some great friends and still didn't have an outlet or plan if I were to leave. Besides, I had already dedicated two years of my life to the Academy, which would essentially go to waste if I departed. Moreover, the benefits and the opportunities ahead were too good to pass up. So, by showing up at the Commitment Dinner, I validated my decision. Commitment Dinner was a hefty milestone I enjoyed sharing with my classmates. The next day would be the official start of my second-class year as a newly devoted cadet. It would also include the dawn of my majors' studies.

I thoroughly enjoyed my majors' curriculum over core classes. As a result, my grades greatly improved. It was easier to internalize the content when I cared more about the subjects at hand. I finished the 2013 fall semester with a 2.54 GPA, but my grades plunged back to a 2.33 GPA the following spring semester mainly because of the D I received in World History. History was not difficult, but it was my least favorite subject. I simply did not enjoy learning about human civilization, so it was decidedly laborious for me to focus. In addition, my instructor's teaching style was averse to my learning style. I am a visual learner, so I retain information better in perceptible form. But when we reviewed readings, my professor would go around the classroom and ask students for their input. This was too subjective for me, and therefore, I did not preserve much of the particulars. Finally, my mind comprehends numbers far greater than fuzzy details such as cultures and societies. Although I strained with history and my overall GPA plummeted, my majors' GPA was 2.85. I was beginning to perceive the manifestation of progress, which served well for my confidence. Athletically, things were a bit different.

My junior year did not go as planned based on my stellar spring football performance and offseason. Foreseeably, I was named the starter for the 2013 season. But my stint was cut short after we began the season 1-3, and I was the odd man out. I was told the change was made because I was not causing enough turnovers or being productive enough. To this day, I've never understood how that was the case when I had recorded 31 tackles, a pass break-up, and an interception in those four games.

On Parent's Weekend, we won our first game handily against D-IAA opponent Colgate, 38-13. I registered four tackles in that game. Unfortunately, we would go on to lose our next three games by an average of 29 points, to no fault of my own. I undoubtedly made mistakes like everyone else, but overall, I was playing well and should not have been benched.

Furthermore, we had won the battle against Colgate but lost the season-long war. Our starting quarterback, Kale Pearson, suffered a season-ending ACL tear in the second quarter. Our second game came against Heisman candidate Chuckie Keeton and the Utah State Aggies. Our defense allowed 52 points against their spread attack, and our offense was only able to muster 20 points with our backup quarterback.

Subsequent to my first concussion in March, I precisely knew the symptoms. In the first quarter, I would take part in a helmet-to-helmet collision and face my second concussion. I was reeling immediately after the hit, and my head was ringing. However, I did not report the collision to the training staff and continued playing. The two bright spots for me were that I made seven tackles and seized my one and only career interception, which came a couple of drives after my concussion. The interception ensued just before halftime as Utah State was threatening to put more points on the board. I was in my half-field coverage reading the quarterback's eyes when he raised up to hit an open receiver screaming down the middle of the field. I had anticipated the throw and dove right under the pass as it sailed over the receiver's head, stalling the Aggie's drive. After the interception, I raced to my team's sideline with a confident flex, welcomed by my exuberant teammates and coaches. The pick certainly felt sweeter because it was against a Heisman candidate, but the loss stung, nonetheless.

Our next game occurred on a nationally televised forum via ESPN at Boise State. I had watched games played on that blue field growing up, so it was a cool experience to actually play there. Boise defeated us 42-20 with the help of two would-be NFL players, Jay Ajiyi and Demarcus Lawrence. We started the first half distinctly well with a halftime deficit of only four, but were unable to get much going in the second half. I recorded a career-high nine tackles in the loss. Ajiyi destroyed us, rushing 17 times for 125 yards and four touchdowns. He was a load to tackle and would cause the same problems in the NFL for years. Lawrence charted nine tackles of his own with two for loss. Lawrence is now one of the better pass rushers in the NFL for the Dallas Cowboys.

My worst defeat as a starter would come the next game against Wyoming, another spread offense. We lost 56-23, and the story was more of the same. After my benching, we would lose four more games before our next win against Army. We were never quite able to get on track that season and finished 2-10, the team's worst record in history. The increase in production never emerged when I was replaced, but I remained positive, and hopeful given the circumstances.

I played through various illnesses while at the Academy. Believe it or not, one of them was even pneumonia. A couple of my teammates had already caught it, and I was suffering the same symptoms, so I decided to get checked out. I was diagnosed on October 8, 2013, by way of an X-ray, but I hardly missed a beat. I continued to practice and play in games, often vomiting between repetitions. I was able to keep playing with the help of an inhaler to facilitate my breathing, along with antibiotics for my acute cough. It was a difficult feat, but I made do. Astoundingly, the X-ray also revealed a mild abnormal curve in my spine. Hence, the reason I had been ailing and playing through back spasms for several years. Thus, I began receiving additional treatment for that as well. Even then, I was wholly dedicated to the football team and wanted to be on the field with my brothers. That was until my season was cut short by a life-changing event.

Several of my teammates and I were out in Denver enjoying some much-needed time away from the Academy. We decided to go to a bar downtown during our bye week in November. One of my teammates had gotten into a confrontation with a stranger, and as most loyal teammates would do, I intervened to defend him. The situation calmed down, and we went back to enjoying ourselves. A short time later, the opposition returned and blindsided me with a vigorous punch to my right eye. Undeniably, my eye was in considerable pain, but I thought I was fine. After stumbling slightly, I quickly regained my balance. By the time I went to defend myself, the man had darted down the stairs and out of the building. I was too distorted to chase him, so I let my teammates ineffectively race after him. The man had somehow gotten away from several Division I football players, and Jordan was nowhere to be found.

Promptly, everyone else in my group was frantically pointing at my eye. I told them I was alright, but they insisted that I sit down. I was told to look at my eye on my phone and was stunned to see blood flowing down my face. I could no longer see out of my right eye as it was now swollen shut. The ambulance was called, and I was rushed to the emergency room. Upon arrival, I took a better look at my eye and could not believe what had transpired; I felt betrayed. Sustaining a wound for shielding my teammate did not sit well with me. To make matters worse, no one was there to look out for me. I had looked out for the friends I was with on countless occasions, but the one time I needed them to have my back, they were absent. There were so many questions running through my head about how the situation befell; I was crushed.

After careful examination and numerous X-rays, I was diagnosed with a skull fracture. The bone under my eye had been broken, in addition to numerous lacerations on my eyelid. The lacerations were stitched together, and an implant was placed in my eye duct for the surgeries I would need soon. Regrettably, my eye would never be the same. Even now, I still suffer complications from my injury. After the initial procedure, I was told I may not be able to play football again. I was distraught by the horrifying diagnosis. Not only that, but my ability to graduate was in jeopardy as well due to the Academy's graduation standards. The undetermined state of my future as a football player and a cadet was worrisome, and profusely stressful.

Several of my friends remained with me at the hospital until I was released the following day. Demario Kohn, who chased after the adversary, stopped by my room to express his remorse. We had a heart-to-heart, and he apologized for my abrasion and the assailant getting away. I recognized his sincerity and instantly forgave him. Demario and I continued to have a great friendship. Jordan also apologized, but I did not trust his genuineness. He told me he was in the restroom during the altercation, which I found hard to believe at the time. Marques Stevenson, who I had defended, also had a questionable excuse in my mind, as well as Miles Fisher.

Consequently, I attributed my trauma to everyone present, except for Demario. I reverted to my old, guarded self because that was the only way I knew how to handle the situation, and I did not want to be hurt by them again. I slowly distanced myself away from the rest of the guys and went back into my shell. That being the case, my last 18 months at the Academy were fairly lonely, and it wasn't until a few years ago that I found it in my heart to forgive them. Upon reexamination, I regret how I managed the plight. My reaction was misguided, and I am remorseful for my approach. I should not have held my affliction against them and forgiven them sooner. Whatever their reasons, they had an oversight, and mistakes happen. I hope they can forgive me for my lapse as well.

The next day was filled with ample paperwork and phone calls disclosing to everyone what took place. My squadron leadership was contrite, my mother was distraught, my coaches were disappointed, and my family and friends back home were outraged. I was also greatly infuriated. My hometown friends wished they had been there to avert an accident like this. After all the conflict I experienced in Tacoma, I had never been attacked off guard. Anytime there was a confrontation, the two parties would talk it out, or more commonly, agree to engage in a fair fight. But sucker-punching someone was considered weak and frowned upon.

Over the next few weeks, my swelling abated, but I still encountered excessively poor vision. My right eye was blurry, and experienced diplopia, or double vision. This led to my first surgery to restore my vision and insert a plate under my eye where the bone had been shattered, which could not be achieved until my swelling declined. The surgery required sedation and was successful for the most part as the eye surgeon, Dr. John Burroughs, was able to expertly position the plate under my eye and erase my blurry vision.

Unfortunately, there was still some diplopia remaining, requiring an additional surgery to repair. Yet, the extra surgery was unnecessary, nor was there any guarantee it would fix the residual diplopia. So, as advised by Dr. Burroughs, I waived the added surgery and still have some double vision today. Currently, my eye has swelling and is easily irritated, which I will endure the rest of my life.

Posterior to my lucrative surgery, the next few weeks were spent rehabilitating my eye to determine if I would be competent to play football again. My overhaul was conducted in the sports training section of the Human Performance Lab (HPL), across the street from the Field House. The U.S. Air Force Academy's HPL applies sports science principles to improve Academy athletic teams and individual cadet performance. Coaches, cadet-athletes, and cadets receive specific physiological information through testing, research, training, and education. The Performance Lab also provides expertise on the Air Force fitness program and human performance, offering scientific data through research and exercise science principles. As a result, the HPL provides a venue for cadet researchers and qualified exercise physiology interns to complete independent study research in exercise physiology, biology, biochemistry, and biomechanics. The HPL tests and trains more than 2,000 cadets and approximately 200 faculty, staff, and active duty members annually.[136] The sports vision training encompasses the following:

- Depth perception - the ability to quickly and accurately judge the distance and speed of objects.
- Eye-tracking - the ability to stay focused on an object in motion.
- Peripheral vision - the ability to see objects in the periphery while concentrating on a fixed point.
- Eye focusing - the ability to change focus quickly and accurately from one object to another.
- Binocular vision - the ability to keep both eyes working together.
- Fusion flexibility/stamina - the ability to keep both eyes working together under visually demanding conditions.
- Eye, hand, body coordination - the ability to appropriately use your body when responding to visual information.
- Visual concentration - the ability to stay focused on visual tasks for increased awareness and fewer distractions.[137]

I took part in each of these activities daily, which became overly tiresome. But I knew I wanted to play football again, so I was inordinately motivated. Midway through my rehabilitation, I was given an exam to determine my eye's recuperation. I knew I'd made progress, but I was still nervous about the outcome; my entire football career hung in the balance. When it came time to test, I put my best foot forward, and the results were staggering. I passed comfortably. I cannot thank the vision staff enough for the innumerable hours put in, resulting in the strides I made. My eye was healthy enough for me to return to the field. In fact, the vision training had gone so well that my eyesight improved from 20/20 before my injury to 20/13. 20/13 vision is when one can see from 20 feet away. The average person would have to be 13 feet away to perceive the same object. This was another moment where I was abundantly grateful to God for enabling me to recover. Following that victory, I went back to work.

The second semester of my junior year incorporated the selection of my AFSC, which is known as a dream sheet. AFSCs are broken up into two categories: rated and non-rated. Rated AFSCs encompass pilots and career fields related to flying aircraft. Non-rated AFSCs are non-flying jobs such as acquisitions, finance, and contracting. Rated jobs demand ancillary medical qualifications; I elected not to go that route because I did not want to fly or incur an additional five-year service commitment. The job-selection process is based on four criteria: needs of the Air Force, cadet qualifications, cadet preferences, and the board rankings.[138] I listed my top six jobs, with acquisitions being number one.

Acquisitions officers manage defense acquisition programs covering every aspect of the acquisition process, including integrating engineering, program control, test and deployment, configuration management, production and manufacturing, quality assurance, and logistics support. They also perform functions essential to acquisition programs involving major defense acquisition programs and other than major systems or subsystems.[139]

Acquisitions in the Air Force is essentially program management, the field of study most aligned with my major; thus, it would be a smooth transition for me. The main reason I chose acquisitions was because it is the AFSC most compatible with the corporate world when one decides to separate from the Air Force. I had planned to complete my five-year commitment and then dodge, also known as "five and dive," amongst Academy graduates, so this was in line with my scheme. The nuance with career choices is that the needs of the Air Force take priority over cadet preferences. Laurie Carroll, the Academy's Manpower, and Personnel director, voiced, "When the Air Force classifies cadets into their career field, preference is considered as an important factor. However, Air Force needs take precedence. Ensuring Air Force mission needs are met sometimes means fewer cadets receive their top career field choices, but where possible, we consider individual preferences."[140] With my dream sheet submitted, I anxiously waited until the ensuing fall to find out what my Air Force career would be. In the meantime, I was set to partake in my last spring football as a cadet.

It was the spring heading into my senior season, and my career hadn't gone as I'd hoped. We'd had a horrendous junior season, much to the fault of our senior leadership. So going into my last year, that was a focal point of mine. I gave my last shot all I had. To add to the pot, there was a defensive backs coaching change as Coach Warren took a job at Nebraska. My new position coach would be Steve Russ, former USAFA football player, and Denver Broncos linebacker. Coach Russ, now the linebackers coach for the Washington Commanders, was an awesome coach to play for. He was extremely knowledge and galvanized the defensive backs with a fervent mentality. Dexter, my competition from the preceding year, had been moved to linebacker during the offseason so a golden opportunity opened.

Leading into spring football, where I thrived again, Dexter's position change gave me a clear advantage to become the starter. That was until I endured my fourth concussion during practice. Each successive concussion took longer to recover from, which was particularly derailing. This one would keep me out for the majority of spring ball. Overall, though, my senior season was much different than years past, and it manifested. We did a great job providing leadership to the team as seniors, we were focused, and had an identity. The defensive back group gave ourselves the name "Money Team." The logic was that we would be putting money in the bank through hard work and repetition at practice and then getting paid on game days by enjoying the fruits of our labor.

The end of my second-class year concluded with the momentous Ring Dance. Ring Dance is a formal ball exclusively for second-class cadets held during graduation week, before the second-class cadets become first-class cadets, and is where they receive their class rings and unveil the class crest. The rings are traditionally placed in a glass of champagne and are caught in the teeth following a toast.[141] The class crest is a treasured representation of class unity and pride. The Academy crest is placed on the left side of the ring. The bezel surrounds a stone or inset with the words "U.S. Air Force

Academy." A chain of 59 links circles these to represent the Academy's first graduating class and the bond each class shares. These elements remain constant throughout the years and serve as another bond all classes share. My class's ring contains multiple representative symbols:

- Graduation year - "2015" is boldly displayed at the top of the crest.
- Class motto - The Class of 2015 in Latin is "Una Pugna, Una Caterva," - "One fight, one team." The Class of 2015 carried this motto from BCT, the struggles of our four-degree year, and through the intensity of Recognition.
- Eagle - The crest's centerpiece, the eagle, is an honored symbol of the U.S. known for its power and grace in flight, qualities future Air Force officers strive to emulate.
- U.S. flag - The U.S. flag, clutched by the eagle, symbolizes the patriotism and respect Academy graduates have for the U.S. The 15 stars represent the pride in being a member of the Class of 2015.
- Polaris - The North Star, portrayed as a symbol of honor and guidance, is grasped by the eagle's talons. This symbolizes the integrity each Academy graduate possesses in their heart to be an officer of character.
- Orville and Wilbur Wright - The Class of 2015's exemplars, the graduates honor the Wright Brothers with an "O" and a "W" hidden in the beams of Polaris.
- Wright flyer - Powered flight is possible because of the Wright Brothers. The Wright flyer illustrates the creativity and ingenuity that is the basis of the U.S. Air Force.
- Class number - The Class of 2015 is the Air Force Academy's 57th graduating class, represented by the Roman number LVII hidden in the Wright Brother's wing supports.
- Prop and Wings - The Prop and Wings are in the crest to remind the Class of 2015 of the struggles they endured during Recognition and remind them that they can overcome any hardship.
- Saber - The saber is a symbol of leadership and authority. It is placed on the crest to remind Class of 2015 graduates that

officership forms the foundation upon which they will grow in their careers.[142]

My class ring is one of my most prized possessions because it embodies the blood, sweat, and tears I underwent at the Academy. I wear it every day as a token of my endeavor. After Ring Dance, it was time for my last summer at USAFA.

My final summer was spent at home, enacting ESET cadre again, and undertaking the legendary Astronautical Engineering (Astro) course. Astro is debatably the most challenging core class at USAFA. It introduces the history, principles, and challenges of space. Emphasis is placed on understanding the underlying physical principles and the system engineering process used to select orbits, plan maneuvers, and accomplish preliminary design of spacecraft payloads/subsystems to meet mission requirements.[98] Mrs. B again used her mastery and enrolled me in Astro during the summer. One of the main reasons for her effort was that Astro has a reputation for leading seniors to their demise. Several first-class cadets had failed this course during the academic year and were not allowed to graduate on time. Taking this course in the summer gave me ample time to retake it during the schoolyear if I were to stall.

However, retaking Astro was completely unnecessary as I passed with a B+, ironically one of my best grades as a cadet. Part of this was, once more, due to the ability to focus on one class during the summer with tailored instruction. The other driver was that the Astro principles surprisingly made sense to me. Because Astro involved a ton of math, I grasped the material, plus I took it seriously because I knew the potency it could have on my career. That success in the classroom set me up for my concluding football season.

I found myself in another battle in my final training camp, probably the closest one on the team. A huge point of emphasis for the defense during training camp was creating turnovers. Coach Russ was emphatic about it, and I understood the importance. I was quoted in the Gazette expressing, "It's a mindset of stripping at the ball. Even if you don't get it the first time, eventually, during a game, one of those is going to come out. So, we've got to be persistent and keep working at it." The position contest this time around was against freshman Weston Steelhammer (Wes), who too bought into the turnover initiative.

Wes was an abundantly talented kid from Shreveport, LA, who was also highly recruited for baseball. His baseball skills undoubtedly helped him on the football field because he had supreme ball skills. Although we were fighting for the same position, Wes and I became great friends, and I was able to share some of my veteran experience with him. We cordially duked it out until the starters were named a few weeks before our first game. The position could have gone either way, but eventually, Wes was chosen as the starter. I could not fault Coach Russ because it was a laborious decision, but he ended up making the right one. While I wasn't starting, I played a significant role on the team and practiced a lot with the first team. I was one of the smartest players on defense, so I knew all the plays and each player's responsibilities. This paid dividends as it allowed Coach Russ to rotate me between free safety and strong safety, resulting in more playing time. This was not a bad bargain, and I took advantage of it.

Wes and I each had two tackles in our first game of the season against D-IAA opponent Nicholls State. We conquered them 44-16 inside the packed stadium on Parents' Weekend. Our next game came against conference rival Wyoming. Unluckily for me, I would undergo my endmost concussion. Due to my concussion history and the advent of technology, I was presented with a helmet containing shock sensors prior to the season. Each time I was involved in a collision, the sensors would record the magnitude and send it to monitors held by the training staff. The trainers would then be able to recognize the impact's percentile and, if high enough, analyze me for a concussion. The loftiest collision I logged all season registered in the 99th percentile, or the hardest possible blow, but did not result in a concussion.

The concussion I sustained in the Wyoming game did not warrant concern from the training staff because the impact was ordinary. However, the helmet-to-helmet tackle I made left me dazed and wobbly with an excruciating headache. Like the Utah State game my junior year, I did not notify the trainers and finished the game. We had displayed our best outing against Wyoming in years, holding the lead until the last 58 seconds of the game. That was until they scored on a three-yard touchdown pass to seal the game. It was an extremely deflating fashion to lose in, especially since we played so well on the road.

I recorded two more tackles in the game and played good assignment football. Afterward, the concussion had reared its head. By then, my head was throbbing more forcefully, and I was vomiting so copiously that I began to cry. It was at that moment I knew I did not want to endure anymore concussions, and this would be my last year playing football. The trainers came to check on me and discovered I had suffered yet another concussion. This resulted in one more trip to the emergency room.

The doctors performed a customary X-ray and CT scan to see if there was any cerebrum bruising or ambiguities. Happily, neither existed. I was just experiencing symptoms from the collision. One of the trainers, Col McGinty, was kind enough to stay overnight with me in Wyoming while the rest of the team headed back home after the game. He gave me a ride back to Colorado the next morning, then allowed me to stay at his residence and rest. This was such a courteous gesture, and it was greatly appreciated. After the concussion, I began to feel some lasting effects from my head injuries, central of them being insomnia. I started having grave difficulty falling and staying asleep.

Consequently, my productivity and mood were negatively affected. I wasn't as interested in being around others and started spiraling into depression. Although I was taking up enduring symptoms, I was able to complete the return to play protocol fairly quickly and only missed two games: just in time for our annual service academy clash against Navy.

At this point, we were 3-1, but we knew we should have been 4-0. Quarterback Keenan Reynolds was a menacing runner who went down as one of the greatest players in Navy football history. He also remains the NCAA record-holder with 88 career rushing touchdowns, while ranking third in Navy history in passing yards and first in passing touchdowns.[143] Reynolds was selected in the sixth round by the Baltimore Ravens the following year.

Regrettably, for Reynolds, we were clicking on all cylinders and had a great week of practice leading up to the game. Our scout team had done a noteworthy job of running their plays and preparing us. Herschel Walker, arguably the greatest running back in college football history and Heisman trophy winner, stopped by our practice the Wednesday before the game to speak some remarkably inspiring words. It was an honor to be able to meet him. Moreover, before the season, we had moved the empty CIC trophy case into the center of our locker room, which was eminently motivating having to look at it every day.

The contest against Navy yielded incredible energy, though we were able to withstand ours longer. We were starkly sound on both sides of the football. I pitched in three tackles against their triple-option attack. Unfortunately, I also suffered a further ailment in my first game back when I was blocked low by a lineman. I was able to finish the game, but the injury lingered on to the next game against Utah State; I could not catch a break.

Nevertheless, we prevailed over the Goats 30-21 after pulling away in the fourth quarter. It felt like we were on top of the world. This was a huge step towards winning the heralded Commander-in-Chiefs trophy for the first time since my freshman year. Secretary of the Air Force Deborah James was in attendance and led cadets in pushups following one of our touchdowns. Also in attendance was the Joint Chiefs of Staff, Army General Martin Dempsey and the Air Force Chief of Staff, General Mark Welsh. Additionally, General Welsh was happy enough to join the football team in the locker room for our postgame celebration.

After every win, we celebrated by performing the Samoan "Oh Talala" chant. The chant was established by Richard Bell, Chris Gizzi and Jeff Mohr following the 1998 Oahu Bowl.[144] As the team huddles together, the chant begins especially quiet and then gradually grows louder. Towards the end, everyone is at full throttle and Gatorade and water are being projected around the locker room. Everyone's uniforms become drenched, but it's certainly worth the commemoration. It's one of the best parts of winning football games at the AFA. General Welch planted himself in the middle of the celebration, soaking his uniform and loving every minute of it.

A couple of days after the Navy win, the Northwest Guardian, a local newspaper from Tacoma associated with McChord Air Force Base, reached out to me for an interview. The article, titled *Air Force senior got start at McChord Field*, focused on my background and Academy experience up to that point. Here is an excerpt from the article: There are 128 college football teams in the National Collegiate Athletic Association's Football Bowl Subdivision (FBS), each with about 125 total players both on and off the rosters -- a grand total of around 16,000 players. Jamal Byrd, a senior defensive back for the Air Force Falcons, is one of only 375 -- about 2.3 percent of FBS -- who is serving at a military academy and playing against some of the best Division I programs nationally. Byrd was born at the Air Force Academy before moving to Tacoma in 1995 when his father was stationed with the 62nd Civil Engineer Squadron at McChord Air Force Base. Growing up with his mother in Tacoma, Byrd said he was thankful for the coaches and mentors at Foss High School to help keep him motivated and driven while going through difficult times as a child. "I think that helped prepare me that not everything is handed to you," Byrd said. Byrd said he's already excited about where he will be sent after graduation and hopes to pursue a career in acquisitions. But for now, his immediate goal is for the Falcons to go to 1-0 each week of the football season. Despite missing a number of games due to concussions, Byrd has a total of seven tackles, including three in a 30-21 win over Navy to advance one step closer to claiming the Commander-in-Chief's Trophy. Navy held the trophy in 2012 and 2013, but the Falcons hope to claim the title when they face Army November 1st at the Military Academy at West Point, N.Y. Jamal hopes the team can continue to compete for the Mountain West Conference title and qualify for a bowl game. At 5-2, the Falcons just need one more win to clinch a berth.[145] It was uplifting to receive love from my hometown for the success I was having. I soaked up the brief notoriety and then went back to business, preparing for my next opponent.

I left the Utah State game early after being bothered by my prolonged ankle injury, relaying my frustration on Twitter via an in-game tweet. Following that game, we would go on to win five of our last seven games, earning a 9-3 record. Most notable of those games was our triumph over Army, clinching the CIC title for that year. The game was never close as we throttled them 23-6 in their home stadium. We were ecstatic after the win, turning their visiting locker room into a party. Waiting in each player's locker was a card from President Obama, congratulating us on the victory and anticipating his visit with us the following spring. This was a surreal moment for each of us, one that displayed a product of our hard work.

Due to my inability to stay healthy, I became more of a special teams player towards the end of my senior season. Thus, I closed the season with only 16 tackles, 7 of those coming against San Diego State. Individually, my season wasn't what I wanted, but more importantly, my team had turned things around and was having a tremendous year. Wes, on the other hand, earned first-team All-Conference honors. He finished fourth in the Mountain West and

13th nationally in interceptions with six, the fifth most in a season in school history. Part of the reason we had such an illustrious season was that we were unselfish, so each defensive back celebrated his success. At that, our exceptional season netted an invitation to the Idaho Potato Bowl.

I didn't think the gifts were as good as the ones we received from the Armed Forces bowl a couple of years prior, but the game was assuredly much better. We trounced Western Michigan 38-24 on the rainy blue turf in Boise, ID. The game also presented a prodigious benefit. With Boise being a six-hour drive from Tacoma, I was able to have about a dozen of my friends and family see me play in the last game of my college career. On the other side of the ball, we faced would-be NFL receiver Corey Davis. Davis was the fifth overall pick in 2017 by the Tennessee Titans, and his play against us showed why. He shredded us, reeling in eight catches for 176 yards and three touchdowns.

We finished the season 10-3, the team's best record in over 15 years. The eight-game turnaround is the best in school history.[146] My senior season was truly a momentous one. The Falcons entered the bowl season as one of just two teams nationally to have beaten two 10-win teams in the regular season. The Falcons beat Boise State and in-state rival Colorado State, who each won 10 or more games. Air Force's 10-win season is just its sixth in school history. The victory over Boise State was historic, as the Falcons became the first team in the Mountain West's Mountain Division to beat the Broncos. The victory over Colorado State, which was ranked 21st nationally, marked the highest-ranked team Air Force has beaten since 1996. Air Force finished 6-0 at home for just the fourth time in school history.[147]

Although I had already decided my senior season would be my last year playing football, I couldn't help but think about my NFL dream. Several other seniors on the team with NFL ambitions had already chosen to continue working out and test at our school's pro day, where NFL scouts evaluate prospects as they perform position and combine drills. I had even received a letter to attend a combine in Georgia, but my concussion history, the progressive severity of each of them, and the lasting effects I was noticing weighed on me.

Playing time and productivity over a college football player's career are both significant factors for NFL recruitment. Talent, intelligence, testing, and combine performance are all notable as well. Hence, I did not allow my lack of playing time to influence my decision. I knew I was talented enough, smart enough, and had the size to play at the next level. Plus, a handful of athletes make teams every year who play at small schools or even go undrafted; Kurt Warner, Warren Moon, and Antonio Gates to name a few. This made my determination that much more complex. Hereafter, I wisely, yet wistfully gave up on my NFL aspirations. I was compelled to choose my health over my dream, a compromise I still struggle with today. I knew I could have played in the NFL, but God had other plans for me. That swap is what's given me peace over the years.

While I was eager to graduate, I did not allow senioritis to set in; I couldn't afford to. I remained focused on my academics, earning an overall 2.48 GPA with a 2.65 majors GPA during the fall semester. Also, during the first semester, I would discover my operational career. Cadets with rated AFSCs had already been notified of their jobs on October 1, 2014, so the rest of us were anxiously standing by. On November 8th, our AFSCs were posted on our doors while we were at lunch. My stomach was in knots as I proceeded to reveal my occupation. Delightedly, I received my number one pick–acquisitions. I knew God had worked things out for me again, and I was thoroughly grateful. I was one of 70 cadets to receive an acquisition management career.[140] Not everyone was fortunate enough to receive their first selection, or even any of their choices. Roughly half received their first choice, 18% received their second choice, and 9% received their third choice.[140]

Some of my teammates inherited the most unfavorable AFSC of all: nuclear and missile operations. Missile operations is the least desired mainly because of the ghastly working conditions and remote locations of missile bases. Missile operations requires you to work 70-80 feet underground for 24 hours at a time in a room less than 200 feet square. I felt terrible for them because that was much different from the standard workday, but I was also glad I wasn't in their shoes.

After receiving our job assignments, we could now designate our base preferences. Every Air Force base has a different mission, so AFSCs are only available at specific bases. With job assignments in hand, we were now allowed to see the available bases to choose from. The loftiest bases for acquisitions are in Los Angeles, Boston, and Ohio, amid about a dozen other smaller locations. Selecting a larger base gives one a better opportunity of receiving their choice because there are more openings. I've never been a fan of the cold, so it was a no-brainer; Los Angeles was my first option. My remaining preferences contained Northern California and Florida, with Boston bringing up the rear. I apprehensively submitted my dream sheet and prepared to wait another couple of months for my decision. Then I hit a bump in the road.

Since the acquisitions career field is so far removed from conventional Air Force culture, the Air Force will often allot acquisitions officers an operations experience (OpEx). The OpEx program grants officers the chance to take on an operational career field, such as space and missile operations, for two years, prior to beginning their prime occupation. I was selected for one of these positions and consequently set to partake in the space operations career field for two years. This also meant my designated base would change because space operations take place at different bases than acquisitions. That being so, I was assigned to Schriever Air Force Base in Colorado Springs, CO, 30 minutes southeast of the Academy. I was devastated, to say the least. I would now have to spend at least two more years in Colorado. Space operations is a lot like missiles in that it necessitates extended hours of shift work. Nonetheless, I accepted my fate and started looking for homes in Colorado Springs. That was until I sustained one more change of plans.

A couple of the Academy's graduation requirements are to pass the Air Force's fitness assessment and the commissioning physical exam. The final fitness assessment is conducted using the Air Force's easier standards rather than the Academy's. The physical exam ensures cadets are physically healthy and have no lingering injuries that may affect their performance on active duty. I passed both right away, or at least I thought I did. Two months prior to graduation, I was contacted by the Cadet Clinic to come in for additional testing. Succeeding their review of my physical, my physician noticed I had previously failed the color vision exam, so I was called in to retest and confirm the results. Low and behold, I fizzled again with deficiencies for green in both eyes and red in my right eye.

This was widely significant because it meant I could no longer participate in the space OpEx since operators cannot be color deficient because their job details the detection and tracking of missiles and satellite tracking.[148] Thus, I was returned to acquisitions and even given Los Angeles as my duty station. Los Angeles AFB, now known as Space Systems Command, is the center of technical excellence for developing, acquiring, fielding, and sustaining military space systems.[149] I was thoroughly pleased with this latest wrinkle as I ended up exactly where I wanted, albeit by default. I had suffered from color blindness my entire life, but this was the only time it had worked in my favor. Although I had already started house hunting in Colorado Springs, I was more than happy to initiate home shopping in Los Angeles.

Now that my football career was over, I needed to find an activity to fill the void, and I knew just the thing. All throughout my cadet career, I continued playing basketball in the offseason when I landed the opportunity. Since my final football season was over, I could play freely since the risk of injury was less important. After an open run session with Demario and former Falcon basketball player, Phil Mays, the opportunity to play club basketball was discussed. Club basketball was now an option for Demario and me because we were no longer IC athletes.

Clubs are a great opportunity for cadets to enhance their professional development by taking on additional leadership roles or opportunities to manage personnel and financial resources and learn administrative and logistics skills. Many cadets become involved with clubs to find and foster new friendships while pursuing an area of interest. Clubs are run by cadets, for cadets, with oversight from an Air Force officer, senior enlisted member, or civilian on staff at the Academy. These leaders organize meetings, practices, or competitions and serve as role models for cadets.[150]

Club basketball was a good way for me to stay active after my football career and continue contending against other athletes. We played against intramural and club teams from other colleges and earned our way to the 2015 National Intramural Recreational Sports Association (NIRSA) Regional Basketball Championship in Nebraska. We played well enough at regionals to obtain an invite to the national championship tournament. The 2015 NIRSA National Basketball Championship was held at North Carolina State University from April 17-19. The tournament consisted of 65 teams from all over the nation. We went 2-0 in pool play against the University of Delaware and Cornell University. Dejectedly, we lost our next game to Boston College. Boston College lost to Cornell in the championship, the same team we'd already overpowered in pool play. We were dismayed because we knew if we'd beaten Boston College, we likely would have made it to the championship and defeated Cornell again. All in all, the tournament was a good experience prior to wrapping things up at the Academy.

The last semester of my cadet career turned out to be my best academically, resulting in a 2.72 GPA. This pulled my cumulative GPA up to 2.46, slightly better than my Prep School one. I was literally chomping at the bit to finish my last final in anticipation of the infamous fountain jump. Leaping into the fountains of the Air Force Academy's Air Gardens fountains is an informal graduation ceremony that comes ahead of walking across the stage. The tradition - allowed only to seniors who have completed their last test as a cadet - is believed to be as old as the Academy itself, with the first class of graduates taking the plunge in the spring of 1959.[151] I'd witnessed three senior classes carry out their fountain jumps and dreamed of the day my time would come. The day had finally arrived, and I made the most of it. I leapt into the cold fountain with my full uniform on in an invigorating fashion, doing a 360 in the air and generating a sizable splash. I had successfully completed the Air Force Academy's remarkably grueling course of studies, placing me on track for graduation. But before that, I had to stomach the last death of my cadet career.

This casualty was the worst because it involved a fellow classmate of mine just one month before graduation. We were in the home stretch, and to make matters worse, Alexander Quiros' passing entailed the most controversy. Following his death, there were ample rumors going around. One was that the cause of his death was a homicide because of the 28 cuts and stab wounds he suffered, in addition to the amount of blood found at the scene. The entire Cadet Wing was fearful there could potentially be a killer amongst us. Everyone was on edge for the next few weeks as the investigation took place. I was especially cautious, ensuring I kept my room locked at all times. It wasn't until the autopsy was completed a few weeks later that the incident was ruled a suicide.[152] On the brighter side, there was a prime event to look forward to.

Three weeks before graduation, The Falcons football team arrived in Washington D.C. for our CIC presentation at the White House. Entering the massive White House on May 7, 2015, was dreamlike, something I'd never imagined doing. We were given a tour of several rooms prior to our meeting with the president. One of them was the Red Room. The Red Room traditionally has served as a parlor or sitting room; recent Presidents have had small dinner parties here.[153] The room boasted patriotism and possessed some of the nicest furniture I had ever seen.

Our honors took place in the East Room. The East Room is the scene of many historic White House events and traditionally used for large gatherings, such as dances, receptions, concerts, weddings, award presentations, press conferences, and bill-signing ceremonies. It is here that presidents are commonly inaugurated in private before proceeding to the Capitol for an official, public inauguration. It is here also that presidents, vice-presidents, and other dignitaries are sometimes lain in honor prior to their funerals. Richard Nixon announced his resignation to his staff here.[154]

Prior to the awarding, President Obama met the team outside of the East Room and individually shook hands with everyone on the team. It was truly an honorable episode. Aside from being much taller than I'd believed, Obama was very charismatic and just as he appeared on TV. Next, the team was introduced into the East Room in front of a multitude of media. President Obama addressed the media expressing, "Now, last year at this time, most folks did not think that Coach Calhoun and the Falcons would be here today. They'd just come off a less-than-ideal season. But this year, they came back determined to set a new tone."[146] He went on to say, "This is the Falcons' third trip in the last five years. I am told it is a record 19 times that they have earned this unreasonably large trophy. But if anybody can figure out how to get this thing to where it needs to go, it is the Air Force."[148]

President Obama also made sure to congratulate the Falcons for more than just their victorious season, pointing out everything they were doing off the field. He praised the cadets for their leadership and commitment to combating sexual assault on their campus. He also noted that the Air Force Falcons had the highest graduation rate in the conference and that Coach Calhoun recruited players with at least a 3.5 high school GPA. He also commended the cadets for volunteering their time and giving back to their communities - and, of course, their country.[155] General Johnson chimed in, proclaiming, "Winning the CIC Trophy is a great honor for our team, the Academy, and Colorado Springs. Our cadet-athletes thrive on competition on and off the field, and this trophy indicates their dedication to excellence and their commitment to teamwork. I could not be more proud of our cadets and Coach Calhoun and his staff, who helped pave the path for this tremendous success."[147]

Following their remarks, President Obama presented us with the highly coveted CIC trophy. As a result of winning the trophy 19 times, Spears and Kale gifted Obama with a #19 football jersey and a game football on behalf of the team. Obama gave his best wishes and then departed to fulfill some of his other presidential duties. Everyone on the team held the event in high regard. It was one of the most indelible occasions of my life, and instances like this were a large part of why I chose to attend the Air Force Academy. With this trip in the books, graduation was the only thing on my mind.

The graduation requirements for the Air Force Academy are particularly extensive. My 2015 graduating class consisted of 840 cadets, after beginning with 1137.[156] We were one of the smallest recent graduating classes up to that point. The class of 2015 had a 93.5% retention rate, the percentage of first-year students who began their studies in the fall of the academic year and returned the following fall.[157] Our average starting salary was $52,600, as promised by my coaches during recruiting.

Graduation serves as ceremonial commissioning as second Lieutenants in the United States Air Force. I was a part of the 57th graduating class from the Air Force Academy. Our graduation speaker was then Secretary of the Air Force, Deborah James. She was the 23rd Secretary of the Air Force and responsible for the affairs of the Department of the Air Force.[158] Here are a few interesting facts about my graduating class:

- 79% of the graduates were men, and just 21% were women.
- The average cumulative GPA for the Academy's Class of 2015 was 2.98.
- Three-hundred and sixty graduates were scheduled for pilot training, 11 for combat. operator (navigator) training, seven for air battle manager training, and 18 for remotely piloted aircraft training.[159]

For me, graduating from the Air Force Academy was the most significant accomplishment of my life, and I still feel that way today. I was fortunate to have some of my hometown friends and family in attendance including my mother, brother, my dad and his wife Gayle, Coach Cocke, Toni and Chuck, and my grandfather Cordell. Having them make the trip for this once-in-a-lifetime moment meant the world to me. The morning of graduation, my nerves were all over the place as I prepared for the big day. Putting on my parade dress for the final time felt surreal as I made sure my uniform looked perfect. I then went down to Falcon Stadium to meet up with my classmates and assemble into formation.

Though I was not a fan of marching during my time as a cadet, marching onto the field for graduation was different. It felt unreal as I simply reminisced on all that I'd been through up to that point. After marching to our seats, the ceremony promptly began. Listening to our guest speakers was nice, but I was just ready to walk across the stage. It seemed like forever with a class of 840 cadets, but I finally made my way stage front. I anxiously waited for my name to be called, and then I bolted up the platform to greet the awaiting faculty, receive my diploma, and shake hands with the Secretary of the Air Force. I had done it. I exited the stage with my diploma and held it high with the biggest smile of my life.

A few final remarks were made after all the names were called. Then the thrilling Thunderbird flyover commenced while each graduate ceremoniously tossed their cap into the air. Thunderbirds perform for people worldwide to display the pride, precision, and professionalism the U.S. Air Force represents. Through air shows and flyovers, they aim to excite and inspire. In addition to showcasing the elite skills that all pilots possess, the Thunderbirds demonstrate the incredible capabilities of the Air Force's premier multi-role fighter jet, the F-16 Fighting Falcon.[160] I'd witnessed the Thunderbirds before at previous graduations but having them perform at mine was special.

Leading up to graduation, cadets customarily place money in their hats of different amounts in anticipation of the hat toss. After dismissal, gradates seize a random cap with cash from one of their classmates inside. The one I grabbed had $20 attached. After graduation, I said my goodbyes to my peers and found my family in the stands. I was met with an abundance of love and acclaim before we set out for an enjoyable celebratory dinner. The next day, I packed my belongings into my car and commenced my drive home to Tacoma for my 60 days of leave.

CHAPTER SIX

THE FRUITS OF MY LABOR

At the close of graduation, second lieutenants are authorized 60 days of paid leave ahead of reporting to their first duty station. This is a well-deserved reward for surviving the Academy, and I enjoyed every minute of it. 60 days was a blast; it allowed me to recuperate, relax, and revamp my mind. Most graduates go on trips and travel the world to celebrate their enormous accomplishment. I was no different, traveling to Eastern Washington to visit friends and the Dallas area to be a groomsman in Broam's wedding. I also did something out of the ordinary; I bought a vehicle. I determined the greatest achievement of my life should be commemorated in a special way–by purchasing a Corvette. The Corvette has been my dream car since I was a toddler. Initially, I was not set on a Corvette, but I knew I wanted a sports car; I've always loved fast cars. I was not a fan of Mustangs, and the newer model Camaros had poor visibility. The moment I hopped into the driver seat of a Corvette; I knew I would get one. Now it was just a matter of finding the right deal.

I visited several locations which had Corvettes in stock, but they were either too expensive or had too many miles. One day, I made the two-hour drive from Tacoma to Portland and surveyed a black, 2005 C6 Corvette I'd found online. The car only had 49,000 miles, a whopping 400 horsepower, heads-up display, and the standard removable top. I instantly fell in love with it on the test drive. After some negotiation, I lowered the interest rate to 3.69%, bringing the monthly payments to $321 for 84 months on the $20,995 vehicle. Before purchasing, the dealership allowed me to take the Corvette next door and have a diagnostic performed for peace of mind. The inspection came back free of issues, so I had the green light. The total came out to $23,995 after purchasing a $3,000 aftermarket warranty just to be on the safe side. Finally, I averted sales tax by procuring the car in Oregon, saving about 10%.

After purchasing my new vehicle, I sold my old one to my brother for much lower than market value. He was ecstatic with his upgrade, mainly because his 2002 Chevy Malibu was on its last leg. Moving up to a well-kept 2007 Grand Prix was a vast improvement for him. We made a payment plan that included a reasonable down payment and monthly disbursements until the debt was paid off.

Also, during 60 days, I was fit to participate in Desmond (Des) Trufant's annual no-cost football camp. Des is one of the best football players to come out of Tacoma. I competed against Des when we played Wilson High School, one of our inner-city rivals, my junior year. He had a huge impact on the game from his running back and cornerback positions, helping his team secure the hurtful win over us. Des would be named to Washington's All-State team. He then went to the University of Washington as a cornerback and earned first-team All-PAC-12 his senior year.

His production at the University of Washington formed a copious buzz with NFL scouts, aiding him to be drafted 22nd overall in the 2013 NFL Draft by the Atlanta Falcons. There he obtained a Pro Bowl selection and became one of the best cornerbacks in the NFL at one point. Des was able to prove doubters wrong for much of his stint in Atlanta until injuries plagued him. He was released on March 18, 2020, after missing half of the season and was picked up a week later by my favorite team, the Detroit Lions.[161] His first year in Detroit was also filled with injuries allowing him to only play in a few games, forcing the Lions to cut him after the season.

Des has described the purpose of his annual one-day camp, which is for kids to "compete their hardest. This camp isn't about participation trophies and moral victories; instead, it's about hustling and improving." Standout players were given awards at the camp's conclusion—offensive and defensive MVP, and position-based awards.[162] "When we first started, it was more one-on-one stuff with a little bit of skill work whereas now, they get a lot of skill work. And they learn about competition, and how to give it your all every day," said Wilson Rams football coach Amad Robinson, who played in the same Rams' backfield as Marcus Trufant.[163] The three-hour event was great to be a part of alongside some of my high school teammates and other professional football players. I enjoyed being able to coach rising high school football players and bring the best out of them. The camp also confirmed that I would indeed like to coach someday.

Once my 60 days were over, I made the 2,000-mile drive from Tacoma to Los Angeles in my new Corvette. My report date was July 31, 2015, so I departed on Sunday, July 26th. The drive in my packed Corvette was quick and painless. I left on Sunday morning and made the twelve-hour hike to Sacramento that night. I had been in touch with one of my buddies, Dominique Williams, while I was in Tacoma and learned he would be in Sacramento while I was passing through. So, I linked up with him and Isaiah Thomas when I made it. Furthermore, instead of purchasing a hotel, I was able to stay the night in an extra room they had. The next morning, I got back on the road and finished the last leg of my expedition, reaching L.A. by the afternoon.

Since I reached L.A. a few days before my report date, I was able to do some additional house hunting. That Friday, I reported to Los Angeles Air Force Base to begin in-processing. Simultaneously, I was relentlessly house hunting while staying in an Extended Stay funded by the Air Force. Upon my arrival to Los Angeles, I was able to reconnect with Zach Banner, who was playing football at USC. We hung out as often as we could and became best friends. It was good to have someone from my hometown in a new environment.

After attending middle school with my brother and me, Zach wisely went to Lakes High School in Lakewood, WA. He had exceptional careers in both basketball and football while there. Banner averaged 18.6 points and 17.3 rebounds as a senior at Lakes. His team just missed out on advancing to the state tournament when they lost to Lincoln HS, but Banner scored 34 points and grabbed 22 rebounds in the game. He helped lead Lakes to a 24-3 record and the Washington state 3A title as a junior in 2011. In their five-game run to the state title, Banner averaged 9.6 points and 8.4 rebounds per game. In the title game vs. Bellevue, Banner scored 15 points and grabbed eight rebounds in the 71-56 victory.

He also starred for the football team as an offensive lineman. His 2012 honors as a senior tallied almost every nationally recognized team including USA Today All-USA first team, SI.com All-American first team, Max Preps All-American second team, Max Preps All-American Medium Schools first team, and the ESPNU 150. He was also a finalist for the 2012 Watkins Award, given to the nation's top African American high school scholar-athlete.[164]

At USC, Zach started 37 of 39 games played, seeing action at both tackle positions. He started 10 of 10 games as a senior. As a junior, Zach started 12 times at right tackle and twice at left tackle and made the 2015 CollegeSportsMadness.com Third-Team All-American and First-Team All-Pac-12, as well as AP Second-Team All-Pac-12. He also won USC's Offensive Lineman of the Year Award. As a sophomore in 2014, he started all games at right tackle and made College Football News Sophomore All-American honorable mention. Banner played briefly as a backup offensive tackle as a redshirt freshman in 2013, appearing in two early season games before he was sidelined the rest of the year with an injury that required surgery on both hips. Banner also played basketball for USC in 2013 but didn't see any action.

Zach's senior year at USC did not go as well as we thought it would, costing him millions of dollars because his draft stock plummeted. If Zach would have declared for the NFL draft after his junior season, he likely would have been a surefire first round pick. Nevertheless, Zach was drafted 137th overall, in the fourth round of the 2017 NFL Draft by the Indianapolis Colts. I recall hearing his name announced by the NFL commissioner and being euphoric. It was a nerve-racking process waiting for his name to be called. Round by round went by, and he was still on the board. By the time he was drafted, it was the third and final day of the draft, so I was concerned he wouldn't be drafted at all. Either way, I was glad he received an opportunity to play in the NFL.

Zach has had a spotty career up to this point. The NFL draft is held in April, and he was released by the Colts on September 3rd. He then signed with the Cleveland Browns the next day. But the Browns parted ways with him seven months later. The Carolina Panthers acquired him and released him just 15 days after that. With so much movement, we were unsure what was to come of his NFL future. Amidst all the naysayers, Zach never wavered in his faith or lost confidence in himself, and I stood by him the entire way.

It was very quiet over the next few months without teams showing enough interest to make a move. Then, the Pittsburgh Steelers took a chance on him on September 12, 2018, and that's where he would find his groove. Zach loved Pittsburgh right away and could immediately tell the cultural difference of a winning franchise. He was also hugely motivated by his new opportunity and worked his tail off. He did not play much his first year there aside from starting one game but was able to learn a lot behind All-Pro linemen Ramon Foster, David DeCastro, and Maurkice Pouncey.

Zach proceeded with his intense physical training and diet the following offseason and it paid dividends. Zach competed for the starting left tackle spot and came out victorious. Sadly, his occupancy at left tackle was short lived as he suffered an ACL tear in the fourth quarter of his first start. The injury was devastating to watch as he had been playing so well. Not only that, but he had worked tremendously hard to finally get to that point. After his surgery, Zach quickly initiated his rehabilitation and remained motivated to return the ensuing year even better.

The 2021 season, Zach was again named the starter after having a monstrous training camp. In the preseason, he made a strong showing by overpowering defenders and holding up nicely in pass protection. He was labeled as one of the Steelers impact players for his rise to one of the team's best athletes. But Zach's knee was sore afterwards, causing him to miss the first four games of the season. That injury wound up being costly, as he would not earn his spot back that season and ended up being cut afterwards. This was yet another unfortunate turn of events, but I am confident things will work out for him in the end as he continues to train in anticipation of a stronger comeback.

I also reconnected with Shaianne while in L.A. when she visited with her sister Joy and Imar. Due to our sporadic contact, she'd known I was living there and reached out on her trip. We all went to Santa Monica and had a blast. Yet again, Shaianne and I picked up where we'd left off, boasting our special bond. We began conversing more after her visit, but the momentum died down. My reservations were detrimental because I learned of Shaianne's engagement a year later on Instagram. I was bothered by the sighting, but only had myself to blame. To my surprise, the engagement was broken off shortly after.

House hunting in L.A. County during July is exceptionally difficult. The demand for housing is so high that availabilities simply don't last very long. This made my search that much more grueling, on top of being in a whole new city. One of the most problematic parts of looking for a home in Los Angeles is the diversity of neighborhoods. Clearly, the nice neighborhoods are more expensive, and the closer you get to the beaches, the higher the rent. But as you move inland and the prices begin to drop, you are forced navigate areas with more crime. This was relevant in my case because I could not afford to live near the beach as a novel second lieutenant.

Thankfully, I had some helpful coworkers who assisted me with house hunting.

One of them gave me insight into the direction of traffic and which areas in L.A. County are most traffic friendly. He then pointed me to the city he lived in, Culver City. Culver City is just five miles north of Los Angeles AFB and only a 10-15-minute commute because it goes against the traffic. I looked at several apartments in Culver City before finding the one I would ultimately move into. I was able to secure a two-bedroom apartment in the Meadows Apartment complex for a reasonable price of $2,100 in L.A. County.

A couple of weeks after moving into my apartment, my brother and good friend Emily made their way down. Emily accompanied him on the drive and was kind enough to drive my Camaro down for me. Darius drove his Grand Prix, and they made the trip together over a few days. Darius had been having trouble juggling school and work at Eastern Washington University, so he wanted a change. Per his request, Darius preferred to live with me so he could focus on school and not have to labor simultaneously. Though a significant financial sacrifice for myself, I agreed, with the stipulation that he promise to finish his bachelor's degree. In exchange, I allowed him to live with me rent and bill free, including food. Contributing to my brother's education was priceless to me. With housing secured and my brother all moved in, I could now focus on my new occupation as an acquisitions officer.

I'd heard a lot of mixed reviews about acquisitions in the operational Air Force; thus, I had a partial idea of what to expect going in. I was extremely nervous in-processing for my first job as a second lieutenant. While I was presented with a new occupation, some things remained the same. I noticed right away that there was not a lot of minority representation in the higher ranks. The Independent Racial Disparity Review revealed that Black service members are consistently underrepresented in both officer and enlisted promotions at the Non-Commissioned Officer (NCO) and senior field grade officer ranks. Although Black officers receive more nominations to attend professional military education, they are less likely to do so.[66] The majority of officers and senior NCOs I encountered were White. This type of discrepancy is evident at the top as well. An astonishing 64% of Black general officers believe racial bias exists in how leadership provides feedback and counseling. A disturbing 55% of Black general officers agreed that racial bias exists when leadership makes decisions concerning lower-level administrative actions like letters of reprimand.[66]

My supervisor, Rick Einstman, assisted in making my transition especially seamless. Rick was an awesome manager who I enjoyed working for. He had served 20 years in the Air Force and retired as a Lt Col. Following his retirement, Rick became a government civilian. He was immensely knowledgeable about program management and space. Even though Rick was very busy as the Chief of Architecture and Engineering for our branch, he made time to teach me the fundamentals of being a successful program manager, skills I carried with me throughout my career.

After observing and learning the program, Rick gradually gave me tasks to lead. I handled each of them efficiently and was eventually named the program manager of a $1.4M program. Right away, I noticed my USAFA training coming into fruition. My ability to think critically, solve problems, and lead were promptly put on notice. But prior to managing of the program, I attended the Air Force Fundamentals of Acquisition Management 103 course (AFFAM 103) at Wright-Patterson Air Force Base in Dayton, OH. AFFAM 103 is required for all acquisitions officers.

AFFAM 103 is a three-week introductory course that provides a foundational understanding of basic project management skills and an overview of Air Force/DoD acquisition. Because the course is preliminary, it's not meant to be overly difficult. The course is intended to show how acquisitions works in the Air Force and provide a basic understanding of how to perform the duty. Even so, there are quizzes that are meant to test comprehension of the material. Each quiz has a minimum score that must be achieved, and if failed consecutively, the class must be retaken. I found the course to be fairly easy and thoroughly boring. The class was Monday through Friday from 8 a.m. to 4 p.m. I have never enjoyed day-long lectures, and this was no different. Yet, I did not allow that to affect my performance. The best part about the class was that we were free on the weekends, so I was able to visit my Detroit family on both weekend with my rental car. I even went to a couple of football games.

I hadn't seen much of my Detroit family for years, so it was intriguing to see them. They were all overjoyed as well and raved at my growth since the last time they'd seen me. My family treated me like a king, cooking and ordering food the entire time I was there. Conversely, my mom was vastly nervous about my trip because of how treacherous Detroit is, and this was my first time there without her. She made sure to keep in touch with me on both weekends I visited. To be safe, I stayed with my aunt Linda in Southfield, a Detroit suburb. From there, I would drive to Detroit during the day to visit the rest of my family. I, too, was aware of Detroit's danger, but I wasn't too concerned because I knew my family wouldn't let anything happen to me; I was simply using wisdom. So, I made sure to take the proper precautions and constantly maintain awareness of my surroundings.

During my first weekend there, on September 19, 2015, Air Force happened to be playing at Michigan State University, only 20 minutes away from Southfield. I reached out to some of my former teammates and secured enough tickets for myself and a few of my cousins. Air Force played them tough, losing 35-21, but we still had a good time. It was also nice to see some of my former teammates and coaches after the game.

The next weekend after visiting with family, I went to the Cleveland Browns game to see Xavier. Unfortunately, Xavier was not active for the game, so I wasn't able to see him play. But this was the first NFL game I had ever been to; hence I enjoyed every minute of it. Cleveland was not very good that year, but their fans were rowdy, so the atmosphere was electric. After the game, I met up with Xavier via the family pass I received with my ticket. It was good to speak with him for the time we had and catch up with each other.

After the three weeks were over, I returned home to Los Angeles and picked up where I left off. I proceeded with successfully controlling the $1.4M program and this, along with other tasks, garnered recognition from my supervisor. When it came time for my first Officer Performance Report (OPR), Rick and my commander, Col Thomas Rock, rated me #1 of 10 lieutenants, "for being a brilliant, young leader with a bright future." Col Rock is a fellow USAFA grad and Corvette enthusiast as well. He was a decisive commander and great leader to learn from.

OPRs are used to document potential and performance as well as provide information for making a promotion recommendation, selection, or propriety action; selective continuation; involuntary separation; selective early retirement; assignment; school nomination and selection; and other management decisions.[165] OPRs are critical to an Airman's career, and they hold plenty of weight. Generally, Airmen draft bullets of their achievements over the course of the year. Supervisors then review the inputs and make revisions based on their judgment of the Airman's performance. OPRs are meant to be objective but can be subjective when a substandard manager is involved. After the manager's review, he sends it back to the employee for concurrence. Upon agreement, the supervisor will submit the OPR to the divisional commander, and then to base level leadership. OPRs are the primary means promotion boards use to authorize a promotion and distinguish Airmen from one another. The best way to differentiate oneself is to receive a favorable stratification amongst peers. So, collecting a stratification on my first OPR was prodigious, and set me on an esteemed track for my career. Outside of my fast professional start, I was able to enjoy much of what L.A. had to offer.

Living in L.A. was awesome; there was so much to do. With Zach playing for USC, we were able to attend every home game we wanted, in addition to their games at UCLA. It was almost as if we were students at USC. Immersing ourselves into the Coliseum football atmosphere was truly unique. The seating for the player's guests was outstanding, planting us ten rows up from the sideline. We were in a position to meet and get to know some of Zach's big-name teammates as well; to the likes of Ju-Ju Smith-Schuster and Adoree Jackson, both in the NFL today. Another cool part about living in L.A. was that it was only a four-hour drive from Las Vegas. We went there at least once, sometimes twice a year. The first time was for my 24th birthday. Emily obtained a luxurious hotel suite so my brother, Zach, and I stayed in very attractive accommodations.

Anytime I went to Vegas I made sure to link up with hometown friend Brandon Jimenez. Brandon also experienced a lot of the same things as I did growing up in Tacoma, and managed to overcome them as prominent athlete in the city. Brandon is a deep thinker with a clever mind, and extremely knowledgeable regarding investments and life planning. He is currently a real estate agent and investor, who I've been able to lean on when I've needed advice in any area.

The next time I went to Vegas was when, once more, Shaianne and I reconvened speaking to each other. She informed me of her upcoming Vegas trip and invited me to join. I accepted her offer and booked my hotel. When the time came, I made the four-hour trek and the vacation started off on a good note. To my dismay, the trip turned sideways after a deep conversation. Shaianne was tired of my dating apprehension and wanted to know why we hadn't taken the next step after so many years. I asked her if she wanted to know the truth and she affirmed. I told her it was because I wasn't interested in doing a long-distance relationship, nor was I ready to be a stepfather. This was not the answer she wanted to hear, and she instantly began crying. It also became a topic of discussion to be revisited over time.

Another added benefit to living in L.A. was the number of famous people who lived there. Due to the sheer volume of celebrities residing in L.A., one is bound to see one eventually. I was fortunate enough to run into several, most notably my favorite rapper at the time, Nipsey Hussle. I'd learned on social media that he would be attending an alumni basketball game at his alma mater, Crenshaw High School, so I decided to attend. When halftime rolled around, Nipsey indeed showed up and even performed a song. He was only present for 15 minutes before exiting. I stayed for the duration of the game and then headed home.

On my way home, I passed his Marathon Clothing Store and saw him standing outside. I immediately turned into the adjacent parking lot and walked to his store. He'd gone inside by the time I pulled up, so I asked his colleague in front if I could take a picture with him. Sure enough, Nipsey returned to the front of the store and took a photo with me. He shared his satisfaction that I had on one of his shirts and even spoke with me for a few minutes. I told him I was from Tacoma, along with our mutual friend, Isaiah Thomas, and that we were big fans of his up there. He was again pleased and shook my hand as we went our separate ways.

Meeting Nipsey Hussle was a profound moment that I didn't take for granted, mainly because his music had such a sizable impact on me in college. In all honesty, Nipsey's motivational music helped me make it through the Academy. His "Marathon" motto, which focuses on life being a marathon, rather than a sprint, inspired me when I was down and encouraged me to persist. Wistfully, Nipsey was later gunned down in front of his store on March 31, 2019. Though taken far too soon, his legacy and immense influence will live on forever.

BREAKING GENERATIONAL CURSES

On an even darker note, my social drinking habit in college had turned into an addiction. My family's generational curse of alcoholism had made its way into my life. Helen's drinking problem had been passed on to my mother when she was a child. Although my mother gave up alcohol at 18, she had already indulged by that point. Therefore, I carried a natural inclination toward liquor. I had my first drink at a high school party when I was 16. Like everyone else, I would socially drink at weekend functions because it was the cool thing to do. Initially, the strong taste of alcohol wasn't very appealing to me; I just did it because all my friends were. The feeling of being buzzed wasn't particularly captivating either. But over time, I developed a taste for spirits and was no longer bothered by its harshness. Furthermore, I began to like the tipsy feeling and how social it made me as an introvert.

In college, my practice compounded. We were all on our own without parental supervision. In general, people were letting loose because it was the most freedom they'd ever had; I was in the same boat. Weekends became automatic for going out and drinking. Accordingly, I quickly developed a high tolerance because heavy drinking was already in my blood. In college settings, high tolerance is prized and even viewed as a strength. Thus, I gained a reputation for being able to drink a lot, which I soaked up. This resulted in bad experiences such as vomiting, passing out, and hangovers. However, I also noticed I was immensely honest and angry when I became drunk. By the end of college, I would get a bottle and drink on my own, even if I wasn't going out. Alcohol offered a temporary relief from the pain I'd been dealing with for years.

After college, my drinking escalated. I only drank to get intoxicated, but never just to relax or chill. I could drink a whole bottle in a single night when I wanted to, or do 10-second pull no problem. My tolerance was so high that it would take me at least seven-eight shots to get buzzed. Then I progressed from regular alcohol to 100 proof. That's when I started to notice alcohol had become a problem. People began to recognize and praise me for how much I could drink.

Drinking had gotten to the point where it wasn't even fun anymore. I could outdrink almost everyone I knew. As I began to gain weight and accept the facts about being in denial about my drinking, I planned to turn things around. I started to realize that my family's alcohol curse had grabbed ahold of me, and that alcohol wasn't the right solution for dealing with my anguish. Sure, alcohol provided momentary comfort from my pain, but it never eradicated it. I also spoke with my doctor, and he informed me that drinking was certainly not helping my concussion symptoms.

In the late spring of 2018, following a three-month diet without alcohol, I vowed to stop drinking hard liquor altogether after Julian's July wedding. I got all my drinking out of the way during his bachelor party and wedding ceremony and was able to go cold turkey afterwards. Until this day, I have not had a sip of hard liquor. God was able to break the stronghold that drinking had on me. I refused to succumb to alcohol and its lasting effects, making the appropriate choice to conquer it. Giving up hard liquor has been one of the best decisions I've ever made. Now, I only partake in wine occasionally, consuming about one or two glasses a month, and never to get intoxicated.

For any readers dealing with alcohol abuse, I suggest you seek help immediately. The first step is coming to grips with your alcohol problem. Next, you must choose to renounce it. Then, you have to attack it. Overcoming alcoholism alone is difficult, so I would advise you to tell a trustworthy person to help keep you accountable. That's exactly what I had in my future wife. She genuinely cared about my health and hated seeing me drink heavily. She was a large reason why I was able to quit as well. Alcoholism is not only a faulty way of dealing with issues, but it can also be harmful and lead to a dark path; a road I could have ended on if it weren't for God.

The Bible strongly condemns drunkenness. Galatians 5:19-21 states, "Now the works of the flesh are manifest, which are these; Adultery, fornication, uncleanness, lasciviousness, idolatry, witchcraft, hatred, variance, emulations, wrath, strife, seditions, heresies, envyings, murders, drunkenness, revellings, and such like: of the which I tell you before, as I have told you in time past, that they which do such things shall not inherit the kingdom of God!" Although I was aware that drunkenness is a sin, I'd developed a taste for and enjoyed it, which was even worse because I knew I was wrong. There are also countless stories of people in the Bible making mistakes and sinning because they were drunk, including Noah. "And Noah began to be an husbandman, and he planted a vineyard: and he drank of the wine, and was drunken, and he was uncovered within his tent (Genesis 9: 20-21)." God desires for us to be "sober and alert" in 1 Peter 5:8. Nonetheless, alcohol wasn't the only thing I had to overcome.

As most males do, another matter I struggled with was pornography. While I knew it was sinful as well, I was amused by the fantasy films. Today, porn addiction, or problematic pornography use, affects approximately 85% of the adult population.[166] Up to 65% of young adult men and 18% of young women report at least once a week, though this amount can be much higher.

The increasing exposure of children to internet porn also likely contributes to the rise in porn addiction. Age restrictions on porn sites often consist of no more than a button to click claiming to be 18 or older. The median age of first exposure to pornography is now only 14 years old. As many as 93.2% of boys and 62.1% of girls first see porn before they turn 18. Early exposure to porn is correlated with increased porn use and addiction later in life. Many studies have been conducted on online pornography use. These have revealed some interesting facts about porn use:

- 40 million U.S. adults regularly visit internet pornography websites.
- 10% of US adults admit to having an addiction to internet pornography.
- 17% of all women struggle with porn addiction.
- 20% of men and 13% of women admit to accessing porn while at work.
- 70% of women admit keeping their cyber activities secret.
- 1 of 3 visitors of all adult websites is a woman.
- Women favor chat rooms 2x more than men.[167]

Today's infatuation with pornography is an adverse outcome of lust. Lust is the strong sexual desire by our flesh. Surely you can lust after other things such as money and material things, but sex is the main culprit. The problem is, lust leads to sin, and sin leads to death. Even further, lust is never satisfied: "Hell and destruction are never full; So the eyes of man are never satisfied (Proverbs 27:20)." This scripture means that the fulfillment of lust is a never-ending journey. In the pursuit of fulfilling one's lust, it actually leads to a deeper sexual desire because the present gratification becomes inadequate.

Even as a Christian your eyes will always lust, so you must crucify your eyes every day, which is the moral of Luke 9:23: "And he said to *them* all, If any *man* will come after me, let him deny himself, and take up his cross daily, and follow me." This is a foundational scripture for Christianity. The takeaway is that we must deny our fleshly desires and suffer with Jesus in carrying our cross, as he was forced to do before he was crucified. Another key is that lust is involved with our senses, for men it is mainly sight, and women it is hearing. Thus, we need to guard our senses.

Men are enticed by what they see, and women by what they hear because that is the way God created us, and it's been that way since Adam and Eve. When Adam first saw Eve, he was bewildered by her beauty and took her as his wife and named her. After they were married, Eve was first deceived by the serpent's promise that if she ate from the forbidden Tree of Good and Evil, she would become like God. Eve was captivated by satan's discourse and fell into his trap.

I first encountered porn at age 14. My curiosity had gotten the best of me and led me down the wrong street. In adulthood, I was viewing porn as often as I pleased, sometimes multiple times a day. Pornography changes the habits of the mind, the inner private self. Its use can easily become habitual, which in turn leads to desensitization, boredom, distorted views of reality, and objectification of women. There are also numerous clinical consequences to pornography use, including increased risk for significant physical and mental health problems and a greater likelihood of committing a sex-based crime.[168] That obstacle, combined with high school pressure to sleep with girls, was an evil ploy.

A Kaiser survey found that boys face particular pressure to have sex, often from male friends. "There are a lot of expectations for boys to be sexually active," said Julia Davis, senior program officer at the Kaiser Family Foundation, an independent group that studies health issues. One in three boys ages 15-17 says they feel pressure to have sex, compared with 23% of girls.[169] For me, this system lasted through adulthood, and intensified in college.

Even after I decided I would wait until marriage to have sex, it was hard to get on the right track. Furthermore, porn is an uncomfortable topic to admit struggling with to other men. Fortunately, Broam was a strong Christian man who had dealt with some of the same issues. He shared scriptures and books with me that helped my restoration but did not cleanse me altogether. I still dabbled here and there.

Gratefully, I was also introduced to Pastor Stephen Darby in 2017, by way of my brother. The late Stephen Darby, former pastor of Destined Ministries in Louisville, KY, was one of the most powerful men of God I've ever listened to. His sermons are still my favorite. He had a special anointing on his life, allowing him to preach the truth about the Word of God, unlike most ministers. As a child, he grew up in the projects and soon immersed himself in the drug game. After several close death calls, one that landed him in the hospital after being stabbed, he knew God had other plans for him. He soon became saved and started his extensive journey as a Christian.

It was Darby and his convictive messages that delivered me in the end. My mother's guidance also helped. Darby presented pornography and sex before marriage, or fornication, in a way I'd never been exposed to. Growing up, I was always told not to have sex before marriage, but never why: Darby filled in that blank.

Darby explained that God doesn't prohibit fornication because he wants us to be miserable or forgo one of life's greatest pleasures. But it's because he wants to save us from heartache since fornication is much deeper than just hooking up with someone outside of marriage. Fornication is defined as sexual immorality. It includes adultery and pornography, and also involves engaging in any kind of sexual relations before marriage or between two people who aren't married. Jesus mentions fornication in a list of corrupting sins that come from within a person's heart: "For out of the heart proceed evil thoughts, murders, adulteries, fornications, thefts, false witness, blasphemies (Matthew 15:19)."[170] Learning about the magnitude of fornication served as tremendous stimulus in helping me overcome both pornography and sex before marriage. Consequently, I noticed myself feeling stronger mentally, having a clearer mind, and no longer looking at women objectively. It is truly amazing how much God's purity and virtue can benefit one's soul. I am eternally grateful to God for not allowing me to stay in darkness or leaving me while I was living wrong. Instead, he brought me out and exposed me to the life he destined for me, and he can do the same for anyone who elects to live for him.

The sin of fornication violates the seventh commandment which was intended to safeguard the integrity of the family and the marriage union. With the pressure and acceptance of fornication in our society, satan has infiltrated this union because he wants to disrupt God's divine order. The fewer families there are, the more problems we face as a civilization because there is less structure, granting the devil more terrain to operate.

God designed sex for marriage, and marriage to be a holy, prized, and honored institution. The Bible calls husbands and wives to keep themselves exclusively for one another or face God's judgment (Hebrews 13:4). Condemnation of sexual immorality is unanimous in scripture. Those who persistently indulge in fornication will not inherit the kingdom of heaven (1 Corinthians 6:9). The Bible instructs believers to run from every kind of sexual sin, including fornication: "But fornication, and all uncleanness, or covetousness, let it not be once named among you, as becometh saints (Ephesians 5:3)." As with any other sin, God will forgive those who repent and turn away from their sin. The key is to deny oneself and follow God, per Luke 9:23. Another token is self-control. 1 Corinthians 7:9 says, "But if they cannot contain, let them marry: for it is better to marry than to burn," meaning if one is not able to control their sex drive prior to marriage, then they should marry to prevent going to hell in sin. Moreover, marriage is designed for one man and one woman as homosexuality is prohibited by God: "Thou shalt not lie with mankind, as with womankind, it is abomination. (Leviticus 18:22). Leviticus 20:13 expounds, "If a man also lie with mankind, as he lieth with a woman, both of them have committed an abomination: they shall surely be put to death; their blood *shall* be upon them.

PROGRESS IS THE PROCESS

After our first year in L.A., my brother and I packed up and moved to Torrance, 10 miles south of Culver City. The Meadows had raised our rent an unsuitable amount that I was unwilling to pay. With a better understanding of L.A. County's geography, it was much easier to find a place the second time around. Torrance was not against the traffic, so it took a bit longer commuting to and from work, but preserving our $2,100 rent was paramount. The unit we settled into at the Torrance Gardens apartment complex was a comparable two-bedroom unit. Just before our change of scenery, my brother and I joined our mom in Detroit for our family reunion.

It was good to be back in Detroit again after going there the previous year. I had much more time on my hands this time around and was able to see additional people. The reunion took place on two consecutive days. There was a good turnout on both days, and I likely saw about 75 family members. We played football and basketball together, shared good food and laughs, and celebrated our family's unity throughout the event.

While in Detroit for the reunion, the Lions were in the middle of training camp at their practice facility in Allen Park, MI. Myself, Darius, and my mother were all able attend one of their practices. It was bizarre seeing players from my favorite team up close and personal for the first time. During the practice, I obtained an autograph from former tight end Brandon Pettigrew. Overall, the Detroit trip was very fun. We again made sure to be aware of our surroundings although this visit did require some night travel through Detroit. To prevent from sitting at red lights, we drove below the speed limit so the light would turn green before we approached it.

Once back at L.A. AFB, I was given more responsibility and elevated to the deputy program manager of a $145M program. This program necessitated a lot more work, time, and coordination. But I worked well with the prime program manager, a captain, and was able to apply what I'd learned from my previous project. I gained a good amount of experience in this role as well. Although in an upgraded position, I still flourished. This time around, I was rated by my commander as #3 of 24 lieutenants in my annual OPR, "for being a phenomenal officer and leader." I also earned the first quarter support team award of 2017 for my role on the program. I was extraordinarily pleased with my early success in the operational Air Force. At the Academy, there's a stigma that athletes don't make good officers. So, once I had the chance, I set out to prove all the doubters wrong, and that's exactly what I was doing.

That April, Emily's first child, and my Goddaughter, Dion Madison Martin, was born. Becoming a Godparent was rewarding because it was a new experience and allowed me to care for a young person from birth. I was blessed to meet Dion just two weeks after she was born and have had the privilege to watch her grow over the past few years into a beautiful young girl with lots of energy and personality. Back on base, a lot of growth was taking place as well.

I was promoted to first lieutenant after two years. This was not necessarily a merit-based promotion, but rather service time. A promotion in the Air Force is not a reward for past service; it is an advancement to a higher grade based on past performance and future potential. The fundamental purpose of the officer promotion program is to select officers through a fair and competitive selection process that advances the best-qualified officers to positions of increased responsibility and authority and provides the necessary career incentive to attract and maintain a quality officer force. Second lieutenants are eligible for promotion as soon as they have 24-months of time-in-grade. For the promotion to first lieutenant, the commander notifies the officer of the projected promotion effective date at least 30 days in advance and advises him or her to assume the grade on the effective date, unless otherwise directed.[171]

Although the promotion to first lieutenant is essentially automatic unless an egregious act has been committed, I was gratified when I received the notification, as it was still an accomplishment. It entailed a $1,000 monthly pay increase as well. Airmen must also meet all the standards detailed in OPRs and receive concurrence from their commanders. Because my promotion date was exactly two years from my May 28th date of commissioning, it fell on the Sunday of Memorial Day Weekend. Therefore, I elected not to have a promotion ceremony; I was content with my new rank and generous raise.

A few months after my promotion, I unexpectedly ran into my Academy teammates. In 2017, two years after our graduation, I returned to Colorado Springs for Air Force's home service academy game against Army. Oftentimes, countless graduates and former players come out for games against Army and Navy; this game was no different. It was like a reunion and seemed like I ran into every one of my former teammates.

Upon graduation, I had no intentions of ever returning to the Academy, so it was assuredly distinct. It was even more awkward running into my old clan. I hadn't told anyone I would be attending the game, so everyone embraced me in astonishment. The ones who I had stopped speaking to were even more excited, all expressing their sentiment regarding my eye incident. This substantially helped with my emotional healing process. Since then, I have revived my friendship with Jordan, mainly due to his tenacious effort and my spiritual maturity. Jordan was unwavering in his attempt and continued to look out for me over the years. I also plan reach out to the others when I'm ready.

Following my 2017 promotion, we moved to a different city in L.A. County again. I had gotten fed up with being stuck in traffic every day and not having air conditioning. This final maneuver perched us in Hawthorne, a mere ten minutes away from the base. Moreover, no interstate use was required; I could take the streets to work. Our apartment at Chadron Terrace was the nicest one we'd had in L.A because it was new construction. I had found the place online a few months prior and decided to check it out ahead of my upcoming move. My cousin Nick was in town, so he went with me to view them, and we were instantly impressed. The complex had four stories, and each top floor unit had two balconies, one in each bedroom. In addition, Chadron Terrace had a gym and gated parking. Even further, rent would continue to be my desired amount of $2,100.

In terms of my love life, Shaianne and I were still having the same conversation. She asserted her logical rationale as to why she thought things would work with us, which allowed me to see the situation from a different perspective. After much prayer and contemplation, I reached the conclusion that my concerns could be resolved over time, overturning her exclusion I'd concluded years prior. It was wrong for me to base my idea of long-distance relationships on a bad experience. Moreover, now that I was in a more stable place in my life, the idea of being a stepfather wasn't as daunting. I would be able to help instill values and raise a young man. Over the next few months, Shaianne and I began getting closer and developed a more profound relationship. So much so that on December 20, 2017, I decided to make her my girlfriend.

The foundation of our linkage was our bond and friendship; we were friends before anything. What drew me to Shaianne was how much of a fighter she was; she did not give up when it came to things she was passionate about. Shaianne had a similar background to mine as she too came from a broken family. This was vital to me because it signified that she understood struggle and managed to navigate it. She also loved me for who I was; she wasn't dating me because I was a jock or because I went to the Academy. Lastly, Shaianne was gentle and affectionate, the opposite of me. I knew this was what I needed because of my aggressive and indifferent personality.

Following my promotion to first lieutenant, I was given my last assignment at Los Angeles AFB. The captain managing my program had been selected to attend Squadron Officer School, thus his position needed to be filled. His slot was meant for a captain, but because I already had experience in the program and Rick felt I could handle the workload, I was designated as the lead program manager of the $145M program. My job duties included awarding the contract, procuring a facility for classified work, transferring personnel to the contract, managing 20 people, and most significantly, performing a $70M modification to the contract. This modification was necessary because the scope of work had drastically changed from the time the request for proposal was released into industry. It was very extensive, and required a lot of organization, in addition to long days. Ultimately, the team was able to successfully complete the effort and provide the division with the necessary support. This execution drew recognition from my leadership as the #1 of 25 lieutenants, "for proven leadership, top-notch program management and acquisition expert." It also warranted a Meritorious Service Medal, which is awarded to Airmen who distinguish themselves through outstanding achievement or meritorious service.

Not only was maturation happening in the workplace, but in my spiritual life as well. Over time, as I watched more of Darby's messages on YouTube, I began to grow spiritually. To do so, I had to axe my bad habits. God helped me in so many areas of my life, mainly: forgiveness, love, and anger, in addition to the aforementioned fornication and drinking. All these domains were important, but the anger one was life changing. Although I'd forgiven my dad once, I had never healed from the pain. Throughout my life, I was resentful and quick-tempered. Rage was my primary emotion, and I foolishly took my anger out on others at times. But as I learned about temperament and self-control as fruits of the Spirit, I comprehended I was actually weak, or showing traits of effeminacy.

Effeminate means to have feminine qualities untypical of a man: not manly in appearance or manner.[172] This was a perplexing concept for me to maneuver. On one hand, men are expected to be strong, show no emotion, and handle stress with ease. On the other, when men show vulnerability, act nicer, display empathy, express sadness, and exhibit modesty, they're viewed as not adhering to masculine gender stereotypes.[173] Anger is the only emotion that is socially acceptable for men. There are a lot of social prohibitions against men expressing emotions other than anger and a lot of social reinforcement for being angry. We think of angry men as powerful and more masculine, but who express sadness or fear as weak, are less masculine. Men are socialized to express their anger overtly and to use their anger to control their partners and their own emotional experience. Anger appeals to men because they can be angry and remain well-defended and not vulnerable. Being angry not only helps many men to feel more in control of their own emotional experience, but also use anger in an attempt to control their partner's expression of feeling as well.[174]

Uncontrollable anger is actually weak, or effeminate. That's because women were created as more fragile vessels, per 1 Peter 3:7, and thus are more emotional. Men were designed to be logical and handle problems through mental processing. So, the individuals who are quick to lash out or kill another man because they were looked at wrong, are effeminate because their considerable sentiment is displayed as excessive anger due to lack of self-control. This was definitely a lesson in my pain.

By listening to Darby, I understood that self-control, one of the fruits of the Spirit, is the true sign of strength. According to Galatians 5:22-23, there are seven fruits of the Spirit: "But the fruit of the Spirit is love, joy, peace, longsuffering, gentleness, goodness, faith, meekness, temperance: against such there is no law." The fruit of the Spirit is the change in our character that comes because of the Holy Spirit's work in us. Self-control is, of course, the ability to control oneself. It involves moderation, constraint, and the ability to say "no" to our baser desires and fleshly lusts.

One of the proofs of God's working in our lives is the ability to control our own thoughts, words, and actions. Self-control naturally leads to perseverance (2 Peter 1:6) as we value the long-term good instead of the instant gratification of the world. Self-control is a gift that frees us. It frees us to enjoy the benefits of a healthy body. It frees us to rest in the security of good stewardship. It frees us from a guilty conscience. Self-control restricts the indulgence of our foolish desires, and we find the liberty to love and live as we were meant to.[175] As I began to apply this change, I noticed how much happier I was. I no longer displayed fury as my main emotion, nor was I getting mad about things as easily. I was much calmer and most importantly, at peace. Now, when I look in the mirror, I see progression staring back at me.

Peace has been a huge area of improvement for me, although I still have a way to go. My ultimate goal is to obtain the peace of God described in Philippians 4:7, "And the peace of God, which passeth all understanding, shall keep your hearts and minds through Christ Jesus." This is perfect peace, where no impediment can disturb your tranquility. My mother has this peace. She has been through a great deal of hardship, but always remains cheerful and rarely lets anything disrupt her peace. I wish to emulate her calmness one day.

After three years of success at Los Angeles Air Force Base, my tour was up. I enjoyed my time there so much that I requested to stay for an additional year, but the petition was denied. Six months prior to the end of my three-year assignment at L.A. AFB, it was time to submit my base preferences for my next assignment. Again, due to my occupational code, I was only able to choose from certain bases. My hatred for cold weather, along with possessing two rear-wheel vehicles ruled out the northeast. I no longer wanted to endure brutal winters, plus I would need to purchase a new vehicle. I preferred to go somewhere that either had nice weather or was near family. That left my options limited. In order, I proposed the following bases: Eglin AFB near Panama City Beach, FL; Patrick AFB in Cocoa Beach, FL; Seattle; Tinker AFB in Oklahoma City; and Robins AFB in Central Georgia.

I communicated my wish to land at Eglin to one of my mentors, Lt Col Lewis. Col Lewis had contacts at Eglin and did all he could to get me there. Initially, he was under the impression I would be given Eglin as my next assignment, so I started to look at places there. To my dismay, the outlook shifted, and I was given my last option: Robins AFB, located in the middle of Georgia.

I was disappointed at the news, but I took it with a grain of salt. I figured it was God's plan for me to go there and for good reason. As I contemplated my next move, I conceived that God wanted me to move there to continue repairing my relationship with my father. My dad lived in Atlanta at the time, approximately two hours north of Warner Robins, so that made perfect sense.

The drive to Georgia was much more abstract than the one to L.A. It was a 36-hour excursion spread over the course of three days. I had planned my trip in advance and knew I wanted to stay in El Paso and Dallas along the way. I drove twelve hours each day to make it to each checkpoint by dusk. The journey was grueling and required a lot of coffee, but I wanted to make it to Georgia as soon as possible, largely because I was enthusiastic about the home I'd just purchased. My brother left a few days later, taking a week to make the journey.

In anticipation of my July move to Georgia, I had been proactive and flown down there on Memorial Weekend to do some house hunting, this time to purchase. I had already touched base with a local real estate agent and synchronized with him to look at homes on Friday and Saturday. I decided to purchase a home in Georgia frankly because the prices were too cheap not to.

After arriving, I made the two-hour trek to Warner Robins and spent the entire Friday surveying homes. I also learned a good deal in the process of searching for my first home. We looked at twenty of the ones I'd found online. We canvassed homes that he believed I would like as well. The majority of homes we viewed were new construction. We took two steps into a pre-owned home, and I was displeased, so all pre-owned homes were removed from my list. I simply preferred to have a new home that no one else had lived in, based on my encounter with my last apartment in L.A. The warranty on new homes also stood out to me.

I was appalled at the property sizes available for the prices in Georgia. I was looking at mortgages between $1,000-$1,500 for four-bedroom houses priced between $150,000-$250,000, much less than I was paying for my two-bedroom apartment. The homes were beautiful and averaged 2,000 square feet, with huge lawns and two-car garages. I took tons of notes about each property and went to Broam's house, where I was staying, to deliberate. My notes were extensive and allowed me to compare the pros and cons for each dwelling. After several hours, I was able to narrow my search down to three homes. The succeeding day, I assessed the three homes again and was able to make a decision.

I settled on a 2,000-square foot home with four bedrooms and three bathrooms located in Kathleen. Kathleen is a Warner Robins suburb filled with new subdivisions. The home also had a sizable backyard and was in the best school district in the county. This was a priority for me at the time because the plan was for Shaianne and June to move in with me after we eventually got married. Moreover, my new home in Kathleen was only fifteen minutes away from Robins AFB.

I arrived at my new home late on Wednesday, July 25, 2018, a few days ahead of my report date. My realtor had left my key in the mailbox so I could go right in once I showed up. My household goods had been shipped a few days prior to my departure so I would be without my furniture for a while. But I did take the liberty of packing an air mattress with the belongings I brought with me; plus, I was just happy to be in my new home.

My experience at Robins was much different than L.A. AFB. There was much more turnover and disorder. The organization I was assigned to was fast paced, so the personnel were exceptionally busy; they were also overworked and under-manned. The organization also performed classified work in a secure building, disallowing any external media devices, nor did it have windows. This was a complete 180 for me coming from the attractive SMC campus building with windows everywhere. The work was remarkably distinct as well. The program management aspect remained the same, but there were many more processes to work through, and it was madly bureaucratic, making it difficult to be productive.

Culture wise, the people were much more friendly in the south. I was not used to the hospitality I received, spending most of life on the west coast, where most people are unfriendly and keep to themselves. My neighbors, especially Jen, were extremely courteous. My new supervisor, Monika Spurley, was great person as well. She was remarkably helpful with my transition and bringing me on board to a new program.

The base basketball team I decided to play on was also full of easy-going people. I chose to play to stay active and because of my competitive nature, I simply cannot stay away from competition for too long. Coach Burns and Chester were both passionate guys who had also served in the military. They did a marvelous job of putting us positions to compete in the Southeastern Military Athletic Conference (SEMAC). Correspondingly, we won the SEMAC tournament in February of 2020.

Cedric Koonce, one of my teammates, was the primary friend I made in GA, along with Mike Singleton. I was pleasantly surprised to meet a couple of good comrades in my new setting, mainly because I don't typically go searching for friendship. Most of the people in my life have been around for years and that's who I roll with. It normally takes me a while to warm up to people and let them in because of all that I've been through. But Ced and Mike have provided constructive and consistent companionship since I met them, which I'm thankful for.

In terms of my relationship with my dad, things drastically improved. Now that we were only two hours away from each other, Darius and I saw him a lot more often. He even visited us once a week for a few months. It was good spending time with him as adults and making up for the time we missed out on as teenagers. Most of our interaction was lighthearted and fun-filled, but some of it was serious as well.

Darius and I had a few heart-to-heart conversations with my dad letting him know that we'd completely forgiven him and understood that people make mistakes. His biggest issue was that he couldn't forgive himself. Thus, we encouraged him to absolve himself so he didn't continue to feel bad about a mistake he could not go back and change. Nonetheless, my speculation that God sent me to Georgia to repair my relationship seemed to be correct, and I'm glad he did because now, our relationship is better than ever.

HE WHO FINDS A WIFE

My relationship with Shaianne started to get demanding after we began dating. Our relationship as a couple started off great as we were in the lovebird phase, but we soon hit a rocky patch, especially since I was further away. Now that we were courting, things were more serious, and expectations were higher. We also had a lot of individual growth to do in order to mesh with each other. Besides, we needed to learn each other on a more intimate level rather than just being comrades. Most importantly, prior to my spiritual growth, we were living wrong. We were clubbing, drinking, and having sex before marriage. I called myself a Christian, but I wasn't living like one. Shaianne was new to Christianity, so she was following my lead, and I was being a bad example. Admiringly, my mother was able to help us in this area. Her guidance pushed us in the right direction and away from negative influences. I regard my mom as my earthly agnel in adulthood. She always has, and is constantly accentuating theological precepts, helping to guide her loved ones in the right direction. Additionally, one of Shaianne's friends introduced us to a book called *The Love Dare*, which was monumental.

Though we were in a long-distance relationship, we read the book together daily and discussed our takeaways. This book was vital to our relationship. So much so, that I don't believe we would have lasted without it. I recommend this book to any couple, married or dating. *The Love Dare* allows men and women to see topics from both sides through a Biblical perspective. It forces you to reflect on your subscription to the relationship and what scripture says you should be doing. At the end of each chapter, it gives each person a dare surrounding love. For example, at the end of the patience chapter, the book may tell you work on patience with your significant other for the next day, and to prevent from saying anything negative to them. The application of Biblical relationship instruction, in addition to the dares, took our relationship to new heights.

The Love Dare also encouraged us to implement what the book calls a "love tank." The love tank is a scale of 1-10 that measures how loved your significant other feels. Checking on each other's love tank calls for a daily inquiry of how full your partner's love tank is. If their love tank is at a 10, then you should continue doing what you're doing, as they feel fully loved. For any number under 10, you should ask what you can do to fill their love tank and strive to accomplish it. This may sound tedious, but over time it became a profitable habit for us and was a great addition to our routine. It improved our communication and ensured we did our best to keep each other happy.

We noticed so much improvement to our alliance that book reading became a key enhancement to our connection. While courting, we would read *The Five Love Languages, Sex, Jesus, and the Conversations the Church Forgot*, and *The Truth About Men. Sex, Jesus, and the Conversations the Church Forgot*, by Mo Isom was an awesome book. Isom turned out to be the wife of Jeremiah Aiken, one of my former strength and conditioning coaches at the Academy. Following our completion of the book, I reached out to Jeremiah and let him know how much his wife's book had helped our relationship and how appreciative we were. We had been experiencing a lot of the same issues the couple dealt with in their book, so it was encouraging to read literature that provided solutions.

Like any other relationship, ours was filled with ups and downs. But as we learned, grew, respected each other's differences, and continued reading, our relationship flourished. We could see the manifestation from all our reading, mentally and spiritually. With that, we received counseling from the minister at our Good Hope church home in Tacoma, Pastor Carter. Pastor Carter is a powerful man of God who I've known since the fourth grade. He practices what he preaches, and God's hands on his life are evident through his marriage, testimony, and family. Pastor Carter provided us with some remarkably good acumen, answered our questions, and recommended several books, one of them being *The Family Manifesto.*

Shaianne injected the marriage word early in our relationship. Marriage was definitely the end goal, yet in my mind, it was distant, so I didn't provide much insight on the subject. However, once I felt our relationship was at the point where I was ready to pop the question, the conversation became more serious. My main quantification for our relationship being prepared to take that next step and knowing Shaianne was the one was largely based on her walk with God; that was most important to me. There was also her communication and consistency that played a part in the evaluation. Once I realized I did not want to be with anyone else and Shaianne was the best person out there for me, I knew it was time to get engaged. Shaianne was the complete package: she could cook, she was a great mother, she was loyal, and she helped me open up in ways no other woman ever had. This led me to create what I called "the engagement meter."

Shaianne was not very thrilled with the engagement meter, but it was my way of knowing she was ready. The engagement meter was a 0-100 scale built from my desired metrics. Each day, I would disclose where she was on the meter based on her actions. Once we reached 90 out of 100, then I would know the time was right. This was a subjective, yet quantifiable way for me to measure our progress. After some struggle, Shaianne eventually made it to 90 in December of 2018. Unbeknownst to her, I had already purchased the engagement ring on Black Friday because I knew she was the one. I was able to get a massive, $6,000 2-carat diamond ring from Zales for half-off through their Black Friday sale.

We got engaged on January 19, 2019. I planned everything from start to finish. I invited our close friends and family to dinner at Texas De Brazil in Tacoma and told them the surprise that would be taking place. To Shaianne, I made it seem like we were just celebrating the holidays with our loved ones over dinner. My mom was my main conspirator. She purchased greeting cards for each of the women in attendance and wrote personal messages for them to read aloud. Shaianne's card was different; it provided thoughtful words of affirmation, then, at the end it instructed her to turn around. Prior to Shaianne reading her card, I had gotten up and gone to the restroom. From just outside the lavatory, I could see our table and discern how far she'd read. About midway through, I snuck behind Shaianne's chair and got on one knee. When she turned around, I was there with the dashing ring in my hand and asked her to marry me. She burst into tears after accepting, and the whole restaurant applauded. It felt like the end of a Hallmark movie and was an indelible experience.

Soon after the engagement, we started planning our wedding. Being that we're both from Tacoma, we knew we'd have the wedding in the area. Planning a wedding while I was in Georgia and Shaianne in Tacoma was strenuous, yet we made it work. We didn't agree on everything and bumped heads at times, but we always came back together and got on the same page. We were able to find a massive venue located in Puyallup, WA, that had room for both the ceremony and the reception, which was highly convenient and economical. After securing the venue, we appointed January 19, 2020, as the big day.

Clarissa, a family friend of ours, has a catering business, so we solicited her services for a much better price than other caterers. We wanted our photos professionally done; hence, we went with an expensive nationwide photographer. Shaianne picked out an alluring three-layer cake. The decorations were handled in sequence between Shaianne and my mom. Most of 2019 surrounded planning the wedding, but Shaianne and I continued to grow and read our help books. We also conducted our second and third counseling sessions with Pastor Carter and were more confident about our future together.

After 10 months on station in Georgia, I was promoted to captain. This furtherance was far more significant to me. During the winter of 2018, I was overjoyed when I received notification from my commander that I was selected for captain. For a first lieutenant to be eligible for promotion to captain, an Airman must complete 24 months of service as a first lieutenant. Due to the magnitude of this promotion, I held a ceremony. I had only anticipated the commemoration to house around 50 individuals. But on the day of the ceremony, commander Col Menke sent a note to the entire division encouraging them to attend. All-inclusive, there were about 100 people in attendance. Most importantly, I was able to have my fiancé, mother, father, and Paris all there as well.

The function was formal and held at the Museum of Aviation located right outside the Robins AFB gates. My military supervisor, Lt Col Gerard, furnished opening remarks and presented my promotion order. I then repeated the oath of office after him, a customary act at promotion ceremonies. Next, Col Gerard spoke a few words about his encounter with me and my development as an officer. Following his remarks, it was my turn to deliver a speech. Like any other time speaking in front of a crowd, I was thoroughly nervous. I'd been noticing the impact my concussion symptoms were having on my cognitive abilities. Thus, I prepared extensively.

The address was heartfelt and honest. With many in the audience not knowing my background, I spoke about people from Tacoma atypically dreaming of becoming captains in the Air Force; they fantasize about being professional athletes. I also talked about how easy it was for me to go down the wrong route growing up in a perilous environment. Thankfully, I had a praying mother who kept a close eye on me. I then discussed my leadership during sports as an adolescent and my experience at the Academy. I had several light moments in my speech where the crowd burst with laughter. Towards the end, I thanked everyone by name who had influenced me along the way. I finished the discourse by publicly giving flowers to Shaianne, my mother, and Paris. After my speech, I received a standing ovation, culminating an unforgettable moment.

Several weeks later, it was time for my next OPR. There were far less officers in my organization at Robins which made OPRs much more competitive. I was ranked #4 out of 12 all-star company-grade officers by Col Gerard. His comment in my OPRs pronounced, "Proven leader with a record of excellence and pushing capabilities to the operational mission. Dynamic new captain, superb young officer/leader/acquisition professional." He then recommended me for a tough program management job next.

Also, in July, the next-generation mid-engine C8 Corvette was revealed. The event was held in Tustin, CA on July 18, 2019. and live streamed across the world. I, as a Corvette owner, assuredly tuned in. Leading up to the event, I'd seen all the sneak peeks and camouflage-covered test vehicles Chevrolet released, so I was anxious for the official reveal. However, once the C8 Corvette was unveiled I was taken away. The car looked even better than I'd anticipated and possessed a whopping 490 horsepower, generating an itch to obtain one as soon as possible. The sticker price of $59,995 was a bargain for the car, but still out of my reach as a junior captain. Nevertheless, my desire to procure one remained over time.

Meanwhile, I was still undergoing treatment for my concussions as my symptoms worsened. Although I was performing well, I noticed a decline in my abilities and a deficit from my previous aptitude. A conclusive list of my concussion symptoms included frequent headaches, insomnia, balance issues, poor long and short-term memory, speech deficiencies, short attention span, anxiety, lack of concentration, and a short fuse. Consequently, after voicing my concerns to my primary doctors, I was referred to a neurologist and Traumatic Brain Injury (TBI) specialist, as well as prescribed melatonin for my insomnia. The melatonin helped me fall asleep fairly well, but I was yet exceedingly tired throughout the day. I had difficulty waking up and an even harder time staying awake by the middle of the day. Therefore, my primary care doctor referred me to sleep clinic to perform a sleep study. A sleep study, also known as Polysomnography, is a comprehensive test used to diagnose sleep disorders. Polysomnography records your brain waves, the oxygen level in your blood, heart rate and breathing, as well as eye and leg movements during the study.[176]

The sleep study was accomplished overnight at a sleep center. At the center, I was assigned a bed with sensors on it that would monitor my sleep. Needless to say, my night of sleep was rough as usual. It took me a while to fall asleep and I woke up several times. The next morning, I was awakened promptly at 5 a.m. and told my test was over. I received my result weeks later and was shockingly diagnosed with moderate sleep apnea. My Apnea/Hypopnea Index (AHI) was 15.1 episodes per hour, the number of times I stopped breathing an hour. I was astonished because I was completely unaware this was taking place during my sleep. Dr. Thomas further described just how serious sleep apnea is. He explained that if my condition was left untreated, it could have led to death. Additionally, there is no cure for sleep apnea. The only solution is a Continuous Positive Airway Pressure (CPAP) machine, which is a breathing therapy device that delivers air to a mask worn over the nose and/or mouth to help consistent breathing. Without a cure, CPAPs must be worn for one's entire life.

To measure my sleep's improvement with a CPAP, I was called in to do another sleep study. This study was executed the same way, with the addition of CPAP machine and mask. Low and behold, my sleep drastically improved. Literally overnight, I went from 15.1 episodes per hour to 0.6. After a successful final test, I was sent home with my own CPAP machine and supplies. I was glad the CPAP had almost eliminated the number of apneas I experienced, but I was also devastated that I would have to use a CPAP for the rest of my life, at the young age of 27. I soon felt tears of fury flow down my face as I was confronted with yet another drawback.

The first few months with my CPAP were disastrous; I did not sleep through an entire night a single time. My body could simply not get used to sleeping with a mask or the air pressure flowing into my nostrils. Inevitably, I was exhausted at work, making it that much more difficult to fulfill my duties. Some nights I omitted my CPAP. I considered abandoning it altogether, because at least I would get a little more sleep. So, I went to God and asked him to help me with the matter. Jesus instructs us to ask for help in Luke 11:9, "And I say unto you, Ask, and it shall be given you, seek, and ye shall find; knock, and it shall be opened unto you."

Slowly but surely, I noticed progress. After a while, I could sleep for a few hours before waking up. I still wouldn't be able to go back to sleep with the mask on, so I'd take it off for the remainder of the night. Then I made more headway and finally started to sleep through the entire night and my increased energy during the day reflected it. I was grateful for the blessing and began to come to grips with my perpetual CPAP usage. Today, I use my CPAP on a nightly basis, and my wife makes sure of it. I am also faithful that God will miraculously heal me of my sleep apnea one day to add to my testimony and give him the glory, because he is able to do what no man can.

My trust stems from the previous healing wonders he's done in my life, as well as confidence in scripture: "But he *was* wounded for our transgressions, *he was* bruised for our iniquities: the chastisement of our peace *was* upon him; and with his stripes we are healed (Isaiah 53:5)." Through the death of Jesus Christ on the cross who bore our iniquities, our ailments have already been healed by him in the spiritual realm. The manifestation of that healing in our natural bodies is a matter of God's will, our faith, and relationship with him. The other encouraging verse is Isaiah 54:17: "No weapon that is formed against thee shall prosper; and every tongue *that* shall rise against thee in judgement thou shalt condemn. This *is* the heritage of the servants of the LORD, and their righteousness *is* of me, saith the LORD." Weapons against people come from the devil. There are times when God permits bad things to happen to good people for His will, but spiritual attacks are from the devil. Isaiah 54:17 repudiates satan's attacks, which may form, but God will not allow them to come into fruition against his faithful followers.

Besides that, I was set for my neurology appointment. There, I was prescribed citalopram, used to treat anxiety and depression, which proved ineffective against my symptoms. The neurologist diagnosed me with post-concussion syndrome and primary stabbing headaches. I was also scheduled for another MRI because the doctor wanted to see if there were any abnormalities with my brain. The MRI uncovered a small area that was believed to be a cyst. I was traumatized when I received this horrifying news. I didn't know if it meant I would die or how severe the implications were. I told my loved ones, and they were all distraught. My doctor told me not to worry until things were confirmed with a contrast MRI, so I tried to stay the course.

A couple months later, I was able to complete my contrast MRI. The results were very favorable, and the previously found area was determined to be normal and not a cyst. I was so glad to hear this. Either the cyst had gone away, or the initial finding was incorrect. However, it is my belief that God healed the cyst, so I attribute the relief to him. Regardless, my symptoms were still prevalent and stagnant, triggering my doctor to recommend me for a Medical Evaluation Board (MEB). The MEB is a process designed to determine whether a Service member's long-term medical condition enables him/her to continue to meet medical retention standards in accordance with military service regulations. It also provides an opportunity for military physicians to clearly document all care and treatments received prior to MEB referral and any duty limitations their condition may cause.

The MEB is considered an informal board because it does not drive any personnel actions. Instead, the findings of the MEB are referred to the Physical Evaluation Board (PEB), which formally determines fitness for continued service and eligibility for disability compensation. The MEB is convened once the medical retention decision point is reached or when the Service member's physician thinks the Service member will not be able to return to duty for medical reasons. The board evaluates a Service member's medical history and condition, documents the extent of the injury or illness, and decides whether the Service member's medical condition is severe enough to impede his/her ability to continue serving in a full duty capacity.[177]

The main reason I was submitted for an MEB was because my symptoms were impacting my job and they had not improved over the years. The MEB process was especially lengthy and stressful. While waiting on the determination, my entire life was on hold. I was unsure if I would be remaining in Georgia, moving elsewhere, staying in the military, going civilian, or taking a corporate job. I just created plans for every scenario so I could be prepared for the outcome.

The MEB also required a multitude of appointments and uncertainty. As transparent as the military tries to be about the process, there are still many unknowns and inconsistencies with the timelines. Evaluators decide whether they think Airmen should be retained and returned to duty, medically separated, or medically retired, based on their assessment of the Airmen's condition. After this recommendation, Airmen are scheduled to go through Veteran Affairs (VA) appointments for each condition to receive a rating for them, and then the ratings are added together. A 0% rating is return to duty, 10-20% is medical separation, and 30-100% is medical retirement. That rating is then provided back to the Air Force to inform the final decision. The Air Force provides their ratings based upon the VA's findings, but typically they are the same.

The VA appointments took place between October and December of 2019 and were quite peculiar compared to any other doctor's appointments I'd been to. Rather than trying to resolve my issues, the VA doctors were only concerned with finding out details about the conditions and the history behind it, nothing more. Not only does the VA review the condition responsible for the MEB, but also every other condition the service member has suffered in the military. The facts are what guided them to determine a disability percentage. Once my VA appointments were over, I did not receive any updates on my case for months. I continued to see my mental health doctor, Dr. Long, as a part of the MEB process, and could only receive estimates of the timetable. Dr. Long was a huge guide for me throughout the affair by providing much-needed assurance and counsel on how to best prepare myself for the verdict, either way it went.

Time was drawing nearer to my wedding date as well. With all our advancement, Shaianne and I elected not to have bachelor and bachelorette parties. We had given up clubbing and hard liquor, so we did not want to jeopardize our hard work for a weekend of senseless activities. Instead, I took a trip to Miami by myself. I visited South Beach, went to a car show, ate some good food, and relaxed at my hotel. Shaianne didn't do anything at all.

A month before our wedding, a notable event took place; my brother graduated from Washington State University with his bachelor's degree in accounting. Although it wasn't my graduation, it certainly felt like it. I'd sacrificed so much financially to take care of my brother all for this day to come. Seemingly, Darius graduating was one of the proudest moments of my life. Darius took an extended route by attending several colleges over the course of seven years, but he persisted and eventually made it across the finish line. Darius honored our agreement and was sincerely grateful for my sacrifice; he understood its magnitude.

Upon graduation, Darius soon landed on his own two feet. He has since secured a lucrative job with a defense contractor in San Diego. He now has his own apartment and is in the process of looking to buy his first home. Darius has also matured and grown into a strong man of God who will be a great husband and father once he finds the right woman. Our bond is as close as two brothers can get, and we have big plans being devised together. After his graduation, my attention shifted back to the wedding.

I flew into Tacoma on Thursday before the wedding. The entire weekend was packed. On Friday, we held our rehearsal with all the groomsmen, bridesmaids, and flower girls at the venue. Following the rehearsal was the rehearsal dinner with each of the parties involved. Our good friend Jasmine Brown had organized the dinner and decorated everything extravagantly. The dinner was held in a private room at Pacific Grill in downtown Tacoma. Jasmine took the liberty of decorating the room with candles, flowers, balloons, and photos. It was over the top and much more than we had expected. The dinner itself was a blast! Our friends and family thoroughly enjoyed themselves. The food was excellent, the drinks were great, and the fellowship was unforgettable. Zach was in a generous mood and ordered 10 bottles of wine by the end of the night, amplifying the cheer and commemoration.

On Saturday morning, I picked up the rental car for our wedding. Because this was a once-in-a-lifetime occasion, I decided to rent something extraordinary. Therefore, I had reserved a Jaguar F-Type, a luxurious foreign sports car. Driving the car was an exhilarating experience. It possessed a high amount of torque and horsepower, and the exhaust roared like a lion.

That night, our families held a get-together with our out-of-town friends and relatives who were visiting. The event was a continuation of the night before and turned out great. Each person was given a chance to express kind words about Shaianne and myself and commune with one another. After the party, Shaianne and I parted ways and went to our hotels. I laid out all of my groomsman gifts and made sure my tuxedo was ready to go.

On the morning of my wedding, I woke up at 8 a.m. enthusiastic and nervous. It was one of the premier days of my life, and I could not wait to get the show on the road. With the wedding starting at 3 p.m., I had a lot of time to spare, until my phone began blowing up; it seemed like everyone needed something, fueling my stress levels. My first stop was the bride's residence; Shaianne needed me to bring June's wedding clothes over. While there, it behooved me to pray with her, simply to acknowledge God and start the day off appropriately. Since the bride and groom are not allowed to see each other before walking down the aisle, we held hands from around the corner as we went to God in prayer. Afterwards, I headed to the venue. My mother and others were setting up for the event and needed a speaker. I had planned on just dropping the speaker off and leaving, but to my astonishment, preparation wasn't going as planned. Not as many people were helping as my mother expected, so things were going extremely slow. Consequently, I took it upon myself to stay and help, which I did for several hours before it was time for me to return to my hotel and get ready.

The groomsmen came to my suite to change because my hotel was right next to the venue. After everyone arrived, I presented them with their personalized gifts. Each of them was thoroughly pleased by what I had gifted. Midway into getting dressed, the photographer showed up after already snapping photos of the bridal party. We continued having a good time listening to music and watching the NFL playoffs while he took numerous candid pictures.

I felt like a million bucks in my perfectly tailored red tuxedo, along with my immaculate taper. The groomsmen were clothed in black tuxedos with red vests and bowties.

Once everyone was dressed, we departed for the locale. Entering the venue thirty minutes before showtime, I expected everything to be ready to go. Unfortunately, my mother was running late because she was forced to set up longer than anticipated due to the lack of participation from others. After setting up, my mother still had to drive 20 minutes to Tacoma to change and return. Ultimately, she ended up being an hour late, delaying the wedding until she arrived. Shaianne was highly upset by the sequence, so I did my best to ensure her bridesmaids kept her calm. I could tell by the look on my mother's face how disappointed she was that she was so behind. I also understood it wasn't her fault and did not hold it against her, neither did Shaianne.

Eventually, we were able to get the show on the road, and the wedding turned out to be fantastic. Of course, everything did not go exactly as planned, but it was still momentous. At first glance of my gorgeous wife coming down the aisle, I was simply taken away. Shaianne looked more beautiful than I had ever seen her. In advance of the wedding, I wondered if I would cry as I awaited her at the top of the aisle because I'm a person who hardly ever sheds a tear. However, this occasion was an oddity, and tears of joy slowly flowed down my face as she gracefully approached the altar.

The ceremony was officiated by none other than Pastor Carter. When it came to exchange rings, I had forgotten the wedding band that came with Shaianne's engagement ring in the car. I had been running around for much of the morning and forgot to put it in my pocket. Nevertheless, Shaianne already had her engagement ring and band on, so she just placed mine on my finger, and I pretended to do the same to her. We repeated the traditional vows after the Pastor and saved our written ones for the reception. After we kissed, the 150 guests in attendance burst into applause.

Subsequent to the ceremony, we signed the marriage certificates and made it official. Then time was carved out to take pictures. Once we were finally done with obligations, the DJ announced the bridal party to the guests, and the party commenced. The first order of business was for our guests to eat. In the meantime, Shaianne and I sat at the head table as guests congratulated us. We were able to take everything in for a minute as time started to slow down a bit. The head table was decorated wonderfully by my mother. I had not seen it until the reception because she wanted it to be a surprise, and it blew me away.

After eating, we cut the cake, and dessert was served. Shaianne had spent a hefty $700 on the cake, and our guests could tell; everyone loved it. Many of them said it was the best cake they'd ever had. Following dessert were speeches from our esteemed guests. Shaianne had two of her bridesmaids, Paris, and Jasmine, give speeches. Jasmine's speech was on the lighter side and filled with spiritual encouragement. Paris' was strong and heartfelt. From my end, my dad, mom, Darius, who was my best man, and Zach gave speeches. My dad's speech was unexpected, yet insightful. My mom's was full of love, excitement, happiness, and faith. My brother's speech contained gratitude for the things I'd done for him and enthusiasm for our future. Zach's address won the crowd with his charism and humor. After our loved ones gave their discourses, Shaianne and I conveyed ours. Shaianne's vows were eloquently written and touched me with her thoughtful words. My outpouring was last and received the best reaction. My speech was genuine, humorous, honest, and promising. It highlighted what my wife could expect in our holy matrimony.

In the interest of time, we abandoned the games we had planned to follow the discourses and invited everyone to the dance floor. The reception started jumping like Michael Jordan. It was good to see everyone having a blast and enjoying themselves at our wedding. Even our elderly family members were out there having a good time. After the reception, Shaianne and I loaded up the F-Type and headed to our Hilton near the Sea-Tac airport. We had an early flight in the morning, setting out on our honeymoon to Cancun, Mexico.

The flight to Cancun seemed to last forever due to our restlessness. This was our first time out of the country, so we were extremely anxious. All in all, the journey was seamless. A quarter of our $20,000 wedding expenses were spent on the all-inclusive honeymoon package in a penthouse suite. Pointedly, our stay took place at the Beloved Playa Mujeres couples-only resort. The $5,000 trip was worth every penny and one of the best experiences of our lives. To start, the package included a private SUV that transported us to and from the airport. We were surprised to see some of the poor living conditions we encountered on our way to the hotel. Because

Cancun is a tourist location, we expected the whole city to be opulent, but that couldn't have been further from the truth. We were even required to pass through a checkpoint managed by armed militia, which was a bit alarming.

After our arrival, we were pleasantly welcomed by the hotel's kind staff, who provided us with warm wet towels and champagne. The towels are used to refresh and clean guest's hands and face. During our check-in, we were greeted by name and treated like royalty while the bellmen hauled our luggage to our suite. After our orientation, we made our way to our room. On the door was a sash labeled, "Congratulations on your honeymoon!" Once inside, we were flabbergasted; the room was immaculate. The flooring was made of marble. There was a fruit basket on the living room table, a fully stocked mini bar, a separate bedroom, a private pool on the vast patio, and a premium ocean view. Our suite was a top-notch accommodation, and we were thrilled to start our vacation. But that was just our room. The hotel supplied scores of amenities as well.

Every morning, the resort delivered a flier covering its daily events. The resort provided activities at different times of the day including bike riding, games, snorkeling, beach sports, knitting, and nightly live music. The resort also housed an authentic taco truck, fresh fruit and smoothie stand, 24-hour coffee shop, three pools, four jacuzzies, a fitness center, and a world-class spa. Most of our time was spent on the beach and the spa. Although the resort was all-inclusive, the spa was not incorporated into basic reservations. But because we went with the penthouse suite, spa services were included, and it was well worth the upgrade.

Hydrotherapy at the spa was our favorite part of our honeymoon. The Hydrotherapy sessions comprised a Crystal steam hammam, Roman caldarium, a Swedish sauna, an ice glacier room, five sensation showers, Kneipp plunge basins, contrast walk pools, swan-neck massage jets, cascade jets, water massage loungers, and water ab stations. Each session lasted 90 minutes and was one of the most relaxing things we've ever done. Our spa treatments were done in the morning and provided a great beginning to our days.

The day before we left Mexico, we finally decided to leave the resort and go to the traveler's portion of Cancun where the big mall and strip of hotels are. We did what most advised us to and took a taxi, retaining the driver for our entire outing. It was a lot busier in the area, and there was also more to do. We elected to rent a speedboat and go on a jungle tour, as well as go snorkeling. The jungle tour was awesome and showed us a different side of Cancun we didn't know existed. Snorkeling was also a fun experience as we detected dozens of fish. After our tours, we ate authentic tacos in the local area. Our driver even sat down and broke bread with us while he explained some of Cancun's local culture. Next, we went to the market to purchase souvenirs for our family members. The salesmen were remarkably aggressive and hounded us to buy from them. On our way back to the resort, we drove through downtown Cancun and saw the poor quality of life the natives possessed.

We were highly disappointed on Saturday when it was time to go home as we did not want to leave. The hardest part was we would be going our separate ways due to unforeseen circumstances. Leading up to the wedding, we had planned to drive Shaianne's car down to Georgia with her son upon returning from our honeymoon, but on January 17th, two days before our wedding, June's father served Shaianne with an immediate restraining order preventing her from taking June out of the state. And as any loving mother would do, Shaianne refused to leave without her son. So, our plan of action was foiled, and we were compelled to go through the court's process. While the court process had just begun, my MEB finally concluded.

After much delay, the ruling was made in March of 2020, and Dr. Long called me in to break the news. I was extraordinarily edgy as I was unsure which way the board had voted. Dr. Long sat me down, and I could hardly sit still. Conclusively, she informed me that I was designated 90% for all of my VA ratings, 40% of that for my TBI, meaning I would be medically retired. The other 50% included ratings for conditions such as: left shoulder strain, obstructive sleep apnea, cervical strain (neck pain), flat feet, left and right knee strain, fingertip amputation, lumbar degenerative disc disease (low back pain), right elbow tendonitis, right hip strain, skull fracture, diplopia, acute gastroenteritis, post concussive headaches, and tinnitus. The VA only attributes ratings to conditions that were sustained or exacerbated while serving. Thus, most of my conditions were football related.

Nevertheless, I was surprised by the medical retirement prognosis because MEBs are so unpredictable. I was also relieved because I was finally presented with a decision, allowing me to continue planning my life. Thankfully, I had done adequate preparation in the year leading up to my discharge. I had completed the Air Force's mandatory separation counseling, which incorporated the Transition Assistance Program (TAP). The goal of the TAP is to provide information, tools, and training to ensure service members and their spouses are prepared for the next step in civilian life, whether pursuing additional education, finding a career, or starting their own business.[178] Upon my insertion into the MEB, I scrambled to get this accomplished. TAP was incredibly useful. The course featured a representative from the Department of Labor who provided us with inside information straight from the horse's mouth. The class taught us several resume writing tips, and networking tactics, included a one-year subscription of LinkedIn Premium, interviewing techniques, and so much more. The class prompted me to write my first official resume as well, one that would be essential to my transition.

I had also learned about the Service Academy Career Conference (SACC) from my peers who had already been discharged from the Air Force and attended themselves. The goal of SACC is to create connections. SACC provides a platform that enables organizations and academic institutions to connect directly with an unparalleled pool of highly qualified candidates. Every candidate is a Veteran of the U.S. Military with a proven track record of organizational leadership in the military and in corporate settings. Regardless of your talent acquisition needs, these candidates represent all levels of military and civilian experience. This same platform provides our candidates the opportunity to engage with industry-leading companies and premier academic institutions from across the globe as they navigate career transitions and pursue graduate degrees.[179]

The moment I heard of SACC, I recognized an advantage of going to the Academy come into fruition. While at the Academy, one of the motivations people use is that not only do you have a guaranteed job upon graduation, but you are set for life. That's because graduation from the Air Force Academy sets you apart from civilian peers due to the rigor, leadership curriculum, and character that has been built. Therefore, it is claimed that once one's military career is over, the opportunities are endless, and getting jobs is easy. There are even stories of graduates "ring knocking," or tapping their ring on a desk during an interview and receiving the job simply because they went to the Academy. So, the reality that there is an entire conference dedicated solely to service academy graduates, is one example of this phenomenon. Even further, SACC is not just a conference visited by insignificant companies; this conference consists of the big boys.

SACC is coveted by these companies because they know the value of service academy graduates. To name just a few, here is a list of some of the companies that were present: JP Morgan, Amazon, Verizon, Walmart, Wells Fargo, Bank of America, PepsiCo, Citi, Proctor & Gamble, Microsoft, Chick-Fil-A, the CIA, and even the Secret Service. All in all, there were close to 100 companies present. Leading up to the conference, we were offered access to the conference website after paying our registration fee. The SACC website allowed us to create a profile along with our preferences and a resume for companies to see. This preliminary interaction permitted interested companies to review our profiles and contact us before the conference. Two companies contacted me beforehand, Smart Sourcing, and UnitedHealth Group. In fact, they were both so intrigued that they requested interviews with me at SACC. I was elated by the exchange and couldn't wait for the conference.

The November 2019 event was held in San Antonio and gave me plenty of time to register, network, and prepare. Upon registration, my resume generated interest from Nestle and JP Morgan. Consequently, I was able to speak with a talent acquisition manager from Nestle before the conference and schedule an informational interview that took place during the actual symposium.

Representatives from each company who came to SACC were usually veteran recruiters or hiring managers. Many of them were service academy graduates and had even gone to SACC themselves. Some of the companies were even represented by high-level decision makers, providing immense opportunities. The two-day conference itself was intimate. The first day was full of presentations by the most favored companies and schools. My informational interview with Smart Sourcing was also held that day. Although it was informal, this was essentially my first interview as an adult, thus I was exceptionally nervous. The interview went surprisingly well though, to the point where I thought I'd soon be receiving my first job offer.

During the second day of the job fair, we were able to speak with representatives from companies we were attracted to, network with them, hand them our resumes, and exchange contact information. It was overwhelming trying to talk to every company I was drawn to. A couple of hours into the fair, I quickly realized I would not have time to speak with all the corporations I intended to, forcing me to prioritize. Overall, I spoke to about 30 firms and handed out all 20 copies of my resume. The conference was widely successful and even better than I expected. Afterward, I sent a ton of follow up emails to let companies know I was still interested in hopes that they would keep me on their radars.

The conference was so fruitful that I decided to go to the next one in Jacksonville five months later. The next SACC was held on March 26-27, 2020. Unfortunately, due to the COVID-19 pandemic, the conference did not take place in person and was postponed to a virtual conference on April 16-17. The pre-conference agenda was identical and worked the same way. As a result, I drew interest from Synchrony, Lowe's, and Northwestern Mutual. The conference was not as beneficial due to its virtual nature, but I was able to reconnect with several companies from the first one and interact with a few new ones as well.

PANDEMONIUM

The COVID-19 virus was introduced to the world in 2019, with its epicenter in Wuhan, China. COVID-19 stands for coronavirus-2019. This new coronavirus is similar to SARS-CoV; thus, it was named SARS-CoV-2.[180] In one year, SARS-CoV-2, the virus that causes COVID-19, quickly became a global pandemic, infecting 96 million people and killing 2 million, 400,000 of them in the USA. As many as 40% of those who test positive for COVID-19 have no symptoms at all, but 2% of people who get sick die. It's especially deadly in the elderly. COVID-19 has killed one of every 66 people older than 85 in the USA. Among those infected, some percentage – we don't know how many – cope with crippling long-term symptoms that plague them for months. Future health impacts remain unknown.[181]

There has been much controversy as to the origin of the virus but ultimately, researchers determined in March of 2020 that "SARS-CoV-2 is not a laboratory construct or a purposefully manipulated virus," they wrote in the journal Nature. Anthony Fauci, director of the National Institute of Allergy and Infectious Diseases, said it may take up to 85% of Americans being vaccinated to protect the population. Reaching those numbers will be challenging considering pervasive vaccine hesitancy and a slow, complicated rollout. In the meantime, public health measures to stop the spread – masking, social distancing, and hand-washing – are essential, experts repeated.[181]

I firmly believe COVID-19 was intentionally created based on my extensive research, primarily on the National Institute of Health's website. Via their contract registry, one can find a list of their contracts, including one with EcoHealth Alliance, Funding Opportunity Announcement PA-11-260. This contract dates to 2014 and focuses on the risk of future coronavirus emergence from bats and other animals in China. It also consists of six projects and has been funded a total of $3.7M since its inception. EcoHealth is a nonprofit research organization concerned with the study of infectious diseases. With government-funded research on coronavirus caused by bats, the very same way experts say COVID-19 began, initiating in 2014, there surely should have been more preparation and vaccines already available if COVID-19 truly was an accident. There is much more research to support my claim, but in the interest of time, I will save the rest of my COVID-19 evidence for another time. Regardless of its intentionality, COVID's blow has been legitimate.

As the COVID-19 situation has evolved, the world continues to be affected. Initially, the virus was not taken seriously by many, including professional athletes. That was until several NBA players became infected, and games were postponed. The conditions unfolded so quickly that eventually, on March 20, 2020, NBA Commissioner Adam Silver decided to cancel the remaining 2019-2020 NBA season. Other sports such as baseball and the Olympics abolished their games as well. The sports world was shocked, and it made the virus that authentic for those who had their doubts.

As the virus compounded and impacted the world, its brunt became increasingly deliberate. More people were contracting the virus and dying, hospitals were becoming overcrowded with victims, and the government implemented numerous lockdowns. Curfews were also enacted, businesses closed, and travel restrictions were arranged around the world. The National Guard was even deployed in some U.S. cities. This started to make citizens feel confined, and with another unarmed minority killed by a police officer on Memorial Weekend, racial tensions only added fuel to the country's fire. The killing of George Floyd on camera in cold blood was a horrific scene.

The U.S. was a ticking time bomb and exploded when riots broke out in cities across America.

COVID-19 also directly impacted my life and the matters I was going through. The MEB process was grueling, and adding a global pandemic only made it worse. As organizations throughout the country implemented social distancing plans and more people tested positive, the timeline continued to extend. Offices were closed, and employees were forced to work from home, a phenomenon that became popular around the nation. Consequently, my MEB decision was hampered for longer than I'd hoped. Ironically, now that I had my results, things moved extremely quickly.

TRIUMPH OVER TRIALS

Medical retirement is granted the same benefits as traditional retirement in terms of terminal leave. Terminal leave is chargeable leave taken in conjunction with retirement or separation from active duty. A member's last day of leave coincides with the last day of active duty.[182] I possessed 10 days of leave and was given the standard 20 days of permissive leave for a total of 30 days. My last official day of active duty was assigned May 10, 2020. This meant my final day of work and out-processing deadline were both April 10th, the day my terminal leave started. Eventually, I was able to hand off my workload to the lucky new program manager, Mike Singleton, and complete out-processing on the morning of April 10th. A couple of days later, I departed for Tacoma, where I would spend the bulk of my terminal leave.

In conjunction with out-processing, I also had to ramp up my transition to obtain income after retirement. I applied for several veteran transition assistance programs, signed up for company job alerts, sent out my resume countless times, and reached out to my widely advantageous Academy network. The AFA has a Facebook group called the "USAFA Alumni Careers and Networking" with over 10,000 members. This network is a professional tool for USAFA graduates to connect, learn, and network for their careers post-military service. This group was started to provide a forum for graduates to share ideas, network, and help each other in their careers.[183]

Oftentimes, one can find jobs, opportunities to apply for, and career advice all posted there. I made a post in the group on September 10, 2019, once I found out I was going through an MEB and received valuable advice. After I received my MEB decision, I posted in the group again, updating them on my situation and seeking assistance with job hunting. I received over 80 comments that led to job referrals, resume revisions, veteran transition companies, links to job applications, and heaps of additional direction. The USAFA network is truly invaluable.

As time drew nearer, my anxiety skyrocketed. I had faith in God and knew he would direct my path, but I was still under a great deal of stress. Seeking employment in new industries was difficult by itself, but that, combined with COVID, made my search terribly challenging. Companies were suffering losses, facing unpredictability, and citizens were being laid off all over the country. While I was networking and attempting to secure a job in the corporate world, one of my mentors, Demetrius ("D") Brown, was working to provide an opportunity as a government civilian there on base. I hadn't considered this alternative, but after discussions with D, he convinced me that it would be smart to keep the door open. D, an NH-04, equivalent to a General Schedule (GS) 14-15 and a Colonel, is the Senior Director at Robins. In other words, he is one of the base's highest-ranking civilians with a lot of power. I was introduced to D by way of Col Lewis, who are good friends and worked together extensively in the past.

Shortly after my arrival to Robins, one of the first things I did was meet with D. Our introduction was great; I could tell right away that he was very clever and loved to mentor others. He vowed to assist me with my career and life moving forward. From then on, I met with D periodically and developed a great relationship with him. Throughout my tenure at Robins, I kept him apprised of what was going on in my life and my plans. Once he learned of my medical retirement, he did all he could to help with my transition. Col Morris was another great mentor at Robins as well.

On April 3rd, one week before my terminal leave started, I received my first job offer. I was delighted by the news. By this point I had conducted several interviews and seemingly improved with each one. My dilemma was that companies wanted to wait until I was closer to my retirement before they offered me a job because of the ambivalence surrounding COVID. This inflamed my angst, but it also made me work that much harder to attain employment. Regarding my first offer, it was from Lynch Consulting. The first interview had gone well enough for them to invite me to a second one with their CEO. That interview confirmed their aspiration, and they sent me an offer letter the next day. The job entailed the work of a consultant to the government with respect to program management activities. So, the nature of the work was somewhat familiar, but Washington D.C. was not enticing to me. My preferences were to either be back on the west coast, Arizona, Texas, or stay in Georgia. Furthermore, the salary was not up to my expectations. With so much uncertainty going in, I did give the offer some thought, but eventually declined three days later; I had faith it wouldn't be my only one.

After my initial offer, new interviews commenced, and more offers started reeling in. The next came on April 16th from Tecolote, a defense contractor in Los Angeles. This offer was close to ideal. It was in a preferential location for a similar role I'd performed in the military, and the pay was decent. My connection with Tecolote came via LinkedIn. About 90% of my networking had taken place on LinkedIn, proving its power. LinkedIn allows you to find hiring managers/recruiters and message them directly. It permits you to search for jobs by company, location, job type, etc. LinkedIn is a focus for companies looking to hire talent. Therefore, I updated my profile and made sure companies knew I was searching for employment.

A recruiter from Tecolote reached out, notifying me that they were looking for candidates like myself. After affirming that I would like to learn more, a phone call with a few of their technical managers went well enough to warrant an interview. A week later, I crushed the interview and was given a job offer. I responded with a few questions, a counteroffer, and an extension so I could have more time to contemplate. My counteroffer was accepted by Tecolote a day later.

In the meantime, I also received a contingent offer from Booz Allen Hamilton (BAH). I had previously interviewed with them in the winter, and they followed up with me down the road with an offer. After much prayer and deliberation with my wife, family, and mentors, I accepted Tecolote's offer. Although BAH's offer was more alluring because it was in San Diego, had a higher relocation bonus, and they matched Tecolote's counteroffer, I declined because it was contingent. The offer was conditional because of the pandemic circumstances, but BAH would allow me to accept later if I chose to. Nevertheless, I was exultant to have accepted a job offer, ensuring post-military employment. Now that it was the beginning of May and I only had a few days left in the military, I finalized the shipment of my household goods and the rental of my home.

I'd been studying real estate investing for a couple of years, so I was familiar with a lot of the logistics. My dream is to become a real estate investor. I enjoy real estate and it is one of the keys to financial freedom. In fact, Over the last two centuries, about 90% of the world's millionaires have been created by investing in real estate.[184] To get there, I'd had a short-term goal of acquiring my first rental property. Unfortunately, I had just refinanced my mortgage in February, so it was too soon for me to sell. My position allowed me to rent my home out without having to purchase an investment property; I was able to use my primary residence as my first rental property.

Since I would be moving to a new state, I examined the idea of hiring a property manager, yet I was discouraged when I learned that most of them charge one month's rent as their acquisition price in addition to the average 10% monthly fee. Therefore, I conducted some research and decided I would find tenants on my own. This involved taking pictures, listing the home for rent on rental websites such as Zillow, and screening applicants. Furthermore, I analyzed the local market and discovered a sweet price point for my property.

My refinance reduced my mortgage from $1,530 to $1,310. "Comps" are rental prices for comparable homes, which were $1,900 to $2,200. I decided to list mine for $2,000. I received my first inquiry just hours after listing and immediately realized that my property was a hot commodity. Not only was my house in a great neighborhood, but there weren't very many places available to rent. In all, I received upwards of 30 inquiries. I personally handled each call, responded to every message, and handled all showings. I digested a lot throughout the endeavor as well. I reviewed credit reports, rental history, verified employment, and reached out to references.

After much probing, I carefully selected a family man who owned a local daycare. I felt he was the most qualified tenant and would keep my home in the best shape. After I notified him of my decision, we scheduled a time to finalize the lease. On Saturday, May 9th, he stopped by my home to make everything official. We conducted the typical pre-walkthrough and went over the lease agreement I'd drafted. Even though I'd had a dog, I did not plan to allow pets from my tenants. I made an exception for the gentleman because he had a small dog who did not pose a threat to my home. After signing the lease, I handed over the keys and collected his deposit, as well as six-months of advance rent. While the individual did not possess the requisite credit to purchase a home, he did hold the finances to do so, hence why he paid so much rent up front. The first year of owning my rental property was smooth and highly encouraging for my real estate aspirations.

On May 8th, three days before my drive back to California, I received an email from Science Applications International Corporation (SAIC), a company I had also spoken to in January. One of their senior managers, also an Academy grad, was following up to see if I was still in the market for a job. I advised him I had already taken an offer but would still be interested if they could provide a better opportunity. After I made it to California on May 13th, SAIC offered me a job based on my January interview. Moreover, my Academy attendance paid dividends again. The senior manager specifically informed me, "I'm going to give you a shot because you're an Academy grad." I gladly responded with my desired salary and start date and waited for a response.

Conversely, my start date with Tecolote was set for May 21st, but God had opened another door. The same day I arranged my start date with Tecolote, SAIC responded with a more attractive offer. Again, I sought advice from my loved ones, and everyone thought SAIC was the best choice. I agreed and consequently reneged my offer with Tecolote to accept the one from SAIC. Instances like this are what validated God's favor in my life. Clearly, as a Christian man, you can live a quality life without being married. But God also promises favor to those who wed: "*Whoso* findeth a wife findeth a good *thing*, and obtaineth favour of the LORD (Proverbs 18:22)." His favor was evident in my job search, medical retirement, and finances, and continues to manifest itself today. I implore every man interested in receiving God's veracious favor to use that as incentive to earnestly pursue a wife.

The most important lesson I learned from my transition was the power of networking. In my opinion, networking is the key to successful job hunting. Networking gets your foot in the door and adds an employee from the desired company to your corner to vouch on your behalf. This gives you a leg up on competitors who coldly apply to companies. The chances of getting a job by applying online are very slim, even if you are well qualified. According to JT O'Donnell, CEO of WorkItDaily.com, you have a 3% chance of getting picked for a job.[185] Networking can also permit you to send your resume to recruiters before applying, allowing you to receive feedback and tips.

Effective resume writing was the other imperative theme I grasped. Of course, everyone knows a good resume is essential to getting hired, but I learned to tailor my resume to the job description for the role I was applying to. The hiring process is lauding, and companies receive flocks of resumes that they can't manually comb through. So, they've implemented the use of computers and algorithms to help select the best candidates. If one's resume does not have vocabulary that matches the job description, they are often discarded.

The search for a home my second time in L.A. was a bit more difficult now that I had a family. We also weren't considering apartments, so that narrowed our options. Furthermore, because I wasn't sure if I'd take the job with BAH in San Diego at some point, I decided it would be better to rent in case the opportunity presented itself. I started looking several weeks before I moved, so I'd reduced the properties I intended to view once I arrived. My preference was to live in the South Bay again, but I considered Orange County because it offered favorable pricing.

Further, house hunting during COVID was far more strenuous than normal as some properties did not allow in-person viewing. Although the search was laborious, I was able to acquire a place in just a couple of days. I had viewed a few homes in Orange County before finding the winner in Long Beach. The three-bedroom house was in a nice, quiet neighborhood with a two-car detached garage and a nice backyard. The $3,300 rent was a bit steep, but within my budget. After examining the home, I hastily completed the paperwork and submitted it to the manager. Everything checked out, and I began moving in on May 15th.

While navigating all these things at once, Shaianne's relocation case was still lingering. It was extremely lengthy and stressful. Essentially, the case came down to a judge's decision of whether Shaianne would be able to relocate out state with her child. The case necessitated loads of paperwork and court hearings. Being unable to be there in person for much of it made it even worse. There was an enormous amount of unpredictability surrounding the case since it was our first time going through a situation like this, plus we didn't know how the judge would rule. Shaianne was more worried than I was because she was so focused on the potential of a negative outcome. While there were moments when I was apprehensive, I did my best to maintain my faith in God and portray that to my wife. In the end, I knew this was just another test from Him and our faith in Him would dictate the result. I continued to remind Shaianne of that fact through the dilemma. The blueprint when facing any obstacle is to have more faith, and less fear.

Along the way, there were pre-trials and intermediary decision points. The most frustrating part of the case was the final trial continued to get delayed due to COVID. Initially, we were set to go to trial in April, then it was pushed to May and finally held in July. This infuriated both Shaianne and I, making it that much harder to hold our confidence. As the trial neared, Shaianne became more and more nervous. We were not very assured when it came to her speaking ability in front of a judge because, as any private citizen, she did not know the right things to say, and she was exceedingly edgy. Consequently, a month before trial, we decided to get a lawyer. That way, we knew things would be done right, and would hopefully not have to revisit the case again.

The day of the trial was nerve-wracking as a witness because I was not allowed to be in the virtual meeting. I had to restlessly wait in the lobby until I was called to testify. Hours passed, and nothing happened. Finally, the meeting organizer permitted me into the trial and the judge welcomed me. Initially, our lawyer, Donald, asked me questions about my employment, family dynamics, and things of that nature. Then I was cross-examined by the child's father, who did not have a lawyer. I was well-prepared as a witness; hence I answered every question eloquently, furnishing pivotal evidence as to why the relocation should be granted. After there were no further questions, I was returned to the waiting room. I was not called on to testify again for the rest of the trial.

Hoping that my wife would call me with an affirmative verdict at the end of the day, I was disappointed to hear that the judge needed more time to deliberate, so the trial was extended another day. I was unallowed to be present for the ruling either, thus I had to wait for Shaianne to present the news. After what seemed like an eternity, she called me crying and told me the judge had ruled in our favor. We were so thankful. We had passed another test and endured another trial, all for God to bless us in the end. His blessings inspire us to give Him the glory he deserves. His favor had also displayed itself again. We were delighted we could finally be together and get on with our lives. The judge also defined the parenting plan detailing that June was to live with Shaianne and me in Long Beach, and visit his father during holidays, in addition to spring and summer breaks.

BLESSINGS ON BLESSINGS

A couple of weeks after the hearing, I flew home to attend June's seventh birthday party and drive Shaianne's car down to California. The drive from Washington to California was much easier now that I had a partner. As it happens, we were able to drive through the night, making it to Long Beach the following afternoon. It was a huge sigh of relief to have finally crowned her relocation.

Through my enterprising, I'd done some exploration into what it'd take to get the new Corvette. I discovered that dealerships had created waitlists because of the car's popularity. Usually, to get on a waitlist, a deposit ranging from $1,000-$2,000 was required. I then investigated which dealership would give me the best chance of securing a Corvette, since waitlists around the nation had already started to extend. I presented this information to my wife, which I thought would turn up void. Amazingly, Shaianne approved of my venture, so I moved out.

I went with MacMulkin Chevrolet in New Hampshire, the #2 Corvette dealer in the country. I placed my $1,000 deposit and was parked at 362 on the list. Over time, I learned that customers were waiting a year on average to take delivery of their Corvettes. This made the wait extremely difficult. I made sure to select every option I wanted with the online visualizer so I would be ready when my allocation was filled. Next, was the process of getting used to cohabitating.

We'd known each other for 11 years, dated for two, and been married for seven months, but this was our first time living together. Even further, this was my first time ever living with a woman, so it took a lot of getting used to. I no longer possessed my own space but had to share it with my significant other. As I write this book after living together for over two years, this is something I'm still getting used to. Overall, though, it's been a seamless transition. While it does require sacrifice, cohabitating is certainly rewarding. The biggest area of contention has been the roles and responsibilities. Shortly after June arrived in late August, I held a family meeting to set expectations for our family. The meeting designated each family member's duties as well as the ground rules.

Leading up to our wedding, Shaianne and I had numerous pre-marital discussions about the way our household would operate. One of our agreements was that Shaianne would no longer work after we married. This is because I believe in following the Bible's gender responsibilities. Moreover, I recognize how beneficial my mother's time at home was to the development of Darius and I. God created men to work, provide for, and protect their family: "And the LORD God took the man, and put him into the garden of Eden to dress it and keep it (Genesis 2:15)." 1 Timothy 5:8 expounds, "But if anyone does not provide for his relatives, and especially for members of his household, he has denied the faith and is worse than an unbeliever."

Woman on the other hand, were created to care for the home by cooking, cleaning, and nurturing the children: "The aged women likewise, that *they* be in behaviour as becometh holiness, not false accusers, not given to much wine, teachers of good things; that they may teach the young women to be sober, to love their husbands, to love their children, to be discreet, chase, keepers at home, good, obedient to their own husbands, that the word of God be not blasphemed (Titus 2:3-5)." Therefore, Shaianne quit her job and became a stay-at-home-mother. The obedience mentioned in the previous scripture stems from God's order in 1 Corinthians 11:3, "But I would have you know, that the head of every man is Christ; and the head of the woman *is* the man; and the head of Christ *is* God." In other words, to be considered a scriptural head of household, not simply by gender, a man needs to be led by God.

These scriptures aren't saying that women can't work, and men aren't responsible for raising their children. It's simply highlighting the primary role for each gender. As I've touched on throughout this book, a father's role is indispensable. Additionally, more women work now than ever before because the amount of single-parent households is at a record high, as well as the cost of the living. So, even a lot of two-parent households need two sources of income to survive. It was a blessing being able to provide for my family and afford for my wife to stay home and take care of our residence.

As everyone settled into our newly blended family, it took time for us to adjust. The transition was difficult for Shaianne initially because she was only used to working. She has since embraced her role as she sees the benefits of having time to invest in her offspring, keep our home in order, spend time together as family, and for personal growth. June had just been uprooted from his hometown where the majority of his family remained. Shaianne has always been primary parent, so June had lived with her and was fundamentally used to being raised by a woman. Shaianne did a great job of raising June by herself but overcompensated for a father not being in the home, and often spoiled him. Although Shaianne was the primary parent, June still had a brother on his dad's side who he was extremely close with. So, the move was difficult for him to handle for a while. For me, jumping into fatherhood as a stepparent was not what I expected. I knew it would be strenuous because raising kids is no easy feat, plus June had already been dealing with some typical disciplinary issues for kids his age. But I did not think things would be as grinding as they were.

During our wedding vows, I promised to treat June as I would one of my own, and that's what I set out to do. I love kids and have taken the pleasure of being involved in the lives of my little cousins and my Goddaughter. June and I got off to a great start. When he arrived in L.A., he was welcomed by a brand-new bed, basketball hoop, bike, and television for his room. We played basketball and catch together, and I made it a point to instill Biblical values in him. But June did not like to be corrected, told what to do, or disciplined. Based on how I was raised, those matters were non-negotiable. So, from his point of view, I was overly harsh on him, but to me I was just attempting to break bad habits and directing him as a strong man.

Although June thought I was hard on him at times, he was always respectful to me, mainly because he was more fearful of men. Correspondingly, when it came to his mother, he was extremely disrespectful, and this was not something I tolerated. We concluded that he blamed her for taking him away from his family and friends in Tacoma and displayed that in the way he treated her. In Shaianne's defense, she was only trying to do what was best for her child and give him a better life with more opportunities. Living in Long Beach, June would be attending one the best schools in the city, playing youth football and basketball, and be 15 minutes away from the ocean which he loved to swim in.

Becoming a parent overnight was challenging and I certainly made mistakes. I also grasped a lot and grew exponentially. I made it a point to avoid the things I learned not to do from my dad and stepdad. I used the Bible as my guide as well. Accordingly, I'm glad I've been able to be a positive influence on June by being a good example and role model by leading and providing for my family. I don't use foul language and stopped listening to secular music. I now only listen to gospel, as I've recognized the power music has, especially derogatory lyrics from profane artists. The biggest mistake I made was not showing enough love and affection. With the strict way I was raised, along with my military background, I focused on discipline because that's all I knew.

I never received affection from the men in my life growing up nor did I think men were supposed show it. I didn't feel I missed manly affection because I didn't know it existed, plus I thought it was a women's role. But I learned that men are not only supposed to be strong and stern, when necessary, but also compassionate, a trait I'm still internalizing. I've since taken it on myself to pray for God to help me gain these characteristics to take my fatherhood caliber to the next level. I've also apologized to June for being too hard on him and explained that I was only doing the best I could based on my understanding and how I was raised. I firmly believe this combination has put us on a constructive trajectory to becoming the father and stepson I know we can be.

Things resolved employment wise as well. Due to my uncertainty about switching to Booz Allen in San Diego, my decision to rent cleared itself up after a few months. It no longer made sense to relocate to San Diego after already planting roots in L.A., plus the job's benefits were not as good. I vowed I no longer wanted to rent because I perceived it as a waste of money. My mindset was to avoid throwing away thousands of dollars every month that will never be seen again when that same money can be put towards a mortgage and incur appreciation and tax benefits. With that concept in mind and our lease up the following May, I decided to get ahead of the ball. The first step was to investigate how much VA loan entitlement I had remaining, and if it would be enough to cover my next home purchase without a down payment. It turned out I did not have enough excess entitlement, so I would have to either sell my Georgia home or save up enough for a down payment in California's expensive housing market.

Thankfully, I uncovered an alternative: The California Department of Veterans Affairs (CalVet). CalVet works to serve California veterans and their families. With nearly 1.6 million veterans living in the state, CalVet strives to ensure that its veterans of every era and their families get the state and federal benefits and services they have earned and deserve because of selfless and honorable military service. CalVet strives to serve veterans and their families with dignity and compassion and to help them achieve their highest quality of life.[186]

CalVet has a program that offers veterans 100% financing even if their VA loan has been consumed. I immediately jumped on this proposition and initiated my pre-approval paperwork. Once that was accepted, we were able to begin house hunting and viewing homes in person. Based on my experience from the purchase of my new construction home, as well as preference, we were only interested in new homes. Because of the costs of homes in Southern California, that did not make single-family homes attainable for the price range and locations we were interested in. That left us with townhomes and condos. I stumbled across a website, www.newhomesource.com, which showed all the new construction homes, counting townhomes, in Southern California. I found a property I was interested in and reached out to the listing agent for more information. The agent specialized in new homes, appearing like a great match.

The next week, we looked at a couple of beautiful townhomes in Orange County. Although in our price range, the major pitfall was the commute; I would be looking at over an hour's drive to and from work. Therefore, we continued our search and found another new townhome community, this time in Gardena. Gardena is located in the South Bay, and just 15 minutes from my place of employment in El Segundo. Gardena is an upcoming city 15 minutes away from the beach and a pair of the biggest freeways in L.A. County. Shaianne and I decided to stop by the property one evening after reaching out to the sales manager. The model homes looked much better than we had expected and catapulted the property to our new favorite. Because of its popularity, units were going fast, so we placed our $5,000 deposit the next day.

The deposit took the lot off the market and secured it under our name. The unit we chose had not broken ground yet and was scheduled to finish construction the ensuing summer, matching our timeline perfectly. We selected a four-bedroom, four-bathroom corner lot with a view of the alluring Ranchos Palos Verdes. Each three-level unit comprised a patio, two-car garage, and the ability to customize options for the new construction home. The number of options available was exhaustive. But with a base price of $650,000, we wanted to strike a balance between keeping the price point low and procuring the upgrades we wanted. In conclusion, we ended up spending $25,000 on upgrades for layout improvements, a kitchen island, fiber internet pre-wiring, and more.

On a different note, I was notified by the Air Force's Temporary Disability Retirement List (TDRL) that it was time for my re-evaluation. Although I had been medically retired, it was only temporarily because cognitive issues tend to resolve over time. This meant the Air Force would perform a re-evaluation of my conditions to identify if there had been any improvement. In my case with TBI, my re-evaluation necessitated another neuropsychological test. A neuropsychological evaluation is an assessment of how one's brain functions, which indirectly yields information about the structural and functional integrity of your brain. The neuropsychological evaluation involves an interview and the administration of tests.[187] I had taken two of them while I was in the military as a result of my symptoms and was diagnosed with the following:

- G31.84 Mild Neurocognitive Disorder due to Traumatic Brain Injury and manifest primarily as auditory memory, verbal reasoning, and mild executive functioning defects.
- F07.0 Personality Change Due to Traumatic Brain Injury. Combined Type (paranoid and aggressive features)

My concussions had impacted my ability to remember information and articulate what I was thinking. They had also made me antisocial and disinterested in being around large groups of people. On the third test I took in November of 2021, I was shocked to find that my results had substantially improved. Under normal circumstances I would have been ecstatic, but I was still dealing with the TBI symptoms, and they hadn't resolved. In fact, I still am. I attributed the upswing to familiarity with the neuropsychological test, as many of the sections were the same as the previous ones.

The new diagnosis meant that my medical retirement would be changed to medical separation, as the doctor was now recommending lowering my TBI disability rating from 40% to 10%. It also meant I would no longer have the cost-effective Tricare as my medical insurance, I'd lose my retired military ID and base privileges, and my VA disability pay and percentage would likely be reduced as well. Tricare is invaluable, costing only $50 per month for a family, as opposed to upwards of $1,000 for civilian health insurance.

I was distraught, especially now that my ability to provide for my family was in jeopardy; I'd been relying on my disability income of $3,600 per month. Consequently, the Air Force provided me with two options. I could either agree with the disposition or disagree and have an Air Force appointed lawyer represent my case. Evidently, I chose the latter. I sent my correspondence back to the Air Force and got right down to business. I immediately prayed to God for him to fight yet another battle for me and bring me through this obstacle. Through my spiritual maturity, I knew if I wanted God to work on my behalf, I had to trust him. I also understood I would come out stronger if I was able to withstand my latest test.

After going up to God, I contacted my lawyer. I was promptly tasked to gather my medical history, imaging, prescriptions, and doctor's notes so we could build a case. I hastily did so in advance of my April 2022 hearing. The hearing would involve a presentation from my counsel, a personal statement, and a testimony from one of my witnesses. As my trial drew closer, I continued to grow confident I would come out victorious. That was until I hit a bump in the road.

A month before my hearing, the actual date was set to April 14th. With my lawyer representing multiple clients, he already had a trial scheduled for that day. Thus, I was appointed a new attorney just weeks before my hearing. I felt myself lose hope at that point, but I knew I still had God on my side. God's victory in my trial was not contingent on my lawyer, His will would still prevail if he decided to bring me through. So, I made the most of it with my new counsel and anxiously awaited trial.

A few days beforehand, my new lawyer had me submit a few more documents, including a personal statement to support my summary request. A summary request is similar to a plea deal, where the lawyer requests the medical board to approve an alternative request to what the board is recommending. In my instance, my attorney conceived it made sense to request my symptoms to be rated under the 30% rating criteria for mental health. This rating signified I would be permanently retired, retain my retiree ID card, and Tricare for my family's medical care. Thus, the trial held copious significance.

Conversely, if the summary request was denied, I would be forced to accept the medical board's new rating. So, there was a lot at stake. I took my lawyer's advice because she believed we'd built a compelling case and had a good chance of prevailing. With all my documents in hand, my counsel submitted my summary request. Midday on April 13th, my lawyer emailed me detailing that my summary request had been approved and the hearing the following day had been canceled. Jesus had lighted my path and displayed his favor on my life one more time. And I had triumphed in another battle test. What a blessing.

A STAR WAS BORN

Next on the agenda was the objective of extending our family. Shaianne had wanted to have another child directly after marriage, but I wanted to wait until we lived together so I could physically support her during the pregnancy. We had assumed getting pregnant was as simple as having intercourse, and then we'd be expecting a baby soon after. But as we would promptly find out, we had a lot to learn when it came to family planning. For some people, it is that easy, others try for years and have no luck. Much of it depends on ovulation cycles and when females are most fertile. Thanks to technology, we were able to input Shaianne's cycles into a mobile app that told us the best times for impregnation. After several months and numerous negative pregnancy tests, we became doubtful. We were praying, but we also hadn't been following the app's schedule closely enough. So, we stepped our game up and implemented Maca Root into our supplement intake as a healthy aid with fertility in both men and women.

On November 22, 2020, we were entertaining friends and family in our home when Shaianne decided to take a pregnancy test.

She had been feeling sick earlier in the day and thought a baby could be the reason. We viewed the pregnancy test together, and it finally came back positive. We were jubilant, almost shocked that our dream had come true. Finding out I would become a father was life-changing, and one of the best moments of my life. We were filled with so much excitement that our family overheard us, compelling us to share the great news. They were all extremely happy for our breakthrough.

After our first Obstetrician-Gynecologist (OBGYN) appointment, we learned our baby would be due July 29th of the following year. We chose to only tell our family and close friends in the beginning. We informed them on Christmas through symbolic baby gifts. Everyone was thrilled with the news, principally my mother who would finally become a grandparent.

Next, we awaited the gender reveal. With Shaianne already having a son, she was clearly hoping for a girl. Since this would be my first child, I wanted a boy. As time went on, we spent plenty of time advocating for why we each thought it would be the gender we wanted, as well as entertaining myths about ways to tell the gender. All the speculation fueled the gender reveal we held on January 30, 2021. Leading up to the gender reveal, there were several doctor's appointments where the OBGYN performed ultrasounds, allowing us to hear the baby's heartbeat and see it moving. This was all a first for me, so undergoing these new activities was dreamlike. The last doctor's appointment before the gender reveal also included a blood test which uncovered the baby's gender. We elected to have the results emailed to Broam so he could order the gender-specific items.

The buildup to our gender reveal was intense. After some deliberation, Shaianne and I agreed to reveal the gender by doing a burnout with gender-colored smoke. To make the reveal even cooler, I invited my brother and his Camaro to join in on the exhibition. Due to California COVID restrictions, we were limited to only 15 people who could be present. Consequently, we set up a Zoom for our loved ones who could not attend. Of those who were able to visit was our good friend Jasmine and her husband Luke. Jasmine specializes in videography and design, so we wanted her there to film the event. On gameday, my nerves were all over the place as I could not wait to find out the sex of my child. At showtime, Darius and I aligned our Chevy's back-to-back, and Broam placed the colored powder bags underneath our rear tires. Once the cameras were in place, we were given a thumbs up. Broam counted down from three, and then we let our tires rip. I soon noticed the blue smoke in my rearview mirror and appreciated I would be having a boy. I let out a joyful cheer and then returned to the front of the house. Shaianne was in tears of joy. Although it wasn't the gender she was expecting, she was still excited to be having another child.

More excitement came via news on my Corvette. I received a call from MacMulkin informing me that my Corvette allocation had been accepted by GM and my car would be built! I was ecstatic. Once one's build commences, delivery is only about two months out. My torch red Corvette build and options were confirmed, along with my courtesy delivery, and that was that; I only had a couple more months of waiting. The car started at $59,995, but I optioned it out to $79,388, amassing front lift memory, Z51 package which includes an upgraded exhaust and magnetic ride control, red leather seats and seatbelts, and more. My mindset was if I was going to make a purchase of that magnitude, I needed to do it right and get what I wanted, and that's exactly what I did.

I was able to track the production of my vehicle online and noticed it had finished in March. Thus, I was expecting to take delivery of my car soon. Disappointingly, COVID had delayed car shipments, so my car didn't arrive until the end of April, just after my 29th birthday. This was a birthday gift for the ages. I was just glad my hard work had paid off enough for me to afford something like this. The car was everything I wanted and more. In terms of Shaianne's pregnancy, things weren't going so smooth.

Shaianne's symptoms in the first trimester came on especially strong. She experienced hardy morning sickness encompassing severe nausea, vomiting, and headaches. After the reveal, we constructed a registry on Amazon. Helpfully, one of Shaianne's friends purchased *The New Dad's Playbook*, by Benjamin Watson. This book was instrumental in helping me navigate Shaianne's pregnancy, providing tips, terminology, definitions, and lessons learned. One of the biggest takeaways was how to cope with a woman's morning sickness. I was able to apply this tactic and deliver weighty support to my wife as she endured her symptoms.

As Shaianne's pregnancy progressed, we continued to see the OBGYN regularly. Our appointments gradually went from monthly to biweekly. We elected to have all the available genetic testing done along the way, and the results all came back negative, which was highly encouraging. Even more heartening, Shaianne's morning sickness began to ease up during the second trimester. Another upside was our baby's placenta was posterior, or one that attaches itself to the back of the uterus, allowing us to feel our baby's movement early on.[188] It was invigorating to see our son's motions so early.

The third trimester was another story as Shaianne's belly had further expanded to make room for our growing son. This trimester presented lower back and pelvic pain, extreme fatigue, insomnia, discomfort, and pre-contractions. With our child being posterior placenta, his maneuvers were clearly visible and even more robust by this point. There were times when we could depict his limbs right against Shaianne's belly. By the time we reached 38 weeks, the doctor told us we were officially full term, and we could go into labor at any time. This was exceedingly trying for me at work because I was not able to have my cell phone while working in a classified building. So, it was laborious knowing that labor could be imminent, and my wife may have trouble reaching me if I were in a meeting.

Shaianne and I also experienced additional stressors outside of her pregnancy. With our original lease ending in May, we had already coordinated a month-to-month lease with our landlord through July, when our new home was scheduled to be completed. Woefully, COVID and supply shortages delayed the finalization to August. The owner of our home again accepted another extension. But our satisfaction was short-lived because we were soon notified that further setbacks had occurred, and construction would not be capped until October 12th. We requested to stretch our lease a third time, but it was denied. The landlord had chosen to sell his home and needed us out by mid-August. This new turn of events put a wrench in our plans and meant we would have to find another place to stay between August and October.

With our son being due on July 29th, we did not want to move into a novel place with a newborn baby. Hence, we decided to get the ball rolling early to move as soon as we could. Due to our circumstances, we were faced with two options: rent a standard month-to-month home or stay in an Airbnb monthly rental. We were leaning towards Airbnb because the rentals came fully furnished and did not require a security deposit as standard rentals did. But during our search, we learned the Airbnb alternative was not feasible because the prices were significantly higher, and above our price range. That left us with a typical rental. Prices were much more attainable but finding all of our preferences in a single property was daunting.

Our necessities were parking for three cars, an in-unit washer and dryer, a low security deposit, South Bay location, a gym, pool, and air conditioning. After combing through hundreds of properties, we trimmed our search and scheduled tours to see them in person. We favored new luxury properties with amenities. We started our tours in downtown L.A. and were pleased with most of our picks. We kept an ongoing ranking as we visited each property and eliminated ones that no longer made the cut. After visiting several apartments in the downtown area, we hit a couple on the westside of L.A. The first was in Del Aire, only five minutes from my job. This self-tour was the best yet and immediately became our new favorite. We visited one last apartment in Marina Del Rey, but it did not compare. We then got in touch with the property manager of Pacific Place in Del Aire and applied the same day.

After submitting our application on Friday, we ceased our search. The following week, we received approval from Pacific Place and signed the lease. It was incredibly relieving to collect authorization from our favorite apartment. The initial lease term was month-to-month for three months and was set to begin on July 10th.

My brother and several friends helped us move since my eight-month pregnant wife was not in shape to assist. The move was concluded in one full day as we packed and unloaded the U-Haul I'd rented. This saved a couple of hundred dollars by not hiring movers. Moving all day was taxing, especially since we added a supplemental trip to our necessary storage facility for the bulk of our belongings. Nevertheless, now that we'd successfully moved, our attention returned to our baby boy.

We became so eager for our son's coming that we did everything to hasten his birth. We tried sex, exercise, red raspberry tea, and spicy foods, but it just didn't seem like our boy was ready to come out. As the days passed, the pre-contractions, or Braxton Hicks, became more frequent, but there was still no baby. Contractions are the tightening of the muscles of the uterus. During contractions, the abdomen becomes hard. Between contractions, the uterus relaxes, and the abdomen becomes soft.[189]

We began to get antsy, although we were still six days ahead of his due date. That was until Shaianne started experiencing recurring Braxton Hicks 10-12 minutes apart on Friday, July 23rd.

This signaled that Malachi may soon be ready to be evicted, so we dashed to the childbirth center in Orange County. Doctors examined Shaianne and monitored her contractions. Ultimately, the contractions were too far apart, and the three-centimeter dilation was not enough for us to be admitted; thus, we headed back home highly discouraged.

We did not give up on expediting the birth of our son. We continued our regime, hoping for the best. Then, on Sunday morning at 3:30 a.m., Shaianne awakened me in an alarming fashion, "Jamal, it's time to go to the hospital!" This time, she was in much more pain, elevating my sense of urgency. Shaianne had already been up for 90 minutes after being aroused by her excruciating contractions. These contractions were no longer Braxton Hicks, but the real deal, and also more consistent. So, we dashed to the car and zipped to the hospital. Because of Shaianne's acute pain, we decided to go to the nearest hospital in our insurance network, which happened to be much closer in Long Beach.

Doctors performed the same examinations as Friday, quickly admitting us this time. Shaianne's contractions were now occurring every seven minutes, and she was dilated to five centimeters. By this point, Shaianne's contractions were so bad that they became unbearable as she shrieked in the delivery room. As a result, she diligently accepted an epidural the moment it was offered. An epidural is an injection in your back to stop you from feeling pain in part of your body.[190] I was forced to leave the room during the procedure but was pleased to find it was successful upon my return. The epidural was a game-changer as Shaianne could no longer feel the contractions. Now, we just had to wait for her contractions to occur closer together and for her cervix to dilate to at least 10 centimeters.

The nurses continued to check on us throughout the night as we fell in and out of sleep. Finally, at around 9:00 a.m., Shaianne's cervix was dilated enough, but her contractions were still too far apart. To expedite this process, the doctor administered Pitocin. Pitocin (oxytocin injection) is a natural hormone that causes the uterus to contract to induce labor, strengthen labor contractions during childbirth, or to control bleeding after childbirth.[191] Soon enough, her contractions had sped up to four minutes apart, quick enough to initiate the delivery process. From then on, things moved expeditiously. The medical team suited up and prepared for our son's birth. Because Shaianne had already given birth before and knew how to push, the doctor only had her do one round of practice pushes. They went well so that the doctor decided it was time for the real thing. During her next contraction, Shaianne began to push. From my position at the top of the bed near Shaianne's shoulders, I alertly kept my eyes fixed between her legs. The baby had not protruded yet, but the doctor mentioned she could see his hair. Then we ran into a complication; the baby's heart rate was beginning to drop.

Therefore, the doctor made the expert decision to immediately start pushing again rather than wait for the next contraction. Midway through the next push, the doctor guided our child's head out. Following the final push, the rest of his little body popped out, and Shaianne had delivered Malachi Shaquille Byrd on July 25, 2021, at 9:55 a.m. I was in complete awe after witnessing the birth of my first child.

The medics quickly cleaned up, wrapped my wax-covered son up in a blanket, and placed him on Shaianne's chest. She immediately burst into tears as the procedure was now over. All in all, active labor only lasted a few minutes and was pain-free thanks to the epidural. The only thing Shaianne felt was the pressure from thrusting. I was shocked at how smooth things went as I envisioned she would have been ailing like in cinema. Either way, I was finally a father and grateful God allowed a healthy and successful delivery.

We were all amazed at how easily Malachi was born after seeing how big he was. We were more aghast after the scale measured eight pounds and 13 ounces, much heavier than the seven-pound average. Malachi measured at 21 inches long, only slightly larger than the 20-inch mean. His skin was mightily opaque as he wailed at his first breaths in the world. It was spectacular that I had brought a little person into the world, and I instantly fell in love with him. I allowed Shaianne to bond with him for the first hour before I touched him because he just looked so small and delicate that I did not want to hurt him. But I soon came around and held my little man with the most joy I'd ever felt; he was perfect.

The rest of the morning included monitoring and testing to ensure Shaianne and Malachi were holding up after the birth. Once they checked out, we were moved to the postpartum division until being released the following day. The next 24 hours consisted of Malachi's circumcision, hepatitis B shot, tracking of his bowel movements and breastfeeding's, the birth certificate, and Shaianne's vitals. Then we were discharged and en route to take Malachi home.

Rightfully so, Malachi became the center of our attention over the next few weeks. The feeling of being a father was wondrous. Being able to care for a little human who is totally dependent upon his guardians was so special to me. It was such a joy learning Malachi, seeing him respond to breastfeeding, adjust to bottles, watching him sleep peacefully, and seeing him grow before our eyes. Thankfully, I was able to do so firsthand as the state of California provided me with six weeks of paid family leave to bond with my new child. This leave is standard for all California state employees who pay into the paid family leave fund. Out in the world, COVID continued to rear its ugly head.

BEAUTIFUL STRUGGLE

The COVID-19 situation has evolved greatly since it originated. After its climax, things started to return to normal as cases dropped and individuals started to receive one of several vaccines. I chose to forgo the vaccine as I did not view myself as high risk from the virus, nor was I comfortable with taking something that had been tested using aborted fetal cells, in addition to other questionable ingredients. Following a close return to normal, new variants of COVID emerged and reversed the recovery from COVID. The regression was so powerful that President Joe Biden began to mandate the vaccine. The DoD, states, companies, and local businesses followed suit, requiring all employees to be vaccinated unless they possessed a valid religious exemption.

I chose to submit a religious accommodation for my job that was ultimately denied. I tendered my religious accommodation on September 21, 2021. After following up for a status update, I did not receive a decision until October 14th. My request was declined, not on account of my accommodation, but because, "Granting my request to remain unvaccinated will cause an undue hardship because of the risk of the transmission to fellow employees or customers potentially causing physical injury, hospitalization, or death. All decisions are final unless you have additional accommodations or purpose that were not already considered. Effective October 27th, all employees without an approved accommodation must provide proof of their first dose."

I was bewildered by HR's response for several reasons. First, my company had not even reviewed my sincere request, but coldly denied it because in their opinion, unvaccinated people pose a risk to others. The second reason was it took them almost an entire month to provide me with a verdict when their determination had nothing to do with my request. Lastly, I did not see myself as a risk to anyone else because most were already vaccinated. If anything, I was a threat to myself.

Thankfully, I was prepared for this outcome because I had been diligently reaching out to other companies for opportunities. Since I had already been through this process before, I was much more comfortable with the transition, plus I had a much wider network. With my previous junction in L.A., I also had several contacts who I could reach out to. I informed each company of my religious beliefs towards the vaccine upfront and my stance on remaining unvaccinated. This limited the number of companies I could connect with, but the search still went extremely well. I ended up receiving three job offers, all higher paying than the one I was in, and did not require the vaccine. That's how I knew I'd made the right decision by sticking to my beliefs and trusting in God.

On the other hand, my company's denial created some difficult conversations with my supervisor and put me in a pickle. I was very displeased with the way human resources handled my case, but I liked working for my supervisor. After informing him that I would be moving on because of my disapproved accommodation, he voiced his disappointment and asked me to reevaluate my decision. I put some thought into it but could not go against my faith. In the spirit of honesty and transparency, I also notified him that I planned to put my two weeks in soon for a job that paid $130,000, which was $13,000 more per year. Surprisingly, he contested that SAIC would be able to match the salary. But by that point, I no longer desired to work for a company that was unwilling to take care of its employees. Consequently, I put in my two weeks' notice and accepted a job offer with Ginisis Group Inc.

The founder and CEO of Ginisis, Errol Gorman, is a former colleague of mine as a Lieutenant at L.A. AFB. After my previous job search in 2020, Errol reached out and told me I should have contacted him because he would have taken care of me. That message resonated with me; thus, I circled back with him during this job search. We had several fruitful conversations, including one with the prime contractor's lead, and discovered where I could fit into their program. After a few days, Errol got back to me with an arrangement and primed me that they would be extending an alluring offer. After one round of negotiations, I gladly accepted his offer and was thrilled to begin this new chapter of my life. Errol is a brilliant company president who founded Ginisis in 2009 to support and improve the efficiency and productivity of government processes. He is also a sociable leader who holds quarterly company happy hours and provides unbeatable company benefits, fostering an enticing work environment.

Since the vaccines, offered by several pharmaceutical companies, have rolled out, the Center for Disease Control and Prevention continues to release data that has proved the vaccines to be highly incompetent, even harmful in some cases. There have been numerous reports of individuals suffering sickness and even perishing from the vaccine. It has also been published that the vaccine has reduced the sperm count in males. Furthermore, pharmaceutical companies and government claims that the vaccine was effective against COVID have been found to be erroneous as well. The high protection rates they asserted were only for good briefly after being vaccinated, then declined over time as new variants emerged. Consequently, vaccinated individuals began commonly contracting and spreading COVID.

Withal, five months after the vaccine mandates, the directives were lifted. Thousands of people, like myself, lost their jobs because they refused the vaccine, all for the mandate to be reversed a few months later. With so much controversy surrounding the vaccine, I was delighted that I chose to forgo it, especially with all its downsides. Essentially being forced find a new job a few months after having a son was a sincere struggle. But I've grown to see the beauty in the struggle because without it, I wouldn't appreciate the success. In this case, the beauty resulted in a much better situation.

Once we were within a couple of weeks of our home's completion, the paperwork ramped up extensively. During the construction of our home, we were given periodic walkthroughs by the construction manager to showcase the progress. After completing the relevant paperwork, it was time for our final walkthrough. The construction manager gave us an overview of all the technology, home warranties, and special features in the home. That put us only a couple of days away from moving in. In advance of the move, I'd planned to hire movers this time around since we'd just moved a few months ago, plus I did not want to ask for help again. I changed my mind at the last minute and decided to move everything myself.

While this was a hefty task, I preferred to invest my time rather than money, especially since closing costs were $11,000. Leading up to the close of escrow, our realtor had not been in touch with us, nor had our lender regarding the amount of required closing costs. Thus, I'd planned for closing costs to be around $5,000 based on my first home purchase. So, I was highly surprised when I found out how much closing costs were, forcing me to move some things around. Once moving day came around, there was a huge fumble. Between our lender and escrow, someone had dropped the ball and forgotten to inform us that we needed to secure condo insurance. Initially, we were told this was unnecessary because insurance was covered by HOA. This botch, along with the delayed processing of our closing costs, set closing back two days. This was monstrous because it forced us to rent the U-Haul for additional time and extend our apartment lease.

Closing was a disaster, but on October 20, 2021, everything was finally completed, and we were handed the keys. Shaianne and I were relieved to be in our new home after so much time. I was exceptionally happy for Shaianne because this was the first home she'd owned, so this was a sizable accomplishment for her. We spent the next few weeks moving everything and getting settled in, a process much more difficult with a newborn. Nevertheless, we made it happen, and things started to come together in our new townhome.

HIGHLY FAVORED

After moving to Gardena, I was able to attend my first Detroit Lions game. They'd happened to be playing at the Rams new stadium the first year it was built. Although the Lions were having a horrible year, the game was awesome. The Lions got out to an early lead with explosive plays, leaving the home crowd in utter shock. But in the end, the Super Bowl-bound Rams were too much to handle, defeating us 28-19. The new $5B Sofi stadium was out of this world. The jumbo screen and offerings made the experience exemplary.

A few weeks later, the Lions played at Pittsburgh. When I saw this game on their schedule, I knew it was a guaranteed trip; I'd be able to see my favorite team play against one of my closest friends. I told Darius about the upcoming game, and he was instantly on board. This would be our first time in Pittsburgh, and Malachi's first trip. He did exceptionally well on the plane ride. Unfortunately, the game was in November, so the weather was freezing the entire time we were there. Nevertheless, it was good to see Zach, and for him to meet his Godson for the first time. My dad was also able to make the trip from Atlanta and meet his first grandson. Both were especially happy to meet little man.

Leading up to the trip, we kept our eyes on the weather forecast, which was surprisingly expected to be warm on game day. That was until we arrived in Pittsburgh, and the forecast changed to snow via a significant temperature drop. Because of the weather update, Malachi could no longer attend the game, so Shaianne decided to stay back at the hotel with him.

Our Hilton hotel was very nice, situated downtown. Heinz Field is also located downtown, so on game day we only had to make a 20-minute stroll to the game. The game was extremely cold, confirming we made the right decision to keep Malachi back. But the rest of us still enjoyed the game, especially June who savored his first NFL game. Once again, the Lions played well as the underdog road team, leaving Steelers fans in disbelief throughout the game. The Lions fought hard the entire game, forcing the Steelers into overtime. The snowy conditions made for a difficult overtime battle, resulting in a tie.

After the game, we all went to Zach's house for a Guamanian-style BBQ. There was an endless amount of food, and everything tasted great. We all took part in some great fellowship and enjoyed Zach's new multi-million-dollar condo. The outing was a great cap to an eventful trip before taking off the next morning.

The next week, the Steelers were playing at the Chargers, so Darius and I were able to attend that game as well. Frequenting three games in one season was more than I had gone to in my entire life and assured me that I'd like to continue attending more games in the future. On the field, the Chargers were too much to handle for the

Steelers, handing them a tough loss. Afterward, we were able to see Zach momentarily before his team departed for their plane.

With the addition of Malachi, space in Shaianne's compact Chevy Cruze became extremely dense. It was uncomfortable when all four of us rode together, so I started looking for Shaianne a new vehicle. She'd made me aware that she wanted an SUV, so I had a good starting point. After much exploration, I narrowed my search down to four cars she liked: the Audi Q5, Alfa Romeo Stelvio, Mercedes-Benz GLB 250, and the Jaguar F-Pace. My favorite was the F-Pace because of its aesthetic and robust motor. The day before the game, I took Shaianne to drive each of the four vehicles.

The test drives eliminated the Audi and the Alfa Romeo, leaving the Mercedes and Jaguar. She was torn between the two, often changing back and forth between them. The following Monday, she decided to look at the Mercedes again. The second look designated the Mercedes as the winner. As a result, we ended up buying the car that day, and Shaianne walked away with a black, 2020 Mercedes GLB 250. The car only had 15,000 miles and was less than a year old. It was also a great deal, being the cheapest one in the country. While searching, we'd looked around the nation to see if there were any better deals and came up empty. The car was fully loaded and well equipped for $37,000, containing leather seats, heated seats, blind-spot mirrors, a backup camera, ambient lighting, beige interior, brake assist, tons of storage space, and an alluring dash and infotainment center.

Prior to purchasing Shaianne's Mercedes, we received an estimate for her Cruze's trade-in value. Her 2016 Cruze, with 90,000 miles on it at the time and in decent shape, was only worth $3,000. Thus, we elected not to trade it in. Instead, we kept it and rented it out on Turo. Turo is a carsharing service, where vehicle owners loan their cars out as rentals. We'd rented on Turo before, so we were aware of the avenue.

Renting the Cruze out on Turo has been a huge success. The first few months of profit were used to pay off the car's remaining balance. After that, I allowed Shaianne to keep all the proceeds to use as discretionary income because it was her vehicle and she no longer worked. Since listing the car on Turo in October of 2021, Shaianne has made $7,000, more than doubling its trade-in value. She regularly generates $500 per month, evolving into a lovely source of passive income. My new job was pleasant as well.

Working from home in the unclassified world was much better than laboring in a classified building every day. I could sleep in longer, have access to snacks and fluids as I pleased, and relax in comfortable clothing. It took some time to integrate into my new program office, but I soon found myself getting spun up and taking on tasks. I was also able to see Malachi more often.

Malachi has since grown into an energized 14-month-old toddler full of life and love. He's the greatest gift I've ever received, as confirmed by Psalm 127:3, "Lo, children *are* an heritage of the LORD: And the fruit of the womb *is his* reward." We had an indication Malachi would be advanced by how alert he was at birth and how he was trying to hold his head up on the first day. But we were taken aback by how sophisticated he actually was. He began crawling at four months and walking at nine, the same age as me. So, I'm confident my acumen has been passed on to him. Now he is always on the go and has developed the most exuberant personality. He amazes us every day, and we are eager to see what God has planned for our little star.

PLANTING NEW ROOTS

Only a few months after moving into our townhome, an opportunity presented itself. Not only had COVID taken millions of lives, but it also impacted every industry and supply chain around the world, notably real estate. The real estate market spiked dramatically during COVID, averaging a 14% increase around the county, and up to 30% in the hottest areas. Along with the global supply chain crisis, there was not enough supply to meet the housing demand, driving prices through the roof. This dynamic worked in our favor. We had placed the deposit on our home in November of 2020, which locked our price in until we closed in October of 2021. All the while, the market continued to rise. Hence, by the time we closed we walked into $75,000 of equity.

One sunny afternoon I was walking around my townhome community and noticed one of my neighbors was hosting an open house. Out of curiosity, I went on Zillow to see how much they were listing for. To my pleasant surprise, they had listed their home for

$788,000, $100,000 over what we paid for ours. Moreover, their home only had three bedrooms, so I knew ours was worth more. Our dream location of Arizona was our place of choice a few years down the road. But with this chance on the table, it appeared our timeline may have shortened. The first step was to receive approval from my employer.

I reached out to my boy Al Kristianto, one of the leads for Ginisis. Because COVID had forced most companies into a remote posture, my company was working at home full time. I checked with Al to get his guidance and he saw no problem with the move, especially since my role didn't require me to go into the office. He advised me to obtain approval from a government lead in my branch, and if they gave me the green light, so would our CEO. Consent from my government customer was seamless. One of my team members was already working full-time in Connecticut, and the prime contractor on my contract had just hired another employee who would be working remotely in Alabama, so there was precedence. My government customer endorsed my request, and so did Errol, with the caveat that I'd be responsible for my own travel for meetings in Los Angeles. That was no issue since my cost of living would be slashed.

Now that I had authorization, I began looking for homes in Arizona. Conveniently enough, we had planned a couple's trip with some of our friends to Phoenix well before this plan materialized. While there, Shaianne and I spent Saturday morning house hunting. We were blown away by some of the neighborhoods and sizes of homes. Our observations confirmed our desire to make Arizona our new home. Thus, upon returning to L.A. after our vacation, I hit the ground running and ramped up my search. Although the Phoenix Metro area had one of the highest market increases at 30%, homes were still $100,000-$200,000 less than L.A., and they came with significantly more land. With our move looking more and more promising, I reached out to Vicky, a California realtor I knew.

Vicky was able to provide an accurate assessment of what she believed our home was worth, as well as an estimate of the proceeds we would take home from the sale after taxes and fees. These numbers were favorable, so we compiled a thorough spreadsheet of new construction Arizona homes we were interested in and began to schedule virtual tours. I was pleased by the information I was given by builders, but the demand in Arizona was so high that there weren't as many homes available as I'd hoped. Most communities had waitlists, some took the highest bidder, and others conducted drawings.

After securing our pre-approval, I placed ourselves onto several waitlists. One of our favorite communities, Mystic Discovery, held a drawing and informed me one would be taking place the following Wednesday. There was no harm in doing so, so I sent the builder my pre-approval and joined the drawing. The Wednesday of the drawing, I was shocked to receive a call that we'd won. This meant we could select the lot and floor plan of our choosing, based on availability. There had been 15 people in the drawing, and we were drawn in one of the top three spots. But because of the demand, the condition was that we had to sign the purchase agreement within 24 hours.

This huge decision became onerous because it required alacrity. I immediately combed through my spreadsheet to compare the home and affirm it was the one we wanted. It was certainly one of the best homes we'd found with attractive amenities such as a community pool, recreation center, and a basketball court. The home is also located in the metro Phoenix Arizona, and in one of Arizona's best cities to live. Plus, the deposit was only $2,000 since we'd be using a VA loan, as opposed to most communities requiring anywhere from $5,000-$15,000. I spent the next 24 hours praying and completing research before deciding to move forward with the home.

We signed the purchase contract and sent over the deposit, locking us in for our new home that is set to conclude construction in January of 2023. The two-story, 3,398 square foot home is almost twice the size our current home, and loaded with features such as five bedrooms, four bathrooms, two dining areas, a three-car garage, covered patio and porch, 24-foot driveway, massive owner's suite with a two-sided closet, and a backyard big enough to fit a pool if we elect to build one. It is truly a great home. We are highly anticipating the day we can plant roots in our new Arizona home.

While house hunting, working, being a father, and a husband, I was also in the midst of another undertaking. The previous year, I had done some probing to see what my options were in terms of furthering my education. I considered a Master of Business Administration (MBA), which would be hugely beneficial to my job as a defense contractor. But most programs were just too expensive or required a GMAT or GRE score, which I was not interested in taking or studying for. An MBA also didn't align with my long-term goal of becoming a real estate investor. As a result of serving in the military, I was eligible for Post 9/11 Education Benefits. One of these benefits, known as the GI Bill, covers tuition, housing, and book expenses for veterans based on the amount of time served. Because I was medically retired short of five full years of service, I was only allotted 60% coverage. This denoted the VA would pay for 60% of my education costs at any school that accepted the GI Bill, as well as provide me with a housing stipend.

Upon further research, I stumbled upon UCLA's Extension Certificate program after I'd applied to their MBA program. Several universities offer certificate programs which provide 400-level courses in just about every area of expertise from construction and taxation to fitness and photography. UCLA Extension offered the perfect program for me: Real Estate with Concentration in Investments. This suited my immediate goal of studying a subject I was interested in, as well as my long-term real estate investing plan; I was sold. I instantly applied for the 15-month program and was accepted weeks later.

Because COVID was still running rampant, many universities, including UCLA, had shifted their courses to remote. Thus, my courses took place online. The program was exceptionally taxing at times, especially on top of all my other responsibilities. But I learned an abundance of valuable information I was able to apply right away, as well as keep in my toolbelt for when I'm ready to invest in real estate full time. Furthermore, the courses counted towards California's real estate salesperson exam education requirements, an avenue I hadn't even considered until I became aware of the opportunity. Now, I am in the process of studying for my sales agent license to produce another stream of income.

During my last quarter of the program in the spring of 2022, I was informed of my graduation date and that we would be walking, just as degree graduates do. With COVID still looming, it was unknown if this would take place. Nonetheless, I was thrilled for this opportunity. My last class in property management was a good way to cap off the program, leading me right to graduation.

Graduation was truly a novel and rewarding experience. Beholding UCLA's massive and beautiful campus for the first time was a blessing. The campus was full of so much history. There were more than 500 students in my graduating class. Walking on stage with my cap and gown at age 30 was significant because I'd set out on another endeavor and successfully completed it. Moreover, I was awarded distinction for graduating with a 3.57 GPA. Afterward, I was in the courtyard taking photos with my brother, Shaianne, and Malachi when I was stopped by UCLA Extension media and asked for an interview. This was icing on the cake as I was unwitting to the exchange. The interview allowed me to share my experience and describe how I felt about the program. As I reflected on my latest achievement, I noticed how accomplished I felt after adding another feather to my cap, realizing, and sharing with my family, "I'm addicted to success, Lord knows what's to come next.

CONCLUSION

I would like to sincerely thank you for reading my story. Distinctly, I poured my heart and soul into this book. I've learned so much in the first 30 years of my life. Taking over two years to compile, dozens of hours were spent researching to expound my points and validate the information I presented. Late nights were also a common theme. God has done so much to me up to this point, and I can only imagine what he has in store for me as I continue growing through life. I am constantly learning, especially as I spend more time in the Word of God. I know God has a purpose for me, and I aim to unlock its connotation.

At the end of the day, this life, and every possession in it, is temporary and will fade away. Heaven is eternal and where our attention should be focused as we will be judged by God for what we did with our time here on earth, and our heavenly rewards will stem from those contributions. Hell is also real and is designated as the everlasting home for those who deny Jesus.

The most important thing I wanted to share is that God is the key, and it is imperative to keep him first. Prayer is indispensable; my conversations with God are what keep me going. I, like many others, learned some things the hard way and took longer to completely live for God than I should have. The good thing is, as long as you're alive, it's never too late, and there's still a chance to get right with Him. Especially now, in the last days, as things continue to worsen according to Bible prophecy, signaling his second coming. Natural disasters, wars and rumors of wars, pestilence, famine, and lawlessness all taking place now are indications of Jesus' return, so we must be ready.

In terms of life's journey, it's best to follow God's lead and allow Him to direct your path, as advised in Proverbs 3:6. This will save you a great deal of time and prevent you from going through a lot of turmoil. Although, as a Christian, you will definitely go through your fair share of trials and tribulations. It's a part of following God, and worthwhile, as the end result is eternal life in heaven. Thus, the ability to endure is golden.

After traveling more and being exposed to new experiences, I grew to see Tacoma in a different light when I visited as an adult. Growing up, I thought my environment's turmoil was normal because that was all I knew. But as I matured, I realized how detrimental it was for kids to have to endure those conditions, like many other inner cities. I love Tacoma, but leaving was the best decision I could have made. If I chose to stay, I likely would have gotten caught up in the fast life like many people I know.

Sadly, making it out of Tacoma happens less often than it should. The phrase, "Only the strong survive" couldn't be truer for a city like Tacoma because the ones who do overcome it have tenacity and moxie like no other. I embody Tacoma and all the durability it requires, because its pressure turned me into a diamond. I will continue to do so because along with my faith, it's given me the unbreakable courage to not only pursue, but surmount numerous obstacles. Accordingly, I am inordinately proud to be from Tacoma, and I know its proud of me too. Consequently, I aspire to give back to in a meaningful way one day and hope to help redirect the lives and perspective of people in my city.

Naturally, the only thing constant in life is change. So, the best way to navigate dynamism is to learn how to adapt. Adaptation is underestimated and can create peace and stability amid chaos. Ups and downs are a part of everyone's life, but the best way to handle turbulence is to not get too high or too low. That's also what I wanted to showcase throughout this book. Every time I was down, or things looked gray, God brought me out. So, when it comes to suffering, embrace the struggle as King David did in the Lion's Den. I've grown to embrace struggles because I know with God, I will come out victorious. I also haven't gone through a struggle that I didn't smile at later. With the resilience I have now, I feel like I'm built for any storm that may come. Tough times only make us stronger and increase our faith in God. When you declare triumph during a trial, it shows God that you believe He will bring you through. God is greater than any test you will ever face, and with Him, the battle is already won.

NOTES

1. Marklew, Tim. "How Detroit Got Its Nickname: Motor City." *Culture Trip*, 10 July 2017, theculturetrip.com/north-america/usa/michigan/articles/how-detroit-got-its-nickname-motor-city.

2. "Cirrhosis - Symptoms and Causes." *Mayo Clinic*, 6 Feb. 2021, www.mayoclinic.org/diseases-conditions/cirrhosis/symptoms-causes/syc-20351487.

3. "Urge to Rename Cass Tech Heats up: Lewis Cass Was Slave Owner and Helped Cause Trail of Tears." *FOX 2 Detroit*, 1 July 2020, www.fox2detroit.com/news/urge-to-rename-cass-tech-heats-up-lewis-cass-was-slave-owner-and-helped-cause-trail-of-tears.

4. "Tacoma, Washington (WA) Profile: Population, Maps, Real Estate, Averages, Homes, Statistics, Relocation, Travel, Jobs, Hospitals, Schools, Crime, Moving, Houses, News, Sex Offenders." *City-Data.Com*, www.city-data.com/city/Tacoma-Washington.html. Accessed 7 July 2022.

5. Dunkelberger, Steve. "The City of Destiny: Tacoma's Quirky History and the Man Behind Its Nickname." *SouthSoundTalk*, 23 Nov. 2015, www.southsoundtalk.com/2015/03/19/city-of-destiny-tacoma.

6. Creager, Ken, et al. University of Washington, 2001, *The Nisqually Earthquake of 28 February 2001*, https://www.eeri.org/lfe/pdf/usa_nisqually_preliminary_report.pdf. Accessed 30 Dec. 2020.

7. "Angelo Giaudrone Middle School (2022 Ranking) | Tacoma, WA." *Public School Review*, 24 June 2022, www.publicschoolreview.com/angelo-giaudrone-middle-school-profile.

8. Hess, Robert D., and Kathleen A. Camara. "Post-Divorce Family Relationships as Mediating Factors in the Consequences of Divorce for Children." Journal of Social Issues 35.4 (1979): 79–96. Web.

9. Demo, David H., and Alan C. Acock. "The Impact of Divorce on Children." *Journal of Marriage and Family*, vol. 50, no. 3, 1988, pp. 619–48. *JSTOR*, https://doi.org/10.2307/352634. Accessed 8 Jul. 2022.

10. Teachman, Jay D., and Kathleen M. Paasch. "Financial Impact of Divorce on Children and Their Families." *The Future of Children*, vol. 4, no. 1, 1994, pp. 63–83. *JSTOR*, https://doi.org/10.2307/1602478. Accessed 8 Jul. 2022.

11. Higuera, Valencia. "Sarcoidosis." *Healthline*, 22 Feb. 2022, www.healthline.com/health/sarcoidosis#:%7E:text=What%20is%20sarcoidosis%3F,viruses%2C%20bacteria%2C%20or%20chemicals.

12. All4Kids. "A Father's Impact on Child Development." *Child Abuse Prevention, Treatment & Welfare Services | Children's Bureau*, 19 Mar. 2021, www.all4kids.org/news/blog/a-fathers-impact-on-child-development/#:%7E:text=Behavioral%20problems%20(fatherless%20children%20have,%2C%20resentments%2C%20anxieties%20and%20unhappiness).

13. GotQuestions.org. "What Does the Bible Say about Deliverance?" *GotQuestions.Org*, 4 Jan. 2022, www.gotquestions.org/deliverance.html.

14. MacNutt, Judith. "What About Deliverance?" *Christian Healing Ministries*, 2019, christianhealingmin.org/index.php/hl-issue-2019-3/366-magazine/2016-2020/hl-articles-2019-3/1564-what-about-deliverance.

15. Smith, E. M. (2015). Does a Positive Male Role Model Affect the Achievement of Adolescent African American Males? A Case Study. *Graduate Theses and Dissertations* Retrieved from https://scholarworks.uark.edu/etd/1336

16. fathers.com. "The Roadmap to Manhood: 5 Essentials for Raising a Teenage Boy." *National Center for Fathering*, 29 July 2020, fathers.com/featured-resource-center-page/just-give-your-son-the-roadmap-to-manhood-just-be-dad.

17. Galla, Sean. "Male Role Models: A Complete Guide on Positive Role Models for Men." *MensGroup.Com*, 9 Sept. 2021, mensgroup.com/male-role-models.

18. Smith, Elphin Maxwell Jr., "Does a Positive Male Role Model Affect the Achievement of Adolescent African-American Males? A Case Study" (2015). Theses and Dissertations. 1336. http://scholarworks.uark.edu/etd/1336

19. Tacoma Public Schools. "About - Foss High School." *Tacoma Public Schools*, foss.tacomaschools.org/about#:%7E:text=Foss's%20IB%20P

rograms%20offer%20internationally,at%20university%20and %20life%20beyond. Accessed 23 Nov. 2020.

20.   ABC News. "Tacoma Death Linked to Sniper Suspect." *ABC News*, 7 Jan. 2006, abcnews.go.com/US/story?id=91096&page=1#:%7E:text= Oct.,for%20Muhammad's%20auto%20repair%20business.

21.   "Taste of Tacoma." *Festivals.Com*, 2019, www.festivals.com/taste-of-tacoma-2248.

22.   CBS News. "Cops Seek Motive In Wash. School Shooting." *CBS News*, 4 Jan. 2007, www.cbsnews.com/news/cops-seek-motive-in-wash-school-shooting.

23.   Woodward, Curt. "Shooting Suspect Offers No Motive." *Spokesman.Com*, 5 Jan. 2007, www.spokesman.com/stories/2007/jan/05/shooting-suspect-offers-no-motive.

24.   Cafazzo, Debbie. "Ten Years after, a Fatal Shooting Still Echoes in a Tacoma High School" [Tacoma, WA]. *The News Tribune*, 28 Jan. 2017, cqrcengage.com/neamn/app/document/18589776.

25.   "Foss." *SchoolDigger*, www.schooldigger.com/go/WA/schools/0870001466/school .aspx. Accessed 8 July 2022.

26.   Frothingham, Scott. "Hematoma in the Leg." *Healthline*, 8 Mar. 2019, www.healthline.com/health/hematoma-leg.

27.   Hardison, Chaitra M., Susan Burkhauser, and Lawrence M. Hanser, United States Service Academy Admissions: Selecting for Success at the Air Force Academy and as an Officer. Santa Monica, CA: RAND Corporation, 2016. https://www.rand.org/pubs/research_reports/RR744.html. Also available in print form.

28.   Safier, Rebecca. "New SAT Format: What It Means for You." *PrepScholar*, 19 Mar. 2016, blog.prepscholar.com/new-sat-format-2016#:%7E:text=How%20Is%20the%20New%20SAT,rang es%20from%20200%20to%20800.

29.   Cheng, Allen. "What Is the Average SAT Score?" *PrepScholar*, 22 Oct. 2021, blog.prepscholar.com/what-is-the-average-sat-score#:%7E:text=National%20SAT%20Average%20Score,T otal%3A%201060.

30.   Zhang, Fred. "New SAT vs Old SAT: Changes You Must Know." *PrepScholar*, 5 Feb. 2018, blog.prepscholar.com/new-sat-vs-old-sat-quick-summary.

31.   "Preparatory School." *United States Air Force Academy*, 28 June 2022, www.usafa.edu/prep-school/#:%7E:text=If%20you%20apply%20to%20the,the%202022%20Preparatory%20School%20graduates.

32.   United States Air Force Academy. "U.S. Air Force Academy Preparatory School." *United States Air Force Academy*, www.usafa.af.mil/About-Us/Fact-Sheets/Display/Article/428289/us-air-force-academy-preparatory-school. Accessed 8 July 2022.

33.   Wilson, Eric. Foundation for Tacoma Students, Tacoma, WA, 2018, pp. 1–41, *2017 Community Impact Report*.

34.   Hardy, Nadia, et al. City of Tacoma, Tacoma, WA, 2016, pp. 1–62, *Community Needs Assessment*.

35.   Publishing, Rockwell, et al. *CA Real Estate Practices 8th Ed*. 8th ed., Rockwell Publishing, 2018.

36.   "Tacoma WA Crime Rate 1999–2018." *MacroTrends*, www.macrotrends.net/cities/us/wa/tacoma/crime-rate-statistics#:%7E:text=The%20Tacoma%20WA%20crime%2 0rate,a%2016.36%25%20increase%20from%202015. Accessed 8 July 2022.

37.   "Property Crime." *FBI*, ucr.fbi.gov/crime-in-the-u.s/2018/crime-in-the-u.s.-2018/topic-pages/property-crime. Accessed 8 July 2022.

38.   Department of Justice, State of California. "Computational Formulas." 2014, https://oag.ca.gov/sites/all/files/agweb/pdfs/cjsc/stats/com putational_formulas.pdf. Accessed 2022.

39.   Areavibes. "Tacoma, WA Crime Rates and Map." *Areavibes*, www.areavibes.com/tacoma-wa/crime. Accessed 11 July 2022.

40.   "Whitman (2022 Ranking) | Tacoma, WA." *Public School Review*, 8 July 2022, www.publicschoolreview.com/whitman-profile.

41.   United States, Congress, National Park Service, et al. *The National Register of Historic Places*, Eysaman + Company, 1994, pp. 1–30.

42. Dunkelberger, Steve. "Ranger Ash Street Shootout Remains Part of Tacoma's Gang Lore." *SouthSoundTalk*, 25 Aug. 2019, www.southsoundtalk.com/2019/04/05/ranger-ash-street-shootout-remains-part-of-tacomas-gang-lore.

43. "25 Years after Bloodshed." *MYNorthwest*, 23 Sept. 2013, mynorthwest.com/65860/25-years-after-bloodshed.

44. Military.com. "That Time Army Rangers Got in a Gunfight with the Crips Street Gang." *Military.Com*, 19 Apr. 2022, www.military.com/history/time-army-rangers-got-gunfight-crips-street-gang.html.

45. Staff, Seattle Times. "A Path to Murder: The Story of Maurice Clemmons." *The Seattle Times*, 12 Apr. 2010, www.seattletimes.com/seattle-news/a-path-to-murder-the-story-of-maurice-clemmons.

46. Carter, Mike, and Christine Clarridge. "A Day That 'Hurt Your Heart': 10 Years Ago, 4 Lakewood Police Officers Were Shot Down." *The Seattle Times*, 29 Nov. 2019, www.seattletimes.com/seattle-news/law-justice/a-day-that-hurt-your-heart-10-years-ago-4-lakewood-police-officers-were-shot-down.

47. Worland, Justin. "America's Long Overdue Awakening to Systemic Racism." *Time*, 11 June 2020, time.com/5851855/systemic-racism-america.

48. Illing, Sean. "George Floyd Protests: Why the Policing Problem Isn't about 'a Few Bad Apples.'" *Vox*, 6 June 2020, www.vox.com/identities/2020/6/2/21276799/george-floyd-protest-criminal-justice-paul-butler.

49. Neily, Clark. "America's Criminal Justice System Is Rotten to the Core." *CATO Institute*, 7 June 2020, https://www.cato.org/blog/americas-criminal-justice-system-rotten-core. Accessed 1 Mar. 2022.

50. Schneider, Andrea, and Cynthia Alkon. "Our Criminal Legal System: Plagued by Problems and Ripe for Reform." *Dispute Resolution Magazine*, 28 Jan. 2020.

51. "The History of Mass Incarceration." *Brennan Center for Justice*, 5 Apr. 2022, www.brennancenter.org/our-work/analysis-opinion/history-mass-incarceration.

52. Youderian, Melissa. "USAF ACADEMY PREPARATORY SCHOOL (USAFAPS) CLASS OF 2022 REPORTING

INSTRUCTIONS." DEPARTMENT OF THE AIR
FORCE, 24 Mar. 2021.

53. Sitterly, Daniel. "AIR FORCE MANUAL 36-2203."
DEPARTMENT OF THE AIR FORCE, 19 June 2018.

54. "Sponsor Program." *United States Air Force Academy*, 17 Mar.
2022, www.usafa.edu/prep-school/prep-school-sponsor-
program.

55. UAMS, Health. "Can Standing Up Straight for a Long
Period Cause Fainting." *UAMS Health*, 8 Mar. 2019,
https://uamshealth.com/medical-myths/can-standing-up-
straight-for-a-long-period-cause-
fainting/#:~:text=Richard%20Nicholas%2C%20one%20of
%20our,%2C%20may%20amplify%20the%20process.%E2
%80%9D. Accessed 30 Nov. 2020.

56. Resnikoff, Paul. "Aretha Franklin Plays the Longest National
Anthem In U.S. History." *Digital Music News*, 5 Dec. 2020,
www.digitalmusicnews.com/2016/11/25/aretha-franklin-
longest-national-anthem.

57. "Prep Academics." *United States Air Force Academy*, 4 May 2022,
www.usafa.edu/prep-school/academics.

58. Gay, Dale. "Student Life." *United States Air Force Academy*, 18
Mar. 2022, www.usafa.edu/prep-school/student-life.

59. "Frequently Asked Questions." *United States Air Force Academy*, 1
Mar. 2022, www.usafa.edu/prep-school/prep-school-faqs.

60. Training, Cadet Wing. "Basic Cadet Training." U.S. Air
Force Academy, 2020.

61. Payne, Brian C., et al. "Minding the Terrazzo Gap between
Athletes and Nonathletes: Representativeness, Integration,
and Academic Performance at the U.S. Air Force Academy."
Journal of Sports Economics, vol. 17, no. 3, Apr. 2016, pp.
302–320, doi:10.1177/1527002514530406.

62. "United States Air Force Academy Diversity: Racial
Demographics and Other Stats." *College Factual*, 16 June 2022,
www.collegefactual.com/colleges/united-states-air-force-
academy/student-life/diversity.

63. Diversity Commission, Military Leadership. "Prep School
Usually Has about 21% African-Americans, According to a
Study Done by the MLDC between 2006 and 2009." Military
Leadership Diversity Commission, May 2010.

64. Pound, Leah, "Sense of Belonging and Racial Diversity at the U.S. Service Academies" (2019). *Doctoral Dissertations*. 2386. https://opencommons.uconn.edu/dissertations/2386

65. Booker, K. (2016). Connection and commitment: How Sense of Belonging and Classroom Community Influence Degree Persistence for African American Undergraduate Women. *Int. J. Teach. Learn. High. Educ.* 28, 218–229.

66. Pipes, Col. Candice. "Consistent, Widespread Racial Disparities Hurt Black Airmen, IG Study Finds." *Air Force Times*, 27 Feb. 2021, www.airforcetimes.com/opinion/commentary/2021/02/27/we-need-radical-change-to-fix-the-racial-disparity-in-our-air-force.

67. Thomas, Dominique & Smith, Chauncey & Marks, Bryant & Crosby, Brandon. (2012). "Institutional Identity and Self-Esteem among African American Males in College." Journal of African American Males in Education. 3.

68. Mcleod, Saul. "Maslow's Hierarchy of Needs." *Simply Psychology*, 29 Dec. 2020, www.simplypsychology.org/maslow.html.

69. Hanselman, Paul et al. "Threat in Context: School Moderation of the Impact of Social Identity Threat on Racial/Ethnic Achievement Gaps." *Sociology of education* 87.2 (2014): 106–124. Web.

70. Genheimer, Elijah, "The Impact of Minority Faculty and Staff Involvement on Minority Student Experiences" (2016). *Master of Arts in Higher Education (MAHE) Theses*. 23. https://pillars.taylor.edu/mahe/23

71. Conahan, Frank. 1993, *Air Force Academy: Gender and Racial Disparities*, https://www.gao.gov/assets/nsiad-93-244.pdf. Accessed 16 Dec. 2020.

72. Means, Billie Howie. "A comparison of academic advising experiences and satisfaction of African American males and other students at a Predominately White Institution." (2014).

73. Thomas, Jackie C., et al. "Examining Relevant Influences on the Persistence of African-American College Students at a Diverse Urban University." Journal of College Student Retention: Research, Theory & Practice, vol. 15, no. 4, Feb. 2014, pp. 551–573, doi:10.2190/CS.15.4.e.

74.   "USAFA Way of Life Committee." *Air Force Academy Foundation*, falconfunder.usafa.org/project/19244. Accessed 12 July 2022.

75.   Uploads, USAFA. "USAF Academy Acronym List." USAFA.edu, 2022.

76.   WebTeam. "What's a SAMI? | USAFA Webguy." *Webguy*, 14 July 2019, www.usafawebguy.com/Blog/Entry/2497.

77.   "The Air Force Academy Extended." *The Lowry Foundation in Denver, Colorado*, Lowry Foundation, 24 June 2020, lowryfoundation.org/lowry-legacy/air-force-academy/extended.

78.   United States Air Force Academy. "The Contrails: Class, Building Colors." *United States Air Force Academy*, 15 Mar. 2016, www.usafa.af.mil/News/Features/Article/693742/the-contrails-class-building-colors.

79.   "So Much Gold, a Class Color Lesson | USAFA Webguy." *Webguy*, 30 June 2019, www.usafawebguy.com/Blog/Entry/2461.

80.   Greenbrier Outfitters. "Exemplar Dinner." *USAFA 2022 Spirit Mission*, Sept. 2018, usafa2022spiritmission.com/milestones/exemplar-dinner/#:%7E:text=The%20Cadet%20Exemplar%20Progra m%20is,heritage%20with%20our%20boundless%20future.

81.   History.com Editors. "Wright Brothers." *HISTORY*, 13 Nov. 2020, www.history.com/topics/inventions/wright-brothers#:%7E:text=Wilbur%20and%20Orville%20Wright %20were,the%20first%20fully%20practical%20airplane.

82.   Team, Web. "Drill Time." *Webguy*, 5 July 2019, https://www.usafawebguy.com/Blog/Entry/2475. Accessed 15 Dec. 2020.

83.   Branum, Don. "Academy Officials Treating Sick Cadets, Staff for Stomach Flu." *United States Air Force Academy*, 26 July 2011, www.usafa.af.mil/News/Article/428693/academy-officials-treating-sick-cadets-staff-for-stomach-flu.

84.   Forster, Liz. "Air Force Academy Cadets Culminate Basic Training with Big Bad Basic Tournament" [Colorado Springs, CO]. *The Gazette*, 6 Aug. 2017, gazette.com/military/air-force-academy-freshmen-cadets-culminate-basic-training-with-big-bad-basic-

tournament/article_5eb83a87-2031-530d-bd08-bde2bfd4cb7a.html.

85.   Peterson, Patti. "Air Force Cadet Shares Life at the Academy" [Fremont, NE]. *Fremont Tribune*, 28 Dec. 2016, fremonttribune.com/cass-news/news/air-force-cadet-shares-life-at-the-academy/article_2c6e91b1-3eb9-5fc0-b912-c6b667a633ed.html.

86.   Air Force. "Cadet Wing Accepts Class of 2015." *Air Force*, 4 Aug. 2011, www.af.mil/News/Article-Display/Article/112640/cadet-wing-accepts-class-of-2015.

87.   Thompson, William. "Parent Handbook." Association of Graduates, 2012.

88.   Stoddard, Justin R. "UNDERSTANDING RESILIENCY—THE RELATIONSHIP BETWEEN USAFA CADET GRIT-S SCORES AND CADET DEVELOPMENT." (2019).

89.   Johnson, Richard. "The Commander-in-Chief's Trophy, Briefly Explained: Army-Navy-Air Force Rivalry." *SBNation.Com*, 9 Dec. 2017, www.sbnation.com/college-football/2017/12/9/16756074/commander-in-chief-trophy-army-navy-air-force.

90.   Alessandrini, Mike. "Air Force Books Commander-in-Chief's Trophy Series as Only 2020 Games." *theScore.Com*, 13 July 2022, www.thescore.com/ncaaf/news/2021107.

91.   Do, James Joon Woo. *Crossing Into the Blue: Cadet Culture and Officer Development At the U.S. Air Force Academy.*

92.   Air Force Academy, United States. "What to Expect in the First 10 Weeks A Parent Guide." United States Air Force Academy, 2019.

93.   Goodwin, Kristin. "Class of 2023 Appointee Booklet." Department of the Air Force, 1 Mar. 2019.

94.   "The Terrazzo." *United States Air Force Academy*, 28 June 2022, www.usafa.edu/facilities/terrazzo.

95.   United States, Congress, National Park Service, et al. *National Historic Landmark Nomination*, 1 Apr. 2004. https://archives.iupui.edu/bitstream/handle/2450/674/National%20Landmark%20USAFA.pdf?sequence=1&isAllowed=y. Accessed 1 Dec. 2020.

96.   United States Air Force Academy. "Academics." *United States Air Force Academy*, 7 May 2022, www.usafa.edu/academics.

97. "United States v. Virginia." *Oyez*,
www.oyez.org/cases/1995/94-1941. Accessed 12 Jul. 2022.

98. Abair, Paul. "Curriculum Handbook." United States Air
Force Academy, 2011.

99. Gay, Dale. "Governance." *United States Air Force Academy*, 22
Apr. 2022, www.usafa.edu/about/governance.

100. "Athletics." *United States Air Force Academy*, 14 Apr. 2022,
www.usafa.edu/athletics.

101. Roeder, Tom. The Gazette. "A BROKEN CODE: Air Force
Academy Athletes Flouted Sacred Honor Code by
Committing Sexual Assaults, Taking Drugs, Cheating and
Engaging in Other Misconduct." *Colorado Springs Gazette*, 23
Oct. 2019, gazette.com/sports/a-broken-code-air-force-
academy-athletes-flouted-sacred-honor-code-by-committing-
sexual-assaults/article_97b9e453-fcab-5ee7-a577-
7743c03260f3.html.

102. Academic. "Prop and Wings." *Academic Dictionaries and
Encyclopedias*, Wikimedia Foundation. 2010, en-
academic.com/dic.nsf/enwiki/2766318. Accessed 13 July
2022.

103. Team, Web. "Class of 2022- Recognition." *Webguy*, 8 Mar.
2019, https://www.usafawebguy.com/Blog/Entry/2392.
Accessed 14 Dec. 2020.

104. Bowden, Raymond. "Air Force Academy's Class of '22 Gets
'Recognized.'" *United States Air Force Academy*, 15 June 2022,
www.usafa.edu/air-force-academys-class-of-22-gets-
recognized.

105. "Jacks Valley." *United States Air Force Academy*, 28 June 2022,
www.usafa.edu/facilities/jacks-valley.

106. Federal News Network Staff. "Air Force: Up to 78 Cadets
Cheated on Math Test." *Federal News Network*, 7 June 2012,
federalnewsnetwork.com/defense/2012/06/air-force-up-to-
78-cadets-cheated-on-math-test.

107. "Physical Education." *Air Force Academy Athletics*,
goairforcefalcons.com/sports/2018/6/21/ot-afa-phys-ed-
html.aspx. Accessed 13 July 2022.

108. "Boxing Instills Warrior Mindset at Academy." *United States
Air Force Academy*, 6 May 2022, www.usafa.edu/boxing-instills-
warrior-mindset-at-academy.

109. Briggeman, Brent. "Air Force Academy Adds Women's Boxing to Keep up with New Gender Equality Rules in Combat Roles." *Colorado Springs Gazette*, 1 Oct. 2016, gazette.com/sports/air-force-academy-adds-womens-boxing-to-keep-up-with-new-gender-equality-rules-in/article_8c3877f8-907e-53b9-9a36-f43868421e99.html.

110. Baillie, Amber. "Boxing Equips Cadets with Courage, Resiliency to Finish the Fight." *United States Air Force Academy*, 10 Feb. 2015, www.usafa.af.mil/News/Features/Article/619680/boxing-equips-cadets-with-courage-resiliency-to-finish-the-fight.

111. "Management." *United States Air Force Academy*, 26 Jan. 2022, www.usafa.edu/academic/management.

112. "Military." *United States Air Force Academy*, 28 June 2022, www.usafa.edu/military.

113. "New ESET training to wrap up next week." *United States Air Force Academy*, 24 July 2014, www.usafa.af.mil/News/Features/Article/619730/new-eset-training-to-wrap-up-next-week.

114. U.S. Air Force. "Survival, Evasion, Resistance and Escape Specialist - Requirements & Benefits - U.S. Air Force." *U.S. Air Force*, www.airforce.com/careers/detail/survival-evasion-resistance-and-escape-sere. Accessed 13 July 2022.

115. Oates, Russ. "Air Force Vs. Michigan 2012: Game Time, TV Schedule, Odds And More." *SB Nation Denver*, 8 Sept. 2012, denver.sbnation.com/air-force-falcons/2012/9/8/3288194/michigan-air-force-2012-schedule-game-time-spread.

116. Go Air Force Falcons. "GoAirForceFalcons.Com - Official Site of Air Force Athletics Official Athletic Site - Stats." *Go Air Force Falcons*, airforce_ftp.sidearmsports.com/custompages/sports/m-footbl/stats/112412aaa.html. Accessed 13 July 2022.

117. Las Vegas Raiders. "Davante Adams (WR): Bio, News, Stats and More." *Las Vegas Raiders*, www.raiders.com/team/players-roster/davante-adams. Accessed 13 July 2022.

118. Las Vegas Raiders. "Derek Carr (QB): Bio, News, Stats and More." *Las Vegas Raiders*, www.raiders.com/team/players-roster/derek-carr. Accessed 13 July 2022.

119. Mauss, Jeremy. "College Football Bowl Swag, Who Got What." *Mountain West Connection*, 6 Dec. 2012, www.mwcconnection.com/2012-mountain-west-bowl-news/2012/12/6/3735918/college-football-bowl-swag-who-got-what.

120. Impact Vision Therapy. "ImPACT Concussion Testing." *Impact Vision Therapy*, www.impactvisiontherapy.com/eye-care-services/neuro-optometric-rehabilitation/impact-concussion-testing/#:%7E:text=ImPACT%20stands%20for%20Immediate%20Post,about%2025%20minutes%20to%20complete. Accessed 13 July 2022.

121. Wallet, The Military. "How to Smartly Use the USAA Career Starter Loan." *The Military Wallet*, 10 Mar. 2022, themilitarywallet.com/usaa-starter-loan.

122. National Weather Service. "Seasonal Snowfall -- Colorado Springs." *Weather.Gov*, www.weather.gov/pub/climateCosSeasonalSnowfall. Accessed 13 July 2022.

123. Weather Spark. "Colorado Springs Climate, Weather By Month, Average Temperature (Colorado, United States) - Weather Spark." *Weather Spark*, weatherspark.com/y/3685/Average-Weather-in-Colorado-Springs-Colorado-United-States-Year-Round#:%7E:text=In%20Colorado%20Springs%2C%20the%20summers,or%20above%2092%C2%B0F. Accessed 13 July 2022.

124. Walton, Lisa. "Freezing Weather Will Linger in Colorado Springs until 2015." *Colorado Springs Gazette*, 30 Dec. 2014, gazette.com/news/freezing-weather-will-linger-in-colorado-springs-until-2015/article_4503b68d-cedc-5095-9f68-b634ac28d483.html.

125. "Summertime Operations Air Force Program Starts for Academy Cadets." *United States Air Force Academy*, 3 May 2022, www.usafa.edu/summertime-operations-air-force-program-starts-for-academy-cadets.

126. U.S. Air Force. "Security Forces Careers - U.S. Air Force." *U.S. Air Force*, www.airforce.com/careers/in-demand-careers/security-forces#:%7E:text=PROTECTING%20THOSE%20WHO

%20PROTECT%20OUR,and%20handling%20military%20 working%20dogs. Accessed 13 July 2022.

127.   Sheppard Air Force Base. "T-38C Talon." *Sheppard Air Force Base*, 17 Oct. 2012, www.sheppard.af.mil/Library/Fact-Sheets/Display/Article/367538/t-38c-talon.

128.   Space Center Houston. "Meet Our T-38 Jets in Talon Park." *Space Center Houston*, 8 Apr. 2019, spacecenter.org/meet-our-t-38-jets-in-talon-park.

129.   Rivera, Pedro. "Pedro Takes Flight in a T-38, Pulls 5 Gs" [Sacramento, CA]. *Fox40*, 30 Mar. 2018, fox40.com/morning/pedro-takes-flight-in-a-t-38-talon-pulls-5-gs.

130.   Lee, Hasard. "What's It Like To Pull 9 Gs In An F-16? A Fighter Pilot Weighs In." *Sandboxx*, 18 Apr. 2021, https://www.sandboxx.us/blog/g-forces-and-fighter-pilots-whats-it-like-to-pull-9gs/. Accessed 7 Dec. 2021.

131.   Jedick, Rocky. "Be a Better G-Monster: The Anti-G Straining Maneuver (AGSM)." *GO FLIGHT MEDICINE*, 2 Mar. 2020, goflightmedicine.com/agsm.

132.   Shaw, Caitlyn. "This Unclassified Technique Keeps Fighter Pilots Awake and Alert in the Cockpit." *Gear Patrol*, 4 Oct. 2017, www.gearpatrol.com/fitness/a393291/hook-maneuver-agsm-tutorial/#:%7E:text=The%20Hook%20Maneuver%20was%20unclassified,their%20cool%20in%20the%20cockpit.

133.   MedlinePlus. "Gastroenteritis." *Stomach Flu | MedlinePlus*, medlineplus.gov/gastroenteritis.html. Accessed 13 July 2022.

134.   "Matt McGettigan - Football Coach." *Air Force Academy Athletics*, goairforcefalcons.com/sports/football/roster/coaches/matt-mcgettigan/967. Accessed 13 July 2022.

135.   Silveria, Jay. "Parent Guide." United States Air Force Academy, 2020.

136.   "Human Performance Laboratory." *Air Force Academy Athletics*, goairforcefalcons.com/sports/2018/6/21/ot-human-performance-home-html.aspx. Accessed 13 July 2022.

137.   "Sports Vision." *Air Force Academy Athletics*, goairforcefalcons.com/sports/2018/6/21/genrel-011502aac-html. Accessed 13 July 2022.

138. "Cadets Get Job Assignments." *Air Force*, 18 Dec. 2003, www.af.mil/News/Article-Display/Article/137945/cadets-get-job-assignments.

139. Air Force Academy, United States. "Commissioning Codes." United States Air Force Academy, 2019.

140. "Academy Releases Non-Rated Career Field Selections." *Air Force*, 18 Nov. 2014, www.af.mil/News/Article-Display/Article/554533/academy-releases-non-rated-career-field-selections.

141. USAFA EDU. "Traditions." *United States Air Force Academy*, 24 June 2022, www.usafa.edu/about/traditions.

142. U.S. Air Force Academy Association of Graduates. "Class of 2015 Ring Design Elements." *United States Air Force Academy*, 22 May 2015, www.usafa.af.mil/News/Features/Article/619657/class-of-2015-ring-design-elements.

143. Wagner, Bill. "Navy Football Where Are They Now: Catching up With Keenan Reynolds." *Capital Gazette*, 18 Oct. 2019, www.tribpub.com/gdpr/capitalgazette.com/#:%7E:text=Reynolds%20has%20not%20been%20scheduled,14.

144. 247Sports. "Locker Room Celebration." *247Sports*, 28 Sept. 2014, 247sports.com/college/air-force/Board/102854/Contents/Locker-room-celebration-70610504.

145. Siemon, Dean. "Air Force Senior Got Start at McChord Field." *Team McChord*, 31 Oct. 2014, www.mcchord.af.mil/News/Article-Display/Article/767432/air-force-senior-got-start-at-mcchord-field.

146. Air Force Academy Athletics. "President Barack Obama Presents CIC Trophy to Falcons." *Air Force Academy Athletics*, 19 June 2018, goairforcefalcons.com/news/2015/5/7/president_barack_obama_presents_cic_trophy_to_falcons.aspx.

147. Haux, Hailey. "Academy Receives Commander-in-Chief's Trophy from President." *Air Force*, 8 May 2015, www.af.mil/News/Article-Display/Article/588156/academy-receives-commander-in-chiefs-trophy-from-president.

148. Page, Seraine. "7 Of the Coolest Air Force Jobs You Can Have." *Sandboxx*, 7 Sept. 2020, https://www.sandboxx.us/blog/cool-air-force-jobs/. Accessed 10 Dec. 2020.

149. Los Angeles Air Force Base. "About Us." *Los Angeles Air Force Base*, www.losangeles.spaceforce.mil/About-Us. Accessed 13 July 2022.

150. "Clubs." *United States Air Force Academy*, 19 May 2022, www.usafa.edu/cadet-life/clubs.

151. Peck, Tony. "A Watery Tradition Follows Finals for Senior Air Force Academy Cadets" [Colorado Springs, CO]. *The Gazette*, 13 May 2018, gazette.com/military/a-watery-tradition-follows-finals-for-senior-air-force-academy-cadets/article_45daefd9-a482-5c46-b523-6060f3a00a46.html.

152. Stanton, Billie. "Darkness to Diary Entries Convinced Coroner That Air Force Academy Cadet's Death Was a Suicide" [Colorado Springs, CO]. *The Gazette*, 29 June 2015, gazette.com/news/darkness-to-diary-entries-convinced-coroner-that-air-force-academy/article_de2b2def-5c68-5319-836c-6c93c419cb0a.html.

153. White House Historical Association. "The Red Room." *WHHA (En-US)*, 2000, www.whitehousehistory.org/white-house-tour/the-red-room.

154. The White House Museum. "East Room - White House Museum." *The White House Museum*, www.whitehousemuseum.org/floor1/east-room-history.htm. Accessed 13 July 2022.

155. Brayton, Jenna. "President Obama Honors the Air Force Academy Fighting Falcons With." *Whitehouse.Gov*, 13 Aug. 2015, obamawhitehouse.archives.gov/blog/2015/05/07/president-obama-honors-air-force-academy-fighting-falcons-commander-chief-s-trophy.

156. Association of Graduates. "Class Facts | US Air Force Academy AOG and Endowment." *Association of Graduates*, www2.usafa.org/ClassData/Index/2015. Accessed 13 July 2022.

157. "Institutional Research." *United States Air Force Academy*, 16 Mar. 2022, www.usafa.edu/about/institutional-research.

158. WebGuy 2.0. "2015 Graduation Speaker Announced! | USAFA AOG WebGuy." *Webguy*, 30 Apr. 2015, archive.usafawebguy.com/2015-graduation-speaker-announced.

159. United States Air Force Academy. "2015 Graduation by the Numbers" [Colorado Springs, CO]. *United States Air Force Academy*, 29 May 2015, www.usafa.af.mil/News/News-Display/Article/619079/2015-graduation-by-the-numbers.

160. U.S. Air Force. "Overview." *U.S. Air Force*, www.airforce.com/thunderbirds/overview. Accessed 13 July 2022.

161. Players Bio Editor. "Desmond Trufant Bio: Early Life, Stats, Career and Girlfriend." *Players Bio*, 14 June 2022, playersbio.com/desmond-trufant.

162. The Olympian. "Trufant Teaches Importance of Competition as He Prepares for NFL Return" [Olympia, WA]. *The Olympian*, 17 July 2017, www.theolympian.com/sports/article161616038.html

163. Milles, Todd. "NFL Star Desmond Trufant on His Summer Football Camp for Tacoma-Area Youth: 'It Is Only Right That I Give Back.'" *Scorebook Live*, 22 Feb. 2022, news.scorebooklive.com/footballa/2019/07/15/nfl-star-desmond-trufant-on-his-summer-football-camp-for-tacoma-area-youth-it-is-only-right-that-i-give-back.

164. Wikipedia contributors. "Zach Banner." *Wikipedia*, 10 July 2022, en.wikipedia.org/wiki/Zach_Banner.

165. Air Force, U.S. "AF Form 707." U.S. Air Force, 2015.

166. Sillis, Davia. "When Is Porn Use a Problem?" *Psychology Today*, 19 Feb. 2018, www.psychologytoday.com/us/blog/experimentations/201802/when-is-porn-use-problem.

167. Pickering, Anna, PhD. "Pornography Facts and Statistics." *The Recovery Village Drug and Alcohol Rehab*, 6 July 2022, www.therecoveryvillage.com/process-addiction/porn-addiction/pornography-statistics.

168. Marripedia. "Effects of Pornography [Marripedia]." *Marripedia*, marripedia.org/effects_of_pornography. Accessed 13 July 2022.

169. Blau, Justine. "Teen Boys Feel Pressure To Have Sex." *CBS News*, 20 May 2003, www.cbsnews.com/news/teen-boys-feel-

pressure-to-have-
sex/#:%7E:text=%22There%20are%20a%20lot%20of,with
%2023%20percent%20of%20girls.
170. "What Does the Bible Say about Fornication?"
GotQuestions.Org, 4 Jan. 2022, www.gotquestions.org/Bible-
fornication.html
171. Sotallaro, Mark. "AFI35-101." Department of the Air Force,
20 Nov. 2020.
172. Merriam-Webster. "Effeminate." *The Merriam-Webster.Com
Dictionary*, www.merriam-webster.com/dictionary/effeminate.
Accessed 21 Dec. 2020.
173. Mayer, David. "How Men Get Penalized for Straying from
Masculine Norms." *Harvard Business Review*, 9 Oct. 2018,
hbr.org/2018/10/how-men-get-penalized-for-straying-from-
masculine-norms.
174. Hagan, Ekua. "Men and Anger." *Psychology Today*, 3 Nov.
2019, www.psychologytoday.com/us/blog/fear-
intimacy/201911/men-and-anger.
175. GotQuestions.org. "The Fruit of the Holy Spirit – What Is
Self-Control?" *GotQuestions.Org*, 4 Jan. 2022,
www.gotquestions.org/fruit-Holy-Spirit-self-control.html.
176. Mayo Clinic Staff. "Polysomnography (Sleep Study) - Mayo
Clinic." *Mayo Clinic*, 1 Dec. 2020, www.mayoclinic.org/tests-
procedures/polysomnography/about/pac-20394877.
177. Health.mil. "Medical Evaluation Board." *Health.Mil*, 26 May
2017, www.health.mil/Military-Health-Topics/Access-Cost-
Quality-and-Safety/Disability-Evaluation/Medical-
Evaluation.
178. Air Force's Personnel Center. "Transition Assistance
Program." *Air Force's Personnel Center*, www.afpc.af.mil/Airman-
and-Family/Transition-Assistance-Program. Accessed 19 Jan.
2021.
179. SACC. "Service Academy Career Conference." *Service
Academy Career Conference*, sacc-
jobfair.com/event?id=34#:%7E:text=For%20more%20than
%2028%20years,Academy%2C%20and%20the%20U.S.%2
0Merchant. Accessed 19 Jan. 2021.
180. Center for Disease Control and Prevention. "Coronavirus
Disease 2019 (COVID-19)." *Centers for Disease Control and
Prevention*, 11 Feb. 2020, www.cdc.gov/coronavirus/2019-

ncov/science/about-epidemiology/identifying-source-outbreak.html.

181. Weintraub, Elizabeth Weise And Karen. "Where Did COVID-19 Come From?" *USA Today News*, 20 Jan. 2021, eu.usatoday.com/in-depth/news/health/2021/01/16/covid-one-year-anniversary-unknowns-remain-coronavirus-origins/6582961002.

182. Fedrigo, John. "AFI36-3003." Department of the Air Force, 24 Apr. 2020.

183. "USAFA Alumni Careers and Networking." *Facebook*, www.facebook.com/groups/USAFAcareersANDnetworking/about. Accessed 27 Jan. 2021.

184. Yates, Jonathan. "90% of the World's Millionaires Do This to Create Wealth." *The College Investor*, 24 Oct. 2021, thecollegeinvestor.com/11300/90-percent-worlds-millionaires-do-this.

185. O'Donnell, J. "The (Depressing) Truth About Applying To Jobs Online." *LinkedIn*, 9 Sept. 2019, www.linkedin.com/pulse/depressing-truth-applying-jobs-online-j-t-o-donnell.

186. CalCareers. "LVN Memory Care Unit." *CA.Gov*, www.calcareers.ca.gov/CalHrPublic/Jobs/JobPosting.aspx?JobControlId=296867. Accessed 13 July 2022.

187. UNC Department of Neurology. "Neuropsychological Evaluation FAQ." *Department of Neurology*, 1 Feb. 2021, www.med.unc.edu/neurology/divisions/movement-disorders/npsycheval.

188. Targonskaya, Anna. "Posterior Placenta Location: Is Posterior Positioning Good for the Baby?&inline=1." *Flo.Health - #1 Mobile Product for Women's Health*, flo.health/pregnancy/pregnancy-health/complications/posterior-placenta-location. Accessed 6 Aug. 2021.

189. Bhargava, Hansa. "Signs of Labor." *WebMD*, WebMD, LLC, 7 June 2004, www.webmd.com/baby/labor-signs.

190. NHS website. "Epidural." *Nhs.Uk*, 11 Mar. 2020, www.nhs.uk/conditions/epidural

191. Cunha, John. "Side Effects of Pitocin (Oxytocin Injection), Warnings, Uses." *RxList*, 12 Oct. 2021, www.rxlist.com/pitocin-side-effects-drug-center.htm.

ABOUT THE AUTHOR

Growing up in the rough city of Tacoma, Jamal has played sports his entire life, helping him circumvent a negative environment. Jamal capitalized on his athletic ability, earning a football scholarship to the United States Air Force Academy. There he received his bachelor's degree in management from the Air Force Academy in 2015. Upon graduation, Jamal served five years in the Air Force as an acquisitions officer before being medically retired. He then began his next career as a defense contractor supporting the Space Force, where he currently works as an acquisition analyst.

Jamal never envisioned becoming an author. The endeavor manifested as result of his life's unprecedented outcomes. After graduating from the Academy, Jamal desired to share his collegiate experience with the world because of its uniqueness. This desire led Jamal to begin composing his work. Originally designed to be a memoir, Jamal's book evolved into an autobiography as necessary background information expanded to include the rest of his life.

Jamal is a prodigious family man. After God, he cherishes his loved ones before everything else. He is currently married to his beautiful wife, Shaianne, with a 1-year-old son (Malachi) and a 9-year-old stepson (Derek). Jamal enjoys traveling with his family and cherishes a good steakhouse. He still loves sports and is an avid Detroit Lions and Air Force fan. He also enjoys playing Call of Duty in his spare time and working on his cars. Jamal owns a 1985 Chevrolet Camaro I-Roc Z28 and a 2021 Chevrolet C8 Corvette. He appreciates eschatology as well, as Biblical prophecy unfolds before our eyes.

Outside of his family and hobbies, Jamal provides football training to young athletes, owns a Christian clothing business, and is a real estate investor. He plans on taking his real estate sales exam soon to become a salesperson which will aid his real estate investing goal. Moreover, he is striving to build capital to acquire more rental properties and increase his portfolio. Lastly, he is aiming to become financially stable enough to embark on his high school football coaching career. Jamal and his family currently reside in the Golden State as they await the construction of their new home in Arizona.